THE STRUCTURE OF THUCYDIDES' HISTORY

THE STRUCTURE OF
THUCYDIDES' HISTORY

Hunter R. Rawlings III

PRINCETON UNIVERSITY PRESS

PRINCETON, NEW JERSEY

Published by Princeton University Press, Princeton, New Jersey
In the United Kingdom: Princeton University Press, Guildford, Surrey

Library of Congress Cataloging in Publication Data will be found
on the last printed page of this book

Publication of this book was assisted by a grant from the
Publications Program of the National Endowment for the Humanities
This book has been composed in Linotype Granjon

Clothbound editions of Princeton University Press books
are printed on acid-free paper, and binding materials are
chosen for strength and durability

Printed in the United States of America by Princeton
University Press, Princeton, New Jersey

For my parents

Contents

CONTENTS

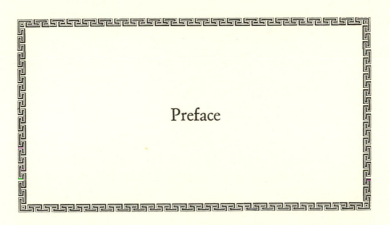

Preface

This book has been a long time in the making. In writing my doctoral dissertation in 1969-70, I was struck by several correspondences between Books I and VI of Thucydides. At the time, I was concentrating my attention on the historian's peculiar uses of *prophasis*, a term that recurs frequently in these two books in his analyses of the causes of the Peloponnesian War and of the Sicilian Expedition. It seemed to me that Thucydides was, intentionally or not, drawing comparisons and contrasts between the motivations leading to war in Greece in Book I and to the invasion of Sicily in Book VI. Though I alluded to some of these parallels, I did not explore them to any significant extent (*A Semantic Study of* Prophasis *to 400 B.C.*, Hermes Einzelschriften, vol. 33 [Wiesbaden 1975], 97-103). A couple of years later I returned to this idea and, after a preliminary review of the text, concluded that the notion of parallelism between two parts of Thucydides' *History* might repay further study. I was fortunate enough to spend the academic year 1975-76 as a Junior Fellow at the Center for Hellenic Studies in Washington D.C., where I was able to conduct the major part of the research for this book. In the Center's superb library and working environment I composed the first draft, part of which benefited from the helpful criticism of the Director, Bernard M. W. Knox, and the other Junior Fellows. I am most grateful for the opportunity to work in such a congenial and productive atmosphere.

To move from first to final draft has been a lengthy, but enjoyable process. I have had the pleasure of conducting seminars on my ideas at Princeton, Oxford, Berkeley, and Chapel Hill. For these opportunities to solicit responses from colleagues whose opinions I value I thank W. Robert Connor, George Forrest and Hugh Lloyd-Jones, Erich Gruen, and George W. Houston. Their hospitality made these occasions memorable as well as informative for me.

I owe a considerable debt of gratitude to Mrs. Joanna Hitchcock, Managing Editor of Princeton University Press. She has provided encouraging and sensible advice over an extended period of time, as well as three careful readers of the manuscript, all of whom contributed to its improvement. As an editor myself, I appreciate the generosity of those who lend their time and judgment to someone else's work.

For assistance with the preparation of the manuscript, I should like to acknowledge the support of the University of Colorado's Council on Research and Creative Work. Eloise V. Pearson typed the first draft skillfully and expeditiously, and Mrs. Luzie Mason lent valuable portions of her time to its revisions. Mr. Carl Huffman, on another grant from the Council on Research and Creative Work, helped with the initial stages of research on the text of Thucydides.

The end of a decade's work is a convenient time to bid an author at least a temporary adieu. Thucydides has been a demanding and difficult subject: complex, reticent, troubled by his times, his own point of view is often impossible to identify with any certainty. The reason is that he shapes his readers' judgments with such subtlety and skill that he makes them their own. To penetrate his mind we must understand his literary composition. In Thucydides' case the artist frequently overshadows the scholar. There need be no apologies in an historical work for the addition of art to accuracy. After ten years, I am convinced that we learn more of permanent value from Thucydides' dramatic intensity than from his reserved precision. That is one irony I am not certain the "austere" Athenian aristocrat would have appreciated.

Boulder
December, 1979

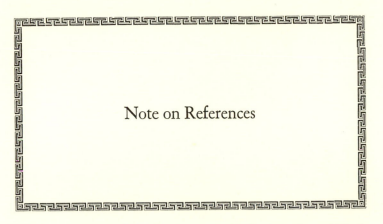

Note on References

The text of Thucydides I refer to in this book is that of H. S. Jones, *Thucydidis Historiae*, with apparatus criticus corrected and augmented by J. E. Powell, Oxford University Press (Oxford 1970). This Oxford Classical Text, in two volumes, will be cited throughout the book as *OCT*. Most of the translations of this text are my own. I have noted the instances when I have used the translation of R. Crawley, *The Peloponnesian War by Thucydides*, Random House, (New York 1951). My renderings have on several occasions been influenced by Crawley, who first published his translation in 1874. For the other classical authors cited I have used the standard editions and commentaries. Thucydides' work, which has no title, is referred to as the *History*.

Abbreviations

AJP	*American Journal of Philology*
L'Ant. cl.	*L'Antiquité classique*
Beloch, *Gr. Ges.*	J. Beloch, *Griechische Geschichte* (Berlin 1912-1931)
BICS	*Bulletin of the Institute of Classical Studies*, London University
Busolt, *Gr. Ges.*	G. Busolt, *Griechische Geschichte bis zur Schlacht bei Chaeroneia* (Gotha 1893-1904)
CJ	*The Classical Journal*
Classen-Steup	J. Classen, *Thukydides*, revised by J. Steup (Berlin Bks. I-II, 5th ed. 1914-1919, Bks. III-VIII, 3rd ed. 1892-1922)
CP	*Classical Philology*
CQ	*Classical Quarterly*
CW	*Classical World*
Comm.	A. W. Gomme, A. Andrewes, and K. J. Dover, *A Historical Commentary on Thucydides* (Oxford 1945-1970)
von Fritz, *Gr. Ges.*	K. von Fritz, *Die Griechische Geschichtsschreibung* (Berlin 1967)
FGrHist	F. Jacoby, *Die Fragmente der Griechischen Historiker* (Berlin and Leiden 1923-1958)
GRBS	*Greek, Roman and Byzantine Studies*

HSCP	*Harvard Studies in Classical Philology*
Hist. Zeit.	*Historische Zeitschrift*
JHS	*Journal of Hellenic Studies*
LSJ	H. G. Liddell and R. Scott, *Greek-English Lexicon*, revised by H. S. Jones (Oxford 1940)
OCT	H. S. Jones, *Thucydidis Historiae*, revised by J. E. Powell (Oxford 1970).
Rh. M.	*Rheinisches Museum*
TAPA	*Transactions of the American Philological Association*
Wege	*Thukydides. Wege der Forschung*, ed. by H. Herter (Darmstadt 1968)
WS	*Wiener Studien*

THE STRUCTURE OF THUCYDIDES' HISTORY

CHAPTER I

The Two Ten-Year
Wars

THE HISTORIAN'S STRUCTURE

The structure of an historical work is not often discussed or
even recognized as an important object of study. The historian's narrative is, after all, determined by the facts or events
he narrates. We are far more likely to pay attention to the
architecture of a play or novel than to that of an historical
work, usually with good reason. The modern historian is himself often quite innocent of reflection or concern with the
literary form of his narrative. Although his unconscious selection and arrangement of facts can, when subjected to rigorous
analysis and criticism, reveal his approach and perspective and
often his prejudices, only rarely does one meet an historian
who gives careful attention to the literary presentation of his
material. The reason for this is that of the two basic methods
open to the historian for marshalling his data, the explicit
method in which he simply narrates and analyzes the data
consecutively is by far the easier and the more common one.
The other, more subtle than the first, is the implicit method,
in which the historian arranges and characterizes the facts in
a manner that brings out or even creates their essential meaning. With this method, the historian judges without seeming
to judge, or, even more subtly, the historian makes the reader
judge, unconsciously, in the way the historian wants, by leading him to form certain impressions about the material. The

historian who masters this method is more than a recorder of facts—he is an artist.

Thucydides belongs to the select company of the second group. He is a great artist as well as a meticulous researcher. The latter we have known for a long time.[1] The former has been generally appreciated only recently, though perspicacious readers have known it for centuries.[2] The reason is that, like most great artists, Thucydides does not mention his own artistry. He lets it speak for itself. This does not make it less effective; quite the contrary, it is for that reason even more powerful. But it does mean that in order to understand Thucydides' artistry one must study it with great care.

Several studies published in the past three decades have helped to reveal the literary structure of Thucydides' narrative. An article by J. H. Finley that appeared first in 1940 made an excellent case for the artistic unity of the *History* and served to shift scholarly attention away from the "composition question" toward the equally important question of the work's structure.[3] J. de Romilly's *Histoire et raison chez Thucydide* (1956), a careful exegesis of several segments of Thucydidean narrative, exposed the methods the historian used to relate one episode to another, to distill the essence of an event or to re-

---

[1] It seems, however, that Thucydides' abilities and care in researching his material are in danger of being underestimated by a new "school" of Thucydidean scholarship. See M. Lang, "Scapegoat Pausanias," *CJ* 63 (1967) 79-85; "Thucydides and the Epidamnian Affair," *CW* 61 (1967-68) 173-176; (for an answer to the latter see Steven Chernick, "Historical Manipulation in Thucydides?" *CW* 65 [1971] 126-130); W. P. Wallace, "Thucydides," *Phoenix* 18 (1964) 251-261; Virginia J. Hunter, *Thucydides: The Artful Reporter* (Toronto 1973). All these works, in my opinion, underestimate Thucydides' historical accuracy. See my Chapter VI, pp. 266-270.

[2] See T. Hobbes, *Eight bookes of the Peloponnesian warre, written by Thucydides the sonne of Olorus* (London 1634), especially the introduction "To the Readers." In antiquity, of course, there were many who recognized Thucydides' artistry: Dionysius and Cicero explicitly, Demosthenes and Sallust implicitly, to mention only a few.

[3] J. H. Finley, "The Unity of Thucydides' History," *Athenian Studies Presented to William Scott Ferguson* (HSCP, supp. vol. 1940) 255-298; reprinted in Finley's *Three Essays on Thucydides* (Cambridge, Mass. 1967) 118-169.

4

construct logically the political and military realities of his time. For the first time we could begin to see Thucydides' mind operating on his material, shaping it for his own purposes and according to his own views. In the fifties there appeared two studies by Hermann Strasburger that refined this technique and exploited its possibilities as a means of fathoming Thucydides' own perspective on important issues.[4] The same scholar's *Die Wesensbestimmung der Geschichte durch die antike Geschichtsschreibung* is concerned, in part, with the same question of Thucydides' art.[5] Kitto's Sather Lectures, published the same year, come to similar conclusions about the artistic care with which Thucydides presents his material.[6]

These scholars and several others as well have studied sections of Thucydidean narrative in an attempt to understand how and why they were composed as they were.[7] It is the aim of this work to analyze the structure of Thucydides' *History* as a whole. While it is thus more ambitious in scope, the present study also takes a new approach to the problem of the structure of Thucydides' *History*. This method incorporates the following principles: that while Thucydides considered the Peloponnesian War to be one great war, he also saw it as comprising two distinct wars; that these two wars were almost identical in length; that they presented similar problems and similar opportunities to the combatants; that the combatants reacted to them in different, sometimes opposite ways. It is the contention of this study that this double vision, this constant comparison and contrast of the events in the two wars, is the principal thematic regulator of Thucydides' work, indeed that

[4] Hermann Strasburger, "Die Entdeckung der politischen Geschichte durch Thukydides," *Saeculum* 5 (1954) 395-428; also in *Thukydides. Wege der Forschung*, ed. H. Herter (Darmstadt 1968), pp. 412-476; hereafter cited as *Wege*, and "Thukydides und die politische Selbstdarstellung der Athener," *Hermes* 86 (1958) 17-40; in *Wege*, 498-530.

[5] Hermann Strasburger, *Die Wesensbestimmung der Geschichte durch die antike Geschichtsschreibung* (Wiesbaden 1966).

[6] H.D.F. Kitto, *Poiesis. Structure and Thought*, Sather Classical Lectures, vol. 36 (Berkeley 1966) 257-354.

[7] See especially H. Konishi, "Thucydides' Method in the Episodes of Pausanias and Themistocles," *AJP* 91 (1970) 52-69.

5

it controls to a very great extent the structure of Thucydides' *History*. In addition, it is responsible for much of the tragic irony in the work and shapes nearly every episode within it. It may not be an exaggeration to say that this double vision is the wellspring of Thucydides' *History*.

Several scholars have adumbrated this view of the structure of Thucydides' work. H.-P. Stahl in his justly-praised book *Thukydides Die Stellung des Menschen im Geschichtlichen Prozess* points out on several occasions Thucydides' tendency to identify "wiederkehrende Strukturmomente des Geschehens," and draws telling parallels between Books I and VI.[8] The same scholar draws similar analogies in his article "Speeches and Course of Events in Books Six and Seven of Thucydides." Stahl suggests a method of analysis similar to that used in the following chapters of this book, but admits that he "cannot carry out that proposed large-scale comparison here, because it lies beyond the scope of this paper."[9] Finally, V. Hunter in her book *Thucydides: The Artful Reporter* comes closest to the results obtained here by concentrating upon certain passages in Thucydides' narrative that prove to be paradigmatic for later episodes and thus serve to reveal Thucydides' compositional techniques more clearly than before. She presents in diagrammatic form the parallels she has discovered between Thucydides' treatment of the Archidamian War and his account of the Sicilian Expedition.[10] Several of her conclusions anticipate my own results, but, as will be seen in the following chapters, the analysis here will be rather different in both approach and scope.

THE WAR AND ITS COMPONENTS

Thucydides' view, explained in 5.26.2, that the Peloponnesian War was a single war of twenty-seven years' duration is well

---

[8] *Thukydides Die Stellung des Menschen im geschichtlichen Prozess* (Munich 1966).

[9] See "Speeches and Course of Events in Books Six and Seven of Thucydides," *The Speeches in Thucydides*, ed. by Philip A. Stadter (Chapel Hill 1973) 76-77.

[10] *Thucydides: The Artful Reporter* (Toronto 1973) 129-131, 145-148.

known. He argues that the peace that separated the Archidamian War from the Decelean War was a peace in name only
because neither side gave back or received what was promised,
because there were other violations on both sides, and because
some Greeks did not observe the peace at all. As Jacoby has
suggested, Thucydides probably wrote this argument in response to the appearance of the *Atthis* of Hellanicus, who
treated the Peloponnesian War as two distinct wars.[11] One
might add that this view allowed Thucydides to strengthen
his case that this war was the greatest and most destructive in
human memory. In 1.23, where he offers this opinion most
explicitly and with substantial argumentation, Thucydides
speaks of the great length of his war. In 5.26.3 he says that the
oracles' prediction that it would last twenty-seven years was
the only one in this war that was firmly substantiated. The
view that the Peloponnesian War was a single war of extraordinary length thus helped to establish the magnitude of Thucydides' subject. So much is true and has been generally recognized.

What has not been fully appreciated is another aspect of
Thucydides' view of the war. He saw it, and says so quite explicitly, as comprising two wars of almost identical length
with an unstable peace in the middle. Chapters 5.20 and 5.24-
26 substantiate this point and reveal an interesting and often
overlooked or disregarded fact about Thucydides' *History*.

In 5.20.1 Thucydides digresses after transcribing the text of
the peace between Athens and Sparta: "This peace was concluded when the winter was over, in the spring immediately
after the City Dionysia; ten years plus a few days had gone by
since the first invasion into Attica and the beginning of the
war." The historian pauses in 20.2 to mount his attack upon
Hellanicus' method of reckoning by archon-years, and then
resumes in section 3: "If one counts by summers and winters,
as this history has been composed, he will find, if each amounts
to half a year, that ten summers and an equal number of winters were contained in this first war." The phrase ὁ πρῶτος

---

[11] F. Jacoby, *Die Fragmente der Griechischen Historiken* (Berlin
and Leiden, 1923-1958), IIIb suppl. vol. 2, p. 16. n. 147.

πόλεμος recurs in 5.24.2 where Thucydides, after recording the text of the treaty made between Athens and Sparta, again sums up the Archidamian War: "This alliance was made not long after the peace, and the Athenians gave back the men from the island to the Lacedaemonians, and the summer of the eleventh year began." ταῦτα δὲ τὰ δέκα ἔτη ὁ πρῶτος πόλεμος ξυνεχῶς γενόμενος γέγραπται ("These ten years, the first war, occurring continuously, have been recorded."). So Thucydides concludes his account of what we call the Archidamian War.

At this point in his narrative Thucydides pauses to consider his subject in its entirety. Chapters 25 and 26 have been called the "second introduction" to Thucydides' history; they have also been used for the so-called composition question. Rather than concerning ourselves with when they were composed, let us examine what they say. First Thucydides refers again to the peace and alliance made between Athens and Sparta after the ten-year war. Then he mentions the Corinthians' and other Peloponnesians' anger against Sparta and the Athenians' growing suspicion of Sparta occasioned by her failure to carry out the terms of their agreements. "And for six years and ten months," continues Thucydides, "they held back from marching upon each other's land, but externally, during an insecure armistice, they harmed each other greatly. Then, however, forced to dissolve the peace made after ten years, they again went to war openly."

Chapter 26 begins: "the same Thucydides has written of these events consecutively, as each one happened, by summers and winters, until the Lacedaemonians and their allies ended the empire of the Athenians, and tore down the Long Walls and the Peiraeus. Altogether there were twenty-seven years of war until this end. And the peace in the middle [διὰ μέσου]. . . ." Section two contains the historian's arguments for viewing the war as one long conflict. In section 3 he again summarizes: "So that, with the first war of ten years' duration and the period after it of uneasy armistice and the later war after that, one will find so many years [27], reckoning by seasons, plus a few days."

We may draw together these statements into a simple form:

I Thucydides have written the history of a war that lasted almost exactly twenty-seven years. That war was composed of the following three elements: a first war of almost exactly ten years; a period of nominal peace in the middle lasting almost seven years; a second war (of almost exactly ten years). Those are the components of the Peloponnesian War as Thucydides himself viewed it.

There are clearly two conceptions of war involved in this view, the "overall war" and the "war(s) within the overall war." Thucydides makes this distinction by his use of the word ξυνεχῶς. On three separate occasions he refers to the first ten-year war as a "continuous war." In 2.1, his announcement of the beginning of the entire war, and also, of course, of the first ten-year war, he says: "The war of the Athenians and Peloponnesians and the allies of each begins from here, when they no longer visited one another without a herald, and starting the war they fought continuously." At the end of the first ten-year war he says, as we have already seen, "these ten years, the first war, occurring continuously, have been recorded" (5.24.2). And in 6.26.2, describing the condition of Athens after six years of "nominal peace," he says "the city had recently recovered from the plague and the continuous war." Thus the first ten-year war was characterized by continuous fighting. By implication, the period of six years and ten months after the ten-year war, which Thucydides calls "unstable" or "suspicious truce" (ἀνοκωχῆς οὐ βεβαίου in 5.25.3 and τῇ ὑπόπτῳ ἀνοκωχῇ in 5.26.3) was not one of continuous fighting, but rather one of sporadic, discontinuous warfare. Also, by implication, the second ten-year war must have been considered by Thucydides to be a continuous war, as indeed it was. In fact, he tells us that it was, if anything, more intense than the first. In 7.27.4 Thucydides contrasts the two ten-year wars:

> For before, the invasions [of Attica] were short and did not prevent them [the Athenians] from having the benefit of their land the rest of the time. But now the enemy was continuously [ξυνεχῶς] camped in Attica and sometimes he attacked in force, sometimes the regular garrison overran the

country and made forays for provisions, and the King of the Lacedaemonians, Agis, was in the field, prosecuting the war constantly. As a result, the Athenians were severely harmed.

Here Thucydides makes it clear that the second war was, if anything, "more continuous" than the first. There is little doubt, then, that the distinction he makes between the overall war and the wars within the overall war is one based upon intensity of fighting.

Thus Thucydides' war was not only precisely twenty-seven years long, but it consisted of two ten-year periods of intensive fighting that he calls the "first" and "second" continuous wars. The advantages of such a view are obvious. First, the length of the overall war, twenty-seven years almost to the day, is significant for two reasons. Oracles divulged at the beginning of the war and throughout its duration predicted that it would last thrice nine years (5.26.4). This was, Thucydides comments, the only oracular prediction "securely confirmed" by the facts. In addition, the number "thrice nine" has special significance for the Greeks. It was often used in prophetic messages or warnings. Indeed, one of the most famous of such cases occurs in the Peloponnesian War itself: when Nicias and the Athenians were finally on the point of leaving Sicily before disaster overtook them, an eclipse of the moon took place and the seers proclaimed that the army must wait "thrice nine days" before moving (7.50.4). In this interim the entire expedition was destroyed by the Syracusans and their allies. Thus a war of twenty-seven years' duration was not only immensely long, but it had what one scholar has called a "geradezu schicksalhaften Charakter."[12]

But if the number twenty-seven had strong overtones for a Greek, the number ten was more significant still: the most famous war in Greek history, compared to which all others paled into insignificance, had lasted ten years. That of course was Homer's war, the war that occupied the central position in Greek history, indeed, the event that was central to Greek

[12] O. Lendle, *Wege,* 674, n. 34.

consciousness. Wars in Greece were automatically measured against the Trojan War. As is well known, Thucydides went to a good deal of trouble to prove that his war was the greatest of all wars in Greek history, especially in terms of its length and the suffering it entailed (1.23.1). Part of his proof involved a careful analysis of early Greek history, which he found to be much less grand than the Greeks generally considered it to be. In particular, the Greek expedition to Troy, upon close inspection, turned out to be quite small, "considering that it was sent out from all of Greece in common" (1.10.5). Thucydides gives his reason for this assessment:

> The cause was not so much lack of manpower as lack of money. For from want of provisions they took a rather small force and only so great as they expected to be able to feed while fighting there; and when they arrived and won a battle, . . . they appear even then not to have used all their forces, but they turned to farming the Chersonese and to piracy from want of provisions. For which reason the Trojans held out by force of arms for ten years against the scattered Greeks, being always a match for those left behind. But if they had come with a supply of provisions and had all together carried on the war continuously [ξυνεχῶς] without farming and piracy, they would have taken it easily in a battle since even when they were not all together they held out with the part that was there at any given time, and they could have pressed a siege and taken Troy in a shorter time and with less trouble. (1.11.1-2)

Given what we know about Thucydides' division of his own war into two continuous ten-year wars, we can better appreciate the nature of his attack upon the received opinion of the Trojan War. It was not, argues Thucydides, a continuous ten-year war in the real sense. It was a more or less sporadic war that lasted ten years only because the Greeks could not use the total force they had brought with them. The result was that the fighting was not intense: the Greeks could not press their siege because of lack of money, nor could they crush the Trojans in a single battle or a couple of battles. Instead, the war dragged on for ten years amid pirate raids and seasonal crop planting and harvesting.

By contrast, Thucydides could argue, his war was not only twenty-seven years long, but it consisted of two periods of intense, continuous fighting each lasting ten years. It was the equivalent of two epic wars. Now if this appears to be a strange way of thinking, we need only look at the tendentious nature of Thucydides' remarks in order to see just how serious he was about this issue. He dismisses Herodotus' war with the following words: "Of the former *erga* the greatest was the Persian War, and this nevertheless had a swift issue in two sea battles and two land battles" (1.23.1). This is, of course, an absurd way in which to describe the significance of the Persian Wars, or even the suffering which they entailed. But it nonetheless reveals Thucydides' method of measuring war, that is, by its length and intensity. His attack upon Homer's war reveals the same concerns and the same bias: Thucydides deduced from what he knew in the epic poems about pirate raids a picture of a Greek force that spent a good deal of its time away from Troy. Thus, while admitting that Homer's war lasted ten years, he is able to argue that they were not a legitimate ten years because the fighting was not continuous and intense. We can see his tendentiousness too in his description of his own first ten-year war as a continuous struggle. The Archidamian War was not fought without interruption, but was broken by about eighteen months of truce, part of it badly kept, but most of it a genuine armistice (see 4.117-119, 5.14-17). It is, at best, exaggerated to claim that the first ten-year war was fought continuously, and yet Thucydides does so with great emphasis on two occasions, at its beginning and again at its conclusion. Furthermore, he calls his first war a "ten-year war" seven times in seven chapters of narrative: 5.20.1, 5.20.3, 5.24.2, 5.25.1, 5.25.3, 5.26.3, 5.26.6. Thus while he is unduly harsh in assessing the intensity of the two great Greek wars preceding the Peloponnesian War, he is quite lax in setting standards for judging the intensity of his own. This establishment of a double standard reveals clearly Thucydides' personal interest in the matter of the significance of his war vis-à-vis those of his two famous predecessors, Homer and Herodotus. It also reveals his interest in the length and intensity of wars and leads us to ask how it happens that Thucydides' war consisted of two continuous wars of almost precisely ten years' duration. Was this coincidence the result of chance or manipulation? When, exactly, did the two "wars within the war" begin, and when did they end?

The archai of the two ten-year wars

It is a peculiar fact that Thucydides' method of identifying the beginnings of wars has never been adequately explained.[13] When we try to discover just when the two ten-year wars in his *History* commence, we run headlong into two of the oldest and most perplexing problems in the text of Thucydides. One reason for these difficulties is, quite simply, that the problems have never been studied together. It has not occurred to anyone, so far as I can see, to examine the difficulties presented by chapters 2.1-2 and 5.25 simultaneously, to recognize, that is, that the two passages might best be treated together. The reason for this failure is also clear: no one has taken Thucydides' second war seriously, or rather, no one has even treated it as a separate war in and of itself. This is due in part to the fact that the narrative is unfinished, truncated, and in part to the fact that the brilliant dramatic unity of the Sicilian expedition has focused attention primarily upon Books VI and VII as an independent unit of narrative and thus obscured the integrity of the second ten-year war. It seems best to approach the problems raised by the beginnings of the two wars together. If this method proves to be useful in solving problems, then we have some confirmation that Thucydides consciously compared his two ten-year wars.

[13] For recent attempts see O. Lendle, "Die Auseinandersetzung des Thukydides mit Hellanikos," in *Wege*, 661-682, especially his bibliography.

We begin with the second war because the difficulties raised by its *arche* are clearer and simpler than those of the first. Let us take another, closer look at 5.25.

After the treaty and the alliance of the Lacedaemonians and the Athenians, which were concluded after the ten-year war in the ephorate of Pleistolas at Lacedaemon, and in the archonship of Alcaeus at Athens, there was peace for those who accepted the treaty, but the Corinthians and some of the cities in the Peloponnese began to disturb the agreements, and immediately *another* disorder of the allies against Lacedaemon occurred. And in addition, the Athenians became suspicious of the Lacedaemonians as time went on because in some cases they did not do what they said they would do in the agreements. For six years and ten months they held back from invading each other's territory, but outside [their territory] they did a great deal of harm to each other in an unstable truce. Then, however, forced to break the treaty made after the ten years, they *again* went into open war. (my italics)

The words "another" and "again" are italicized because they emphasize that Thucydides is thinking here of the second of two wars. This was the second time that a disorder had arisen in Sparta's alliance—the first was that of 432/431 when, also led by Corinth, Sparta's allies had come to her with complaints about Athenian aggression and thus instigated the first ten-year war.[14] Now, Thucydides says, the process began anew. It was eventually to lead to a second ten-year war, though this time it would take six years and ten months for open war to arise from the disorder. This period of six years and ten months is the heart of the problem to which we have referred: when did it start and when did it end? This apparently simple question has no simple answer. Rather, it has produced two different and equally problematic answers.

It would appear that the period should begin with the Peace of Nicias, which Thucydides had mentioned at the beginning

[14] See J. Classen, *Thukydides*, revised by J. Steup, 3rd ed. (Berlin 1892-1922) on 5.25.

of chapter 25 and which was the logical starting point for the interval between the two wars. If one counts six years and ten months from the beginning of spring, 421 (5.20.1), one arrives at midwinter 415/414. But during the entire winter neither side invaded the other's territory at all. The only event of importance was the Spartans' decision to "give their attention to the fortification of Decelea and for the time being to send some help to those in Sicily" (6.93.2). In fact, the invasion of Attica and the fortification of Decelea did not occur until the spring of 413, over a year later, and eight years after the signing of the Peace of Nicias. As a result, it seems incorrect to designate the spring of 421 as the *terminus a quo* for the period of six years and ten months.

A second solution has therefore been offered. W. Jerusalem noted that the first real incursion by Athens or Sparta into the other's territory was made in the summer of 414, an event described in 6.105:

> At the same time this summer both the Lacedaemonians and their allies invaded Argos and ravaged most of its territory, and the Athenians assisted the Argives with 30 ships. These ships most clearly broke the treaty which they had made with the Lacedaemonians. For before they had made piratical raids from Pylos and at other points in the Peloponnese rather than disembarking on Laconian territory, fighting together with the Argives and Mantineans, and though the Argives had often asked them to take whatever force they had and make a landing in Laconia and ravage at least *some* land with them before going back, they had not been willing. But now with Pythodorus and Laispodius and Demaratus as commanders they made landings in Limeran Epidaurus and Prasiae and ravaged the land, and did likewise wherever else they landed, and furnished the Lacedaemonians with an even better reason for retaliation against the Athenians than they had before.

Jersualem argued that this incursion into Laconian territory occurred about six years and ten months after the Lacedaemonian ephors began to try to disturb the treaty made with the

Athenians by conducting secret negotiations with the Boeotians and the Corinthians in the winter of 421/420.[15] Thucydides says that the summer before this had been for both sides a period of calm and free access to one another: τὸ μὲν . . . θέρος τοῦτο ἡσυχία ἦν καὶ ἔφοδοι παρ᾽ ἀλλήλους (5.35.8). Thus the period of uneasy or unstable and suspicious peace began only with the winter of 421/420. One can then argue that Thucydides' language in 5.25.2 suggests that some time went by after the peace of spring, 421 before the period of suspicion began: "And in addition, the Athenians became suspicious of the Lacedaemonians as time went on because in some cases they did not do what they said they would do in the agreements. And for six years and ten months they held back." According to this argument, then, one has two distinct periods: a period of real peace between the Peace of Nicias and the ephors' negotiations (spring, 421 to winter, 421/420; a period of unstable and suspicious peace from those negotiations to the Athenian landings in Laconia (winter, 421/420 to summer, 414). This latter period is approximately six years and ten months long and is thus the one meant by Thucydides in 5.25.2.

This solution has been approved by most scholars who have examined the problem, including Classen, Widmann, Steup, and Busolt.[16] Yet there are at least three major difficulties with it. First, Thucydides says quite specifically in 5.35.2 that "the Athenians and the Lacedaemonians began to be suspicious of one another immediately [εὐθύς] after the treaty because of the failure to give back territory to each other." According to this explicit statement the period of suspicion began in the spring of 421, not in the following winter. Note also εὐθύς and καὶ ἅμα in 5.25.1-2, both of which tie the suspicion directly to the time of the treaty. There is an apparent contradiction, it is true, between this statement and the one in 5.25.2 where Thucydides says that "the Athenians became suspicious of the Lacedaemonians as time went on because in some cases they

---

[15] *Wiener Studien* 3 (1881) 287-290.

[16] See A. W. Gomme, A. Andrewes, and K. J. Dover, *A Historical Commentary on Thucydides* (Oxford 1945-1970), on 5.25.3. Hereafter cited as *Comm.*

did not do what they said they would do in the agreements."
But the phrase προϊόντος τοῦ χρόνου does not mean "after
some time had gone by"; that would require an aorist parti-
ciple. It only implies that the Athenians grew more and more
suspicious of the Spartans "as time passed" (present). There is
thus no real contradiction between the two statements, only a
difference in point of view. It seems difficult, if not impossible,
to avoid the conclusion that Thucydides believed that the period of mutual suspicion began immediately after the signing
of the treaty in spring 421 and that Athenian suspicion of
Sparta grew more intense as time went by, becoming quite
serious after the winter of 421/420 when indeed there was good
reason for it. It would thus appear to be wrong to see two
distinct periods of time in Thucydides' conception, one of
"real peace" and one of "suspicious peace."

The second difficulty with Jerusalem's solution arises over
the actual dating of his two *termini*. The negotiations conducted by the ephors seem to have begun at the very beginning of
winter, 421/420, just after they had taken office (5.36.1). Six
years and ten months from that date should take us to the
autumn of 414, September at the earliest. But the Athenian
landings on the Laconian coast, though they are difficult to
date with any precision, seem to have taken place in the height
of summer, 414, not toward the end of that summer. In order
to put them as late as September, it takes a great deal of manipulation, not only of Thucydides' narrative but of independent evidence outside the text as well.[17] It appears, in short,
quite likely that the period from the ephors' negotiations to the
Athenian landings in Laconia is considerably shorter than six
years and ten months, and any attempt to put the date of the
"suspicious peace" earlier than those negotiations makes nonsense of Thucydides' attempt at precision in 5.25.

The third difficulty is most concisely and forcibly stated by
Andrewes: "The conclusion of the Peace of Nikias, in which
the parties swore not to bear arms against one another, is in-
trinsically the most likely *terminus a quo* for the six years and
10 months, and *the only one for which the reader has been in*

[17] Andrewes, *Comm.*, 7-8.

17

any way prepared" (my italics).[18] The last part of this statement is, to my mind, the most serious objection to Jerusalem's
interpretation. If we are to believe his argument, then we must
convict Thucydides of having employed the most misleading
kind of language imaginable in that very passage where he is
trying to be most precise and clear. Anyone reading 5.25 would
naturally think of the treaty as the starting point for the period
of six years and ten months. It was there that Thucydides had
temporarily stopped his narrative in 5.24 to digress on what he
had just completed and what he was about to embark upon in
the remainder of his work. The peace treaty and alliance were
the *terminus ante quem* for the first ten-year war and thus the
logical *terminus a quo* for the period following that war.
Unless he explicitly designated another *terminus a quo* for that
period, and that he certainly does not do, Thucydides could
hardly expect the reader not to take the peace as his starting
point. Finally, when in 5.26.3 Thucydides explicitly divides his
entire twenty-seven year war into three segments, the first ten-
year war, the suspicious truce after it and the later war after the
truce, he is without question thinking of three intervals of
time and not four.

There are thus serious objections to both identifications of
the *termini* of the period of six years and ten months. We are
left with a dilemma so perplexing that some have been led to
cut the knot and emend the figures. Before turning to this
solution, we should examine Thucydides' starting point for the
first ten-year war in order to see what light, if any, it might
shed upon this question. This approach has the advantage, at
least, of adducing evidence that has never before been used in
attempting to solve the problem of the *arche* of the second war.

Discussion of the *arche* of the first ten-year war (and of the
Peloponnesian War taken as a whole) generally begins with an
examination of the first two chapters of Book II, Thucydides' formal announcement of its commencement.

Here begins the war of the Athenians and Peloponnesians
and the allies of each, in which they no longer continued to

---

[18] Ibid., 8.

visit each other without heralds and, having started the war they fought continuously. It has been composed successively, as each event occurred, by summers and winters.[19]

For the thirty years' treaty made after the capture of Euboea lasted fourteen years. In the fifteenth year, in the forty-eighth year of the priesthood of Chrysis at Argos and in the ephorate of Aenesius at Sparta and in the archonship of Pythodorus at Athens, which had still two months to run, in the sixth month after the battle in Potidaea, at the beginning of spring a little more than 300 Thebans . . . came at the first watch with arms into Plataea, a Boeotian ally of the Athenians.

This formal and detailed statement seems to leave no doubt that, for Thucydides, the Theban attack upon Plataea marks the beginning of the war between the Athenians and the Peloponnesians. The phrase ἐνθένδε ἤδη in 2.1 anticipates the event reported with such precision in 2.2. The war begins with this specific event. Though this interpretation has been accepted by all commentators on Thucydides, it can hardly be correct. Just as we found in the case of Thucydides' *arche* of the second ten-year war, so here we encounter major, perhaps insurmountable objections to the *communis opinio*.

First there is Thucydides' remark in 5.20.1: "This treaty was made as the winter was ending and spring came on, immediately after the City Dionysia; ten years and a few days had passed since the first invasion of Attica and the *arche* of this war." This assertion raises two problems: Thucydides had said in 2.1 that the Theban entrance into Plataea occurred "at the beginning of spring." The treaty was concluded "as the winter was ending and spring came on." The most plausible interpretation of this expression is that it took a few days to conduct the discussions leading to the treaty; during this period winter turned into spring.[20] But in that case Thucydides should have said that his first war lasted a little less than ten years. It is, of

---

[19] One should accept the reading found in Π[8], θέρη καὶ χειμῶνας; see 5.20.3 and 26.1.

[20] See Gomme, *Comm.* on 5.20.

course, easy to say, with Gomme, that Thucydides might have in mind here that the treaty did not actually take effect until after the negotiations were over, a few days after spring had begun. But Thucydides does not say this and we must remember that he is, at least apparently, trying to be as accurate as possible here. He tells us in 5.20.3 and again in 5.26.3 that he calculates periods of time by seasons. Why then would he say that it was ten years plus a few days from the beginning of spring, 431 to the end of winter, 421? If we are content, as most scholars appear to be, with the assumption that Thucydides really meant in 5.20.1 that the treaty was finally concluded and took effect a few days after the spring of 421 began, then we must be prepared to argue that Thucydides expressed himself quite imprecisely in the very passage in which he is attempting to obtain great precision.

A far greater problem arises from the second part of 5.20.1, and that is, of course, the expression ἡ ἐσβολὴ ἡ ἐς τὴν Ἀττικήν. The first invasion of Attica took place at the height of summer, 431, "on about the eightieth day after the action in Plataea" (2.19.1). Thus not only does 5.20.1 conflict with 2.2 on the first event of the war, but it cannot be ten years plus a few days from the invasion of Attica to the peace named after Nicias. Since Thucydides seems to say quite explicitly and formally in 2.1-2 that Plataea is the beginning of the war, and since it is (almost) ten years plus a few days from Plataea to the Peace of Nicias, most scholars accept E.H.O. Müller's excision (*de tempore quo bellum Peloponnesiacum initium ceperit*, Marburg Dissertation 1852) of the words ἡ ἐσβολὴ ἡ ἐς τὴν Ἀττικὴν καί from 5.20.1. It appears that the beginning of the war can have nothing to do with the first invasion of Attica, and so the offending words must be removed. "But," as Gomme says, "it is not an easy correction, both because the offending words do not look like a later supplement or comment, and because in themselves, that is, apart from the difficulty of the date, they would suit the description of the invasion in ii.19.1."[21] For the time being, we might only second Gomme's objection: how can one account for this intrusive gloss?

---

[21] *Comm.* on 5.20.1.

So much for the problems raised by 5.20. But there are problems in 2.1-2 as well. Steup in his little-read *Thukydideische Studien* pointed out that the connection between these two chapters is not so strong as Classen and others believed. In particular, Steup does not accept the argument that ἐνθένδε in 2.1 refers to the Theban entrance into Plataea, described in 2.2: "Gegen diese Auffassung des Eingangs des zweiten Buches spricht aber entschieden die weite Entfernung der Worte τέσσαρα μὲν γὰρ κτλ. von ἐνθένδε und ferner der Umstand, dass Thukydides sich auch in dem mit jenen Worten beginnenden Satze noch keineswegs beeilt, das Ereigniss, welches nach der gewöhnlichen Annahme durch ἐνθένδε angedeutet wird, zu erwähnen."[22] This objection to the *communis opinio* is not decisive but it is at least worth noting. If Thucydides had meant the Plataean affair when he said "the war begins from here," one would have expected him to make his point clearer. Steup went on to contend, following a suggestion of Ullrich, that the first sentence of Book II is in fact an announcement by Thucydides that he begins here his description of the war proper, or, as Ullrich puts it: "Diese Stelle gehört zu den wenigen, in welchen sich Thukydides über sein eigenes Werk äussert, und ist der endlich anhebenden Darstellung des Krieges selbst gewissermassen als Aufschrift vorausgestellt."[23] The first sentence thus serves as a title of the *History* that follows. Ἄρχεται is taken as a real present rather than as an historical present and the sentence is read in close combination with the following words: "It has been composed successively, by summers and winters, as each event occurred." On this interpretation, ἐνθένδε does not refer to the following historical beginning

[22] "Against this interpretation of the beginning of the second book, however, speaks decisively the wide distance between the words τέσσαρα μὲν γὰρ κτλ. and ἐνθένδε, and furthermore, the fact that Thucydides is in no hurry in the sentence beginning with those words to mention the event which is, according to the usual assumption, implied by ἐνθένδε." J. Steup, *Thukydideische Studien* (Freiburg 1886) 61.

[23] F. W. Ullrich, *Beiträge zur Erklärung des Thukydides* (Hamburg 1846) 65. "This passage belongs to the few in which Thucydides speaks about his own work, and is placed, almost as an introduction, before the (at long last reached) presentation of the war itself."

of the war but to Thucydides' historiographical beginning, the commencement of his description of the actual war. Though Steup does not say so explicitly, he appears to take the Plataean affair as the historical beginning of the war; he simply believes that it is not referred to in 2.1.

Albert Dammann a few years later accepted and supported the first part of Steup's argument but drew quite a different conclusion from it.[24] Dammann believed that Ullrich and Steup were correct in holding that 2.1 does not refer to Plataea but to Thucydides' own description of the war. But he then went on to argue that the real beginning of the war for Thucydides was the Peloponnesian invasion of Attica in summer, 431, and not the Theban attack upon Plataea. He thus accepts the phrase ἡ ἐσβολὴ ἡ ἐς τὴν Ἀττικήν in 5.20.1 as genuine and as a clear indication that Thucydides considered the invasion of Attica as the first act, the *arche*, of the war. Dammann has not found many followers, which is not surprising given the fact that his interpretation makes nonsense of Thucydides' explicit statement that the first war lasted exactly ten years plus a few days. Such a claim is completely at odds with a view that the war began in mid-summer, 431. On this point Dammann did not even see fit to comment! And yet, it completely negates his argument.

It thus seems impossible to accept Dammann's extension of Ullrich's argument, and Ullrich's point itself seems to be of little value: we are left with the problem of taking the Theban attack upon Plataea as Thucydides' *arche*, and Ἄρχεται δὲ ὁ πόλεμος ἐνθένδε ἤδη is, in any view, a strange way in which to say "I begin here my account of the war." We should not, however, dismiss Steup's criticism of the *communis opinio* so lightly. It is quite correct to point out that Thucydides is in no hurry to get from ἐνθένδε ἤδη to the Plataean *erga*, to object, in other words, to the assumption that "from here" in 2.1 necessarily refers to the events described in the following paragraph.

[24] A. Dammann, "Der Anfang des peloponnesischen Krieges," *Philologus* 58 (1899) 132-147.

These observations should awaken our suspicions about the generally held view of Thucydides' *arche* of the Peloponnesian War. The most telling objection to it was raised almost a century ago, ironically enough, by a scholar who nonetheless believes in the traditional opinion. In an article published in 1883, H. Müller-Strübing argued that at best Thucydides was grossly inconsistent, and at worst dishonest, in determining the *arche* of his war.[25] This was because he had decisively denied that the actions taken at Sybota and Potidaea constituted the beginning of the Peloponnesian War on the grounds that those events did not involve Sparta and the Peloponnesian League. In both cases Thucydides makes it quite clear that Athenians and Corinthians fought with one another: in 1.49.7 he says, speaking of the Battle of Sybota, "it came to the point of *ananke* that the Corinthians and Athenians attacked each other"; in 1.66 he summarizes the consequences of the Potidaean affair: "These were the charges of the Athenians and Peloponnesians against one another: the Corinthians accused the Athenians of besieging Potidaea, a colony of theirs which had Corinthian and Peloponnesian men in it; the Athenians accused the Peloponnesians of causing a city allied and indeed subject to themselves to revolt from them, and of having come and openly fought against themselves." And yet, after these events, Thucydides states unequivocally that "war, however, did not yet break out, but there was still truce; for the Corinthians did these things in private." The use of three particles with the verb ξυνερρώγει indicates Thucydides' vehemence: these events cannot be considered war, because they are private Corinthian ventures, undertaken, he implies, without consultation with Sparta. Furthermore, Thucydides in 1.146 terms these actions "charges and disagreements" before the war, and again "a breach of the peace and a *prophasis* of war," but not war itself. But does not this argument apply *a fortiori* in the case of the secret Theban invasion of Plataea? At Sybota and

[25] H. Müller-Strübing, "Das erste Jahr des peloponnesischen Krieges. Ein Beitrag zur Chronologie des Thukydides," *Jahrbücher für classische Philologie* 127 (1883) 577-612, 657-713.

23

Potidaea Peloponnesians and Athenians fought one another; at Plataea neither Peloponnesians nor Athenians even took part.

And yet, points out Müller-Strübing, Thucydides must have chosen this event as the beginning of the war for some reason. "Ich will es nur gerade heraussagen: das ist willkürlich, ist unhistorisch. . . . die grunde, weshalb er das gethan hat, müssen also rein subjectiver natür gewesen sein und entziehen sich daher eigentlich unserer kenntnis, wir sind aufs raten angewiesen, auf vermutungen, und so vermute ich denn dasz es ihm zunächst darum zu thun war, für die dauer seines krieges eine runde, ich möchte sagen eine epische zahl zu erhalten, und die zehn jahre waren ja durch den troischen krieg für die epopöe gleichsam geheiligt. kurzere zeit als der troische krieg dürfte aber sein krieg doch nicht dauern!"[26] Thucydides chose the Theban attack on Plataea as the *arche* of his war for a purely arbitrary reason: so that his war would attain an epic length. In order to arrive at this length he disregarded his own criteria for determining what constitutes a war. He also, according to Müller-Strübing, chose not to accept as his *arche* a far more appropriate and significant event: the Athenian rejection of the demands of the last Spartan embassy. Müller-Strübing asks, "Warum nicht schon von da ab, als bei der letzten gesandtschaft der Lakedaimonier Ramphias dem athenischen volk die fast brutale alternative stellte: die Lakedaimonier wunschen die erhaltung des friedens; er kann erhalten werden, wenn ihr die Hellenen als autonom entlaszt, dh. wenn ihr das athenische reich auflöst (I 139). als dann die Athener diese forderung ablehnten, da könnte man allenfalls sagen, staatsrechtlich sei dadurch der kriegszustand eingetre-

---

[26] Ibid., 669. "I must state it frankly: it is arbitrary, unhistorical. . . . The grounds on which he did so must, then, have been of a purely subjective nature and are, therefore, properly speaking, removed from our knowledge. We are reduced to guesses, to conjectures, and so I conjecture that it was, for Thucydides, primarily a matter of acquiring a round number for the length of his war; I should say an epic number, and ten years had been, as it were, sanctified for epic by the Trojan War. His war should not, however, be of any shorter duration than the Trojan War!"

ten, der krieg habe also angefangen, wenn auch keine un-
mittelbaren thatlichkeiten eintraten."[27] Müller-Strübing's careful analysis of the events leading to the Peloponnesian War
led him to the conclusions that Thucydides passed over the
logically most plausible *arche* of the war and that he selected
instead a most inappropriate *arche* for a purely subjective
reason, namely, in order to obtain an epic length for his first
war. Such a charge represents a serious attack upon Thucydides' historiographical honesty; if it can be maintained, and,
so far as I can see, it has never been refuted, it detracts from
our confidence in Thucydides' intellectual integrity. As
Schmid, who could not refute it, complained, "entschliesst man
sich schwer, dem Thukydides solche Zahlenspielerei zuzu-
trauen."[28]

The answer to the problem of Thucydides' *arche* for the first
war can only come from reading 2.1-2 in its full context, that
is, from reading it as the continuation of 1.145-146, the way in
which it was in fact written. Scholars treating this question
have, almost without exception, failed to perform this simple
task. They have been misled by an Alexandrian scholar's edit-
ing of Thucydides' work into reading the first sentences of
Book II as though Thucydides wrote them separately from
Book I, as a new section of his work. And yet we know perfectly well that he did no such thing. Thucydides did not di-
vide his work into books or even into paragraphs. The sentence beginning Ἄρχεται δέ, our Book II, chapter 1, followed
directly upon σπονδῶν γὰρ ξύγκυσις τὰ γιγνόμενα ἦν καὶ
πρόφασις τοῦ πολεμεῖν ("the events were a dissolution of the

<hr>

[27] Ibid., 665-666. "Why not begin immediately from the point when,
in the last embassy of the Lacedaemonians, Ramphias delivered to the
Athenian people the almost brutal choice: the Lacedaemonians desire
the keeping of the peace; it can be kept if you leave the Greeks autonomous, that is, if you dissolve the Athenian Empire (1.139). When
at that point the Athenians rejected this demand, then one could perhaps say, in diplomatic terms, a state of war had thereby been entered,
war had therefore begun, even if no immediate acts of violence occurred."

[28] W. Schmid, *Geschichte der griechischen Literatur* (München
1948) 5:72, n. 7. "One hesitates to attribute such playing with numbers to Thucydides."

treaty and an occasion for war"), the last sentence of our Book I. The particle δέ in 2.1 furnishes us with the most important clue that the text of Thucydides affords for the solution of our problem. It tells us, in short, to look backwards for the meaning of Ἄρχεται δὲ ὁ πόλεμος ἐνθένδε ἤδη rather than forwards.

If we are properly to understand Thucydides' concept of war, we need to examine his account from 1.139, where he resumes his narrative of the events of 432/431 after his digression on the curses which the Lacedaemonians and Athenians asked each other to drive out. He tells us that the Lacedaemonians later sent embassies (φοιτῶντες) to the Athenians requiring them to raise the siege of Potidaea and to leave Aegina independent, and, above all, to revoke the Megarian Decree. The Athenians acceded to none of these demands, so "finally the last ambassadors came from Lacedaemon, Ramphias and Melesippus and Agesandrus, and made none of their previous, customary demands, but only this: 'the Lacedaemonians want the peace to exist and it would if you would leave the Greeks independent.' The Athenians held an assembly and consulted among themselves, and resolved to deliberate and to give an answer once and for all." This was the last embassy the Spartans sent to Athens; it delivered an ultimatum to the Athenians to give up their empire or face war. The Athenians recognized that they must now deliver their final answer on the issue of war and peace. There is a very strong suggestion in 1.139.3 that both sides knew that after this there would be no more demands, indeed, no more embassies. Both sides were making their final decisions. Thucydides tells us that many Athenians spoke in this assembly, but he gives us only one speech, that of Pericles. The reason for this decision becomes clear when we read Thucydides' remarks following the speech in chapter 145: "Pericles said such things, and the Athenians, thinking that he advised them best, voted for what he requested and answered the Lacedaemonians on his advice, both generally and on specific points." Pericles' advice, of course, was that "we must recognize that it is necessary to go to war" (1.144.3). His advice, to "do nothing, but to say that they were ready to settle the disputes on an equal and fair basis by *dike*, as the treaty said they should be settled," sounds harmless enough, but in the light of the Spartan ultimatum, it amounted to a declaration of war.

The next sentence assures us that the Spartans accepted it as such: "And they went back home and they no longer continued to send embassies." Why did the Lacedaemonians stop sending embassies? Because the Spartans knew that this was the Athenians' final answer to their final question. There was no more need for negotiations. Let us now read what Thucydides says next: "These were the charges and disputes between the two sides before the war, arising immediately from the events in Epidamnus and Corcyra. Nevertheless, during this period [ἐν αὐταῖς] they continued to visit each other and they sent embassies to each other without heralds, but not without suspicion. For the events that had occurred [in Epidamnus and Potidaea] were a breach of the peace and a *prophasis* of the war." Here Thucydides' major point is that the period of charges and disputes was a precursor of war but not war itself, because the Athenians and Spartans had sent embassies to each other without heralds. Immediately following this sentence, Thucydides wrote: "The war begins from this point, at which they no longer continued to visit each other without heralds and, having started hostilities, they fought continuously." Read together with 1.145 and 1.146, 2.1 completes Thucydides' discussion of the distinction between war and nonwar. This distinction depends upon a single criterion: the use of heralds with embassies. For Thucydides, war begins when the last Spartan embassy returns home; from this point on, Athens and Sparta will no longer visit one another without heralds.

The parallelism between the first sentence of our Book II and the last sentences of Book I is extremely close. When the Spartan ambassadors reached home the Spartans ceased sending embassies "any longer" (οὐκέτι); when they "no longer" (οὔτε . . . ἔτι) continued to send embassies to each other, the war began. These two sentences frame two sentences that describe the period before the war (1.146). This period, which

Thucydides calls the "charges and disputes" before the war, was one of great suspicion, but cannot be termed war by Thucydides' definition, since embassies needed no heralds.[29] The phrase ἐν αὐταῖς in 1.146 contrasts with the phrase ἐν ᾧ in 2.1; the clause, ἐπεμείγνυντο . . . καὶ παρ' ἀλλήλους ἐφοίτων ἀκηρύκτως in 1.146 contrasts with the clause οὔτε ἐπεμείγνυντο ἔτι ἀκηρυκτεί in 2.1.

That Thucydides considered the use of embassies crucial to the distinction between conditions of peace and conditions of war can be seen also from two passages describing the period immediately following the Peace of Nicias. In 5.35.2 Thucydides says that "during this entire summer there were ἐπιμειξίαι between the Athenians and the Peloponnesians." This is the same word he had used in 1.146 and in 2.1 to define war and peace. It is used in all three passages in a semitechnical sense.[30] Thucydides emphasizes his point later in the same chapter (5.35.8): "during this entire summer, then, there was ἡσυχία and ἔφοδοι to each other."

The parallels between 1.146 and 5.35 are close: just as in 433-431 there were embassies without heralds, but no lack of suspicion (ἀνυπόπτως δὲ οὔ), so in summer, 421, there were diplomatic visits together with suspicion (ὑπώπτευον δὲ ἀλλή-

[29] Ulrich von Wilamowitz-Moellendorf, Kleine Schriften (Berlin 1969) 3:96-98, argues that 1.146 is not Thucydidean, but rather an insertion by his "editor." This argument is unconvincing and has not been generally accepted. Even if true, it would only serve to confirm our case that the δέ in 2.1 is correlative with the μέν in 1.145.

[30] See 5.78, where ἐπιμειξία is clearly used in this technical sense. In 5.76.3 Thucydides tells us that Lichas, proxenus of Argos, came from Lacedaemon bringing two logoi, war or peace. The Argives decided to receive the proposal for peace (τὸν ξυμβατήριον λόγον). After this (5.77) a peace was established between the Argives and Lacedaemonians. Then, when ἐπιμειξία was reestablished, an alliance was made between the two parties (5.79). Clearly, diplomatic relations were made between Argos and Sparta by virtue of the peace. See also Herodotus 1.68.1 for this "technical" sense of ἐπιμειξία, and, for a telling appraisal of the conditions of interpolis warfare, see Plato, Laws I 626A. Note especially the phrase "herald-less war," an indication that "formally announced" wars were generally conducted with heralds.

28

λους εὐθύς in 5.35.2). These were periods of unstable peace, but peace nonetheless, at least in Thucydides' technical sense. To have war one must have a break in normal diplomatic relations, a situation described in 2.1.

The phrase ἐνθένδε ἤδη requires further discussion. The adverb ἤδη has in Greek the same effect upon another adverb as *demum* in Latin. *Demum* frequently means "finally" or "at last," as in the expression *tum demum*. The phrase τοτ' ἤδη is a close equivalent of *tum demum*. Correspondingly, ἐνταῦθ' ἤδη can mean "da vollends oder: dann erst, tum demum."[31] Ἐνθένδε ἤδη in 2.1 should be translated "then finally" or "then and only then." Thucydides' intent is to create a strong contrast between the two periods described in 1.146 and 2.1. His train of thought is: "the Spartans returned home and ceased to send embassies. Thus ends the period of charges and disputes before the war. During this period there was serious hostility on both sides, and even a breach of the treaty. War was imminent. But the war, properly speaking, begins then and only then, when they no longer visited one another without heralds." Thucydides' emphasis upon this definition leaves little doubt that he is arguing against another point of view. We are fortunate enough to know what that view was: popular opinion believed that the Peloponnesian War began with the Epidamnian and Potidaean affairs. We learn this from Aristophanes' *Peace*, lines 987-990, where the war which ended in 421 is called the thirteen-year war, and from the passage in Andocides (3.3; see Aeschines 2.172), where the Peace of 446/445 is said to have lasted thirteen years. It was natural to consider τὰ Κερκυραϊκὰ καὶ τὰ Ποτειδεατικά ("the events at Corcyra and Potidaea") the first events of the war, given the fact that Athenians and Corinthians had fought against one another in both of those conflicts. Thucydides corrects this common misconception with his careful distinction in 1.146-2.1 between *aitiai* and *diaphorai* before the war on the one hand

---

[31] R. Kühner-B. Gerth, *Ausführliche Grammatik der Griechischen Sprache* (Hannover 1904) 2:121. Kühner-Gerth cites Thucydides 4.35 as an example.

and the war properly speaking on the other. The phrase ἐνθένδε ἤδη accentuates this distinction: "the war begins from this point only, in which. . . ."

The phrase "in which" (ἐν ᾧ) is ambiguous. Does it mean "in which war," "in which time," or what? What is its precise function? One scholiast glosses with πολέμῳ or war. Another, who clearly finds it a typical example of Thucydides' use of "substitute" prepositions believes that the phrase ἐν ᾧ is used ἀντὶ τοῦ ἐξ οὗ καὶ ἀφ᾽ οὗ, "in place of 'out of which' and 'from which.' "[32] The latter is probably correct. "The war begins from this point and this point only, from which they no longer continued to send embassies without heralds." Thucydides wrote ἐν ᾧ in place of ἀφ᾽ οὗ because he wanted to make a clear distinction between the periods of time described in 1.146 and 2.1. For the former he wrote ἐν αὐταῖς, for the latter, ἐν ᾧ. The phrase probably stands for ἐν ᾧ χρόνῳ, as is often the case in Thucydides, and thus defines ἐνθένδε ἤδη, not ὁ πόλεμος: "The war begins from this point and this point only, from which they no longer continued to meet with one another without heralds, and, after they had started hostilities, they fought continuously." The words καταστάντες τε ξυνεχῶς ἐπολέμουν ("and having started hostilities they fought continuously") should be separated temporally from the first part of the relative clause in 2.1. L. Herbst first recognized that the sentence must be read in this way: "Mit dem zweiten relativsatz und καταστάντες bezeichnet er den eigentlichen thatsachlichen beginn des krieges, den einfall der Peloponnesier in Attika, mit dem ersten relativsatz, ἐν ᾧ οὔτε ἐπεμίγνυντο, die zeit, die diesem einfall noch vorausgegangen ist."[33] Though we need not agree with Herbst when he goes on to identify the point at which they no longer met with one another as the day on which the Thebans attacked Plataea, we should accept

[32] For substitute prepositions see D. Mulroy, "Substitution Scholia and Thucydides' Use of Prepositions," *TAPA* 102 (1971) 357-410.

[33] L. Herbst, *Philologus* 38 (1879) 507-508. "With the second relative clause and καταστάντες he designates the actual beginning of the war, the invasion by the Peloponnesians of Attica, with the first relative clause, ἐν ᾧ οὔτε ἐπεμίγνυντο, the time which preceded this invasion."

his principal argument that the ending of normal diplomatic relations and the "thatsachlichen beginn des krieges" were not simultaneous events. As we shall see, Thucydides' normal phrase for go to war, or begin actual military hostilities is καθιστάναι ἐς τὸν πόλεμον.[34] It is this meaning that καταστάντες has here in 2.1. There was in any interpretation a period of time between the diplomatic and the actual military beginning of the war. We need now, in fact, to turn our attention to the period following the diplomatic *arche* of the war and to the language Thucydides uses to describe it.

It may be argued that γάρ[35] in 2.2 links that sentence closely to 2.1 and thus requires us to take the attack upon Plataea as the event referred to in the phrase ἐνθένδε ἤδη. But it is standard for Thucydides, after announcing his intention to describe an historical period, to begin the following sentence with γάρ. Here, after his prescriptive remark, "my account of the war has been composed successively, as each thing happened, by summers and winters," γάρ follows quite naturally.[36] Thucydides begins the narrative of the event ending the thirty years' peace (2.7.1). This act is very precisely dated by six systems of chronology. These two facts—first, that Thucydides explicitly says that this act clearly broke the treaty, and second, that Thucydides goes to great trouble to date this act as accurately as possible—have also contributed to the belief that the Plataean affair is Thucydides' *arche* of the war. But the first point is of little value. Thucydides was aware that each side claimed on several occasions during the period of *aitiai* and *diaphorai* that the other had broken the treaty. The Corinthians accuse the Athenians of violating the treaty after Sybota (1.53.2); both sides make such charges after Potidaea (1.66-67); the Lacedaemonians agree in a vote that the Athenians have broken the treaty (1.87.2, 88; 118.3). Yet, despite these accusations and formal charges, war did not break out, at least according to Thucydides' interpretation. The violation of a treaty does not

[34] See 1.125, 2.13.9, 5.25.3.

[35] The particle is absent or differently placed in some manuscripts, but was almost certainly written by Thucydides.

[36] See the examples cited by Classen-Steup, *Thukydides*, on 2.2.

necessarily imply that war has begun. In and of itself, it has no such meaning. It becomes important only if one or both parties decides that it is important and chooses to treat it as a *casus belli*. The Theban attack upon Plataea was different from the other violations of the treaty only because it was a blatant act: there could be no doubt that it broke the treaty. But, in Thucydides' terms, war had already begun before this act.

As for Thucydides' careful dating of this attack, the reasons for this precision are not difficult to ascertain. It was an event that could be dated with great accuracy because it occurred on a single night, dramatically and suddenly. It was the first great *ergon* of the war. But what of the diplomatic *arche* of the war? How should one date that? From the assembly at Athens? From the return of the Lacedaemonian ambassadors to Sparta? It was difficult, and indeed profitless, to try to pin down to a particular day the point from which they no longer continued to visit one another without heralds. The result is that Thucydides chose to date precisely the first real act of the war rather than the formal *arche* of the war. Such an historiographical decision added a dramatic quality to the narrative of the beginning of the war.

Many scholars have noted that even after Plataea Thucydides continues to write of the war as if it is still in the future. In 2.7.1 he says that the Athenians and Peloponnesians made preparations to go to war (παρεσκευάζοντο ὡς πολεμήσοντες), in chapters 8-10 he describes those preparations, in 12 he describes Archidamus' last attempt to convince the Athenians to give in before suffering an invasion of Attica, and in 13-17 he describes in great detail the Athenians' elaborate resources and defenses. It is not until chapter 19 that he narrates the "formal invasion" of Attica: "then, starting from Oenoe, on about the eightieth day after the events in Plataea, at the height of summer and of the crop, they invaded Attica. Archidamos, son of Zeuxidamos, King of the Lacedaemonians, led them." Some have concluded from these facts that the war, according to Thucydides, did not actually begin until this invasion. Others have argued that Thucydides originally intended this invasion

32

to be the beginning of his war, but that he later changed his mind and moved the beginning to the Theban attack upon Plataea. According to this latter view, Thucydides added 2.1 and parts of 2.2 to an already completed narrative and then failed to remove the statements in the following chapters that reflected his former view.[37] This interpretation has little to recommend it, especially now that we recognize that Thucydides' *arche* of the war is a diplomatic *arche*, not a military one. There is no contradiction in saying, after a war has begun formally and diplomatically, that the two sides now prepared to go to war militarily. Indeed, this is a perfectly natural means of expression. There is no need to construct elaborate theories to account for "two points of view" here, no need to seek clues in the text for Thucydides' reworking of his narrative. We should instead carefully note his terminology. In 1.125 Thucydides says that at the end of the Peloponnesian conference at Sparta the majority of the allies voted to go to war:

> But they decided that it was impossible for them to begin immediately since they were unprepared, but it seemed best for each to assemble what was appropriate and to have no delay. Even so, nearly a year went by while they collected what was necessary, before they invaded Attica and started the war openly. In this time they sent embassies to the Athenians to make complaints, in order that they might have as great a pretext as possible for going to war if they should not give in to their demands.

We may derive several specific pieces of information from this passage. Thucydides did not choose this Peloponnesian decision to go to war as his *arche* of the war because it was a contingent decision. If the Athenians bowed to Peloponnesian demands, there would be no war. If they did not, there would be. We have seen that the Athenians gave their final answer to the Spartan ambassadors Ramphias, Melesippus, and Agesandrus and that the Spartans took that as a final refusal to give in to Peloponnesian demands. Only then, according to

---

[37] See O. Lendle, "Die Auseinandersetzung des Thukydides mit Hellanikos," in *Wege*, 661-682.

Thucydides, when the last diplomatic negotiations had been carried out, did the war begin. Note also what Thucydides says in 125.2 about the Peloponnesian invasion of Attica: it was the act that started the war "openly" (φανερῶς). It was, in other words, the first military confrontation between Peloponnesians and Athenians. It was not the formal *arche* of the war, but rather the visible or manifest *arche* of the war. It is in all probability the event referred to in 2.1 in the expression "and *having started hostilities* they fought continuously" (κατα-στάντες τε ξυνεχῶς ἐπολέμουν; my italics). It was the beginning of open hostilities between the Athenians and the Peloponnesians.

We might now summarize the results of our analysis of the *arche* of the first ten-year war. Thucydides defines four distinct events or sets of events in his discussion of the beginning of this war: (1) the aitiai and diaphorai (also called ξύγκυσις σπονδῶν and πρόφασις τοῦ πολεμεῖν), the period of suspicion and hostility during which, however, the two sides carried on diplomatic relations without heralds; (2) the *arche* of the war, that is, the "diplomatic beginning" of the war, the point at which the two sides ceased to carry on diplomatic relations without heralds;[38] (3) the clear breaking of the treaty; (4) the start of hostilities, the manifest or open beginning of the war.

This interpretation of Thucydides' causal analysis has a number of advantages over the old view. First, the minor problem occasioned by the phrase "ten years plus a few days" in 5.20.1 is eliminated. We do not know precisely when Ramphias, Melesippus and Agesandrus returned to Sparta. But we do know they did so before the Thebans invaded Plataea, and

---

[38] For a decision to go to war considered as the *arche* of that war see Polybius 4.13.6 and 4.26.1. Generally in Polybius the *arche* is the first act of the war, not the decision to go to war. Indeed, in 3.6.7 Polybius explicitly says that "By the *arche* of anything I mean the first attempt to execute and put into action plans on which one has decided." But here in Book IV we have a different case. See P. Pédech, *La méthode historique de Polybe* (Paris 1964) 165: "Il a plutôt voulu solenniser l'entrée en guerre en lui donnant le caractère d'une croisade désidée en commun par les Grecs." This is a possible reason why Polybius here varies his normal practice and calls the decision to go to war the *arche*.

that is all we need to know. It is possible to describe the period between the return of the ambassadors and the conclusion of peace as "ten years plus a few days." Such was not the case with the interval between the Theban attack upon Plataea and the Peace of Nicias.

More significantly, we can answer the major criticism made of Thucydides' causal scheme by Müller-Strübing, who argued that the historian was guilty of inconsistency if not dishonesty in choosing Plataea as his *arche*. It is now clear that Thucydides had precisely the same criteria in mind as Müller-Strübing. Note what the latter says, with some exasperation:

> Why not begin immediately from the point when, in the last embassy of the Lacedaemonians, Ramphias delivered to the Athenian people the almost brutal choice: the Lacedaemonians desire the keeping of the peace; it can be kept if you leave the Greeks autonomous, that is, if you dissolve the Athenian Empire (1.139). When at that point the Athenians rejected this demand, then one could perhaps say, in diplomatic terms, a state of war had thereby been entered, war had therefore begun, even if no immediate acts of violence occurred.

Without knowing it, Müller-Strübing put his finger on Thucydides' own analysis of the *arche* of the Peloponnesian War.

Finally, with the new interpretation we are closer to a solution to the major problem in 5.20. There Thucydides says that "ten years plus a few days had gone by since the invasion of Attica and the beginning of this war." In the old view, which equated the *arche* with the Theban attack upon Plataea, the entire phrase ἡ ἐσβολὴ ἡ ἐς τὴν ᾿Αττικὴν καί had to be excised, on the grounds that it was an intrusive gloss. In our view the *arche* was the breaking off of diplomatic relations between Athens and Sparta. But the Athenian rejection of the final Spartan ultimatum and the return of the Lacedaemonian ambassadors late in the winter of 432/431 had a grave and inevitable implication: that the Spartans and their allies would invade Attica in the following campaigning season. The invasion of Athenian land is the necessary result of the official

35

Athenian reply to Ramphias, Melesippus, and Agesandrus.[39] Hence there is a close connection between Thucydides' *arche* of the war and the invasion. The historian may have originally written in 5.20.1 that "ten years plus a few days had gone by since the invasion of Attica first became inevitable and the beginning of this war occurred." A copyist, misled by Thucydides' frequent references to this invasion as the "beginning of hostilities," and by the fact that this invasion seems, even in Thucydides' narrative, to be the natural starting point of the war, removed the offending word or words and created a sentence that looks a little peculiar but at least seems to make good sense. This kind of correction occurs in manuscripts of all periods and is one of the simplest for a scribe to make. It is easier to account for than an unnecessary intrusive gloss of seven words and makes much better sense of the adverb "first" ($\tau\grave{o}$ $\pi\rho\hat{\omega}\tau o\nu$). Most significantly, we can find confirmation for our view that, to Thucydides, a decision to go to war is the *arche* of that war, by examining his aetiology of the second ten-year war.

When we apply what we have learned about Thucydides' treatment of the beginning of the first ten-year war to the problem of the beginning of the second, the solution to that problem is relatively simple. We need only to recognize two things: that Thucydides does not require a military action for the *arche* of a war and that Thucydides does not consider the breaking of a treaty to be necessarily the *arche* of a war. The treaty may be violated before or after the beginning of the war or even before *and* after the beginning of the war. In short, the violation of a treaty has no necessary connection with the *arche* of a war. With these two points in mind, let us reexamine Thucydides' remarks about the beginning of the second ten-year war.

Thucydides says in 5.25.3 that "for six years and ten months they held back from marching upon each other's land. . . .

---

[39] Note that Sparta does not need to call her allies together for further votes after the rejection of the final demand. The Peloponnesian decision, described in 1.125, is conditional only upon the Athenians' not giving in to demands (126.1).

36

[ἀπέσχοντο μὴ ἐπὶ τὴν ἑκατέρων γῆν στρατεῦσαι] then, however, forced to break the peace made after the ten years they again went into open war." As stated before, six years and ten months from the Peace of Nicias (beginning of spring, 422/ 421) takes us to midwinter, 415/414. What, precisely, happened in midwinter, 415/414? Let us read carefully Thucydides' narrative of this period. In 6.88.7 he tells us that a Syracusan embassy arrived in the Peloponnese asking for aid against the Athenians in Sicily. The ambassadors went first to Corinth, where they were given an enthusiastic reception and promises of assistance. Then, accompanied by Corinthian envoys, they went to Sparta, where they were joined by Alcibiades, who had just arrived in the Peloponnese after escaping from the Athenians in Sicily. In 6.88.10 we learn what these three groups effected at Sparta: "And it happened in an assembly of the Lacedaemonians that the Corinthians and Syracusans and Alcibiades all asking for the same things persuaded the Lacedaemonians. The ephors and the government intended to send ambassadors to Syracuse to prevent the Syracusans from coming to an agreement with the Athenians, but they were not eager to send help. Alcibiades then came forward and inflamed and stirred the Lacedaemonians with the following words." There follows Alcibiades' speech, in which he urges the Spartans to fortify Decelea and to send immediate help to Sicily to save the beleaguered Syracusans. At the end of the speech (6.93) Thucydides describes its results: "Alcibiades said such things, and the Lacedaemonians, intending themselves even before to march upon Athens [στρατεύειν ἐπὶ τὰς Ἀθήνας], but still hesitating and waiting, became much more confident when Alcibiades taught them these things, thinking that they had heard them from one who knew them most exactly. So that they gave their attention to the fortification of Decelea and for the time being to sending some help to those in Sicily." In 7.18 Thucydides tells us that the Lacedaemonians did something else in addition on this occasion: they passed a resolution to invade Attica: "The Lacedaemonians were preparing the invasion of Attica, in accordance with their own previous resolve, and at the instigation of the Syracusans and

37

Corinthians." We learn from these two passages, 6.93 and 7.18 that in the winter of 415/414 the Spartans stopped hesitating and waiting to invade Athens and picked up their courage and resolved in an assembly to do so. Does this not mean that the Spartans "stopped holding back from marching upon Athenian land?" Does it not mean, in other words, that the period of six years and ten months in which "they held back from marching upon each other's land" was over, psychologically at least? The verb ἀπέσχοντο in 5.25 expresses the same psychological state as do the participles μέλλοντες and περιορώμενοι in 6.93: that of holding back, of refraining, of hesitating, and waiting. The verb ἐπερρώσθησαν in 6.93 indicates that the Spartans ceased holding back. When the Spartans voted formally in their assembly to invade Attica, the period of unstable truce ended and the second war began, at least as far as Thucydides was concerned.

Thus the second ten-year war, like the first, began with a decision and not with a military act. But we can go much further in our comparison of the *archai* of the two wars than this. When we examine Thucydides' account of the beginning of the so-called Decelean War, we find that he identifies the same four stages in its inception that he had identified in the case of the first war and that he uses the same language to identify them. In 5.26.6 he says that he will begin with a description of the διαφοράν τε καὶ ξύγκυσιν τῶν σπονδῶν; in 6.93.1 he describes the end of the period of holding back and hesitating to commence hostilities; in 6.105 he describes the event that "most clearly broke the treaty"; and in 5.25.3 he speaks of the actual commencement of hostilities as the beginning of "open war." When we put the two sets of events next to one another, we can appreciate their close resemblance:

(1) disagreements and dissolution of the treaty

1.146:   αἰτίαι καὶ διαφοραί; σπονδῶν ξύγκυσις καὶ πρόφασις τοῦ πολεμεῖν ("complaints and disagreements; dissolution of the treaty and occasion for war");

5.26.6:   διαφορά τε καὶ ξύγκυσις τῶν σπονδῶν (disagreement and dissolution of the treaty");

38

(2) decision to cease hesitating and delaying

1.139.3: ἐδόκει ἅπαξ περὶ ἁπάντων βουλευσαμένους ἀποκρίνασθαι ("it seemed best once and for all, having taken counsel, to give an answer");

6.93: οἱ δὲ Λακεδαιμόνιοι διανοούμενοι . . . μέλλοντες δ' ἔτι καὶ περιορώμενοι, πολλῷ μᾶλλον ἐπερρώσθησαν ("the Lacedaemonians intending . . . but still hesitating and waiting, became much more confident");

with 7.18.1: Παρεσκευάζοντο δὲ καὶ τὴν ἐς τὴν Ἀττικὴν ἐσβολὴν οἱ Λακεδαιμόνιοι, ὥσπερ τε προυδέδοκτο αὐτοῖς ("the Lacedaemonians were preparing the invasion of Attica, in accordance with their own previous resolve");

(3) clear breaking of the treaty

2.7.1: λελυμένων λαμπρῶς τῶν σπονδῶν ("the treaty clearly broken");

6.105.1: αἵπερ τὰς σπονδὰς φανερώτατα . . . ἔλυσαν ("which most clearly broke the treaty");

(4) manifest or open war

1.125: τὸν πόλεμον ἄρασθαι φανερῶς ("to begin the war openly"); see 2.2.3: τοῦ πολέμου μήπω φανεροῦ καθεστῶτος ("the war not yet openly begun");

2.13.9: ὅτε ἡ ἐσβολὴ τὸ πρῶτον ἔμελλε Πελοποννησίων ἔσεσθαι καὶ ἐς τὸν πόλεμον καθίσταντο ("when the invasion of the Peloponnesians was first about to occur and they went to war");

5.25.3: αὖθις ἐς πόλεμον φανερὸν κατέστησαν ("again they began open war"); see 6.88.8: τόν τε αὐτοῦ πόλεμον σαφέστερον ποιεῖσθαι ("to make war here more clearly").

I should also point out here the great similarities between Thucydides' introductions to his narratives of the two wars and the periods leading up to them, 1.23.5-6 and 5.25-26. In 1.23.5 Thucydides says that he wrote first the *aitiai* and *diaphorai* of the war. After then identifying what he considered to be the ἀληθεστάτη πρόφασις of the war in section 6, he

39

goes on to say: "These were the openly announced *aitiai* of each side, from which, breaking the treaty, they went to war" (ἀφ᾽ ὧν λύσαντες τὰς σπονδὰς ἐς τὸν πόλεμον κατέστησαν). In 5.26.6 Thucydides says that he will narrate first the *diaphora* and ξύγκυσις τῶν σπονδῶν after the ten years; in 25.3 he says that the two sides were forced to break the treaty made after the ten years and went again into open war (ἀναγκασθέντες λῦσαι τὰς μετὰ τὰ δέκα ἔτη σπονδὰς αὖθις ἐς πόλεμον φανερὸν κατέστησαν).

The parallelism between these passages helps to explain another well-known difficulty in the text, the so-called second introduction (5.26). In this chapter Thucydides digresses or, more properly, continues his digression begun in 5.24 and 5.25 on the different components of the twenty-seven-year war and on his methods of composing his *History* of this war. In this discussion he makes several remarks that have appeared to some scholars to be out of place except on the assumption that he is here writing with a new plan and conception of his work. Hence this passage is frequently mentioned in the debate over the composition question as evidence that Thucydides changed his mind about the length of the war: before the Athenian expedition to Sicily and the renewal of open war he believed that the Peloponnesian War ended with the Peace of Nicias in 421; later (perhaps by 415/414), when he realized that this view was erroneous, he revised some (but not all) passages in the first part of his *History* and took up his account where he had broken off. Chapter 26 in particular is supposed by this school of thought to represent a second introduction: the historian's personal remarks in sections 1, 4, and 5 of this chapter evince his need to start afresh, while the argument in section 2 is designed to mask his earlier, mistaken impression that the Peace of 421 had brought the Peloponnesian War to a conclusion.

This interpretation will always remain a possibility, but in my view an unlikely one. The demonstration just made of the close parallels Thucydides drew between the events leading to the two ten-year wars offers a more satisfactory explanation for Thucydides' remarks in 5.26. If we compare the statements with which Thucydides opens and closes his account of the first ten-year war and begins the next section of his *History*, we find them to be nearly identical:

2.1. κατασταντες τε ξυνεχῶς ἐπολέμουν· γέγραπται δὲ ἑξῆς ὡς ἕκαστα ἐγίγνετο κατὰ θέρη καὶ χειμῶνας ("and having started hostilities, they fought continuously; and it has been composed in succession as each event occurred by summers and winters"); θέρη καὶ χειμῶνας is adscripted in Π[8] and is probably correct: see 5.20.3 and 26.1;

5.24.2. ταῦτα δὲ τὰ δέκα ἔτη ὁ πρῶτος πόλεμος ξυνεχῶς γενόμενος γέγραπται ("these ten years, the first war, occurring continuously, have been composed");

5.26.1. Γέγραφε δὲ καὶ ταῦτα ὁ αὐτὸς Θουκυδίδης Ἀθηναῖος ἑξῆς ὡς ἕκαστα ἐγένετο κατὰ θέρη καὶ χειμῶνας ("And the same Thucydides an Athenian composed also these things in succession, as each event occurred by summers and winters").

The formal similarity in language suggests continuity and parallelism, not change and a fresh plan. Chapter 5.24 tells us that the first cycle is over, 5.25 that the second war began much as the first had, and 5.26 that Thucydides will treat the components of the war in similar fashion. His methodology will be the same[40] and so will his aim: compare 5.26.5 with 1.22.2-3 (especially προσέχων τὴν γνώμην, ὅπως ἀκριβές τι εἴσομαι with ὅσον δυνατὸν ἀκριβείᾳ περὶ ἑκάστου ἐπεξελθών). What seemed before to be two separate plans appears on the present analysis to be two parts of the same plan. Alert readers will perhaps recall the remark made in the first methodology (1.22.4) about the future's being similar and analogous to the past and will understand what the historian is doing when he repeats his introduction to the first war. One must read 5.26 in its full context. Then its function becomes clearer. The purpose of 5.24, 5.25, and 5.26 is to apprise the reader that one segment of Thucydides' *History* is over and another, similar one is about to begin.

[40] For the meaning of ὁ αὐτός in 5.26.1 see Lowell Edmunds, *Chance and Intelligence in Thucydides* (Cambridge, Mass. 1975) 163-166.

Thucydides was consistent in portraying the beginnings of his two wars. The cases that we have made for their *archai* are more than simply helpful to each other; they are mutually explanatory. Our recognition that Thucydides chose as his *arche* of the first war a diplomatic decision rather than a military act enabled us to accept as his *arche* of the second war another diplomatic decision that had in the past been rejected as an implausible event for the beginning of a war. In turn, Thucydides' clear separation of the *arche* of the second war from the first obvious violation of the treaty insures that we are correct in arguing that they were separate events in the first war, even though Thucydides does not make that absolutely clear in 2.1-2. It turns out, in other words, to be purely accidental that the first clear violation of the thirty years' treaty came directly after the diplomatic beginning of the first war. In the second war, it was several months after the Spartan decision to invade Attica when the thirty Athenian ships clearly broke the treaty by ravaging the Laconian coast. Violations of the treaties were in both cases relatively insignificant events that had nothing to do with the real *archai* of the wars, at least as far as Thucydides was concerned.

That Thucydides consciously compared the events leading up to the outbreak of hostilities in the two wars is clear both from his repetition of language and from his remarks in 5.25. When he says in 25.1 that after the Peace of Nicias "another disturbance of the Peloponnesian allies started against Lacedaemon," we may be confident that he has in mind the first such disturbance, also led by Corinth, described in 1.67. That had been the occasion for the presentation of αἰτίαι καὶ διαφοραί by the allies to Sparta before the first war. After the peace of 421, Thucydides says, this process, which in 5.26.6 he calls διαφορά τε καὶ ξύγκυσις τῶν σπονδῶν, began for the second time. Six years and ten months went by before the *arche* of the second war. But then, forced to break the treaty made after ten years, they again started open hostilities. We are surely meant to compare the two sets of events: the period of accusations and disagreements before the first war with the similar period before the second; the Athenian assembly's decision to give a final rejection to the Spartans' demands after Pericles' speech in winter 432/431 with the Spartan assembly's decision to invade Attica after Alcibiades' speech in winter, 415/414; the Theban attack upon Plataea that "clearly broke the thirty years' treaty" with the Athenian attack upon the Laconian coast that "most clearly broke the fifty years' treaty"; and finally, the invasion of Attica by Archidamus in the summer of 431, the event that began the open hostilities of the first war, with the invasion of Attica by his son Agis in the spring of 414, the event that began the open hostilities of the second war. These sets of events are treated as completely parallel by Thucydides. A comparison of his accounts of these two sequences confirms our identification of the *archai* of the wars.

Thucydides applied similar, but not quite identical criteria to the beginnings of the two ten-year wars. For, we might ask, when did Athens and Sparta break off diplomatic relations before the second war? There is not a word about when the Spartans and Athenians "stopped sending embassies to each other without heralds" before the second war, in fact, not a word about diplomatic relations in general for the year 415/414. Instead, Thucydides dates the beginning of the second war to the resolution of the Spartan assembly, passed in winter, 415/414, to invade Attica and fortify Decelea. It was over a year before that resolution was put into effect and not until the spring of 413 that Agis led the Peloponnesian forces into Attica. Of course, Thucydides could argue, there was fighting in Sicily between Peloponnesians and Athenians before that invasion, and the Spartan decision, passed at the same assembly as the resolution to invade Attica, to send Gylippus as commander of the Syracusan defense constituted an act of war against Athens. That is perhaps a reasonable argument, but there is nonetheless the suspicion that Thucydides chose winter, 415/414 as the *arche* of the later war because it gave him a second (nearly) ten-year war to go along with the first. It is not, I think, unfair to suspect that a desire to have two ten-year wars within the twenty-seven-year war colored Thucydides'

43

historiographical choices of the *archai* of both wars. (Even the Romans could not resist "fated" ten-year wars: see Livy 5.22.8.)

What have we learned from this investigation of the *archai* of the two ten-year wars? First, Thucydides consciously compared the two sets of sequences of events that occasioned these wars: he uses almost identical terminology to describe the steps that led up to the outbreak of the wars, and these steps occur in the same sequence in the two cases. Second, Thucydides intended the *reader* to compare the two aetiologies: in describing the outbreak of hostilities in the Decelean War, he points to the events that had led to the Archidamian War. Third, and most important for the thesis proposed in the following chapters of this monograph, the method of comparing Thucydides' treatments of the two ten-year wars can be a useful means of solving difficult problems presented by the text of the *History*: as we have just seen, a close study of Thucydides' handling of the aetiology of the first war proved to be of great value in interpreting his aetiology of the second, while the evidence of the second aetiology provided important confirmation for our interpretation of the first. The two cases corroborated and elucidated each other. And fourth, the book division made for Thucydides' work by the Alexandrians in this instance (and therefore, perhaps, in others) actually served to obscure a crucial connection between two parts of a single Thucydidean argument. This last lesson should be a most salutary warning against using the eight-book division as if it were Thucydides' division, as if, in other words, it provided a significant criterion for understanding the structure of the *History*.[41] While it is true that the Hellenistic editor of Thucydides' work did not make his divisions between books entirely arbitrarily and that these divisions can be of some use, the student of the *History* can ill afford to rely on these guidelines. In our investigation of the work's structure we shall try to identify Thucydides' own divisions of the war; only then can we hope to comprehend the principles he used to arrange his material.

[41] See L. Canfora, *Tucidide Continuato* (Padova 1970) 17-40, 51-53.

44

THE EXPLICIT CONTRASTS OF THE TWO WARS

Thucydides wrote the history of a great war that was itself composed of two wars of almost identical length. Is there further evidence suggesting that he compared those two wars, either consciously or subconsciously, explicitly or implicitly? Fortunately we have clear proof that he did, both consciously and explicitly. It is contained in a passage which is well known for other reasons, 7.18. In this chapter Thucydides describes at length and in detail the state of mind with which the Spartans in the winter of 414 prepared for the invasion of Attica and the occupation of Decelea. This invasion, carried out under Agis the next spring, constituted the true military ἀρχή of the Decelean war, which Thucydides refers to in 5.26 as the "later war." After describing Syracusan and Corinthian pressure upon Sparta to invade Attica and Alcibiades' urgent instructions to fortify Decelea, Thucydides goes on to portray the Spartan mood: "But what especially gave the Spartans confidence were two realizations: that the Athenians would be more easily defeated since they had to face a double war, against both themselves and the Syracusans; and because they felt that they [the Athenians] had broken the peace first." The first consideration is self-explanatory; Thucydides gives a lengthy explanation of the second:

> For in the former war [they felt] that they themselves had been more at fault, since the Thebans entered Plataea during a time of truce, and since, although it was said in the former treaty that they should not bear arms if arbitration were offered, they themselves had not given in when the Athenians invited them to arbitration. For this reason they thought that they had deservedly suffered misfortunes, those others which occurred and particularly the disaster at Pylos. But when the Athenians set out from Argos with thirty ships and ravaged parts of Epidaurus and Prasiae and other places, and at the same time conducted piratical raids from Pylos, and in addition were unwilling to submit to arbitration although the Lacedaemonians invited them to arbitrate

45

concerning whatever disputes had arisen over disagreements about the treaty, then the Lacedaemonians, thinking that the same fault which they had committed in the previous case was now in turn committed by the Athenians, were eager for the war [πρόθυμοι ἦσαν ἐς τὸν πόλεμον].

There are several things worth noting in this passage, but for our purposes here the most important are these. Thucydides makes several explicit comparisons, or rather contrasts, between the two wars. In the former war (ἐν γὰρ τῷ προτέρῳ πολέμῳ) the Spartans believed that they were themselves at fault; this time, the same fault was committed by the Athenians (αὖθις ἐς τοὺς Ἀθηναίους τὸ αὐτὸ περιεστάναι). In the first case, the Thebans entered Plataea in peacetime; now it was the Athenians who broke the peace by ravaging Laconian land and committing piracy from Pylos. In the former case, the Athenians several times invited the Spartans to negotiate concerning their disagreements, as was provided for in the peace treaty, but the Spartans did not consent; now it was the Spartans who did the inviting, again as the treaty provided, and the Athenians who refused. Finally, and most significantly, the Spartans felt that in a certain sense they deserved their misfortunes, especially the shocking disaster at Pylos, in the former war because they had been at fault in starting the war; now they were eager for the war because the Athenians were the guilty party. The Spartan assumption is clear: the Athenians will suffer unexpected disasters in this war.[42]

All these contrasts are made explicit, not only by the substance of the passage but by the language and syntax in which it is expressed. Thucydides gives the reader in the most explicit terms the Spartans' own thinking about the two wars. In their minds they were beginning the second in a far better position, both militarily and psychologically, than the first. That those advantages were real and not merely figments of the Spartans' imagination, Thucydides soon makes abundantly clear (in

[42] For the fulfillment of this assumption see 7.71.7, where Thucydides explicitly says that the Athenians suffered in Sicily precisely what the Spartans suffered at Pylos.

7.27.3-28.4). But, more importantly, these contrasts in the Spartans' attitude are immediately strengthened by another in the actual report of the invasion. The very next chapter (19) begins: "At the very beginning of the following spring the Lacedaemonians and their allies invaded Attica. Agis the son of Archidamus, King of the Lacedaemonians, led them." These two statements, expressed in formulaic language, remind us of the first invasion of Attica under Archidamus, reported in 2.19.1: "at the height of summer and of the crop, they invaded Attica. Archidamus the son of Zeuxidamus, King of the Lacedaemonians, led them." Archidamus was the father of Agis; one is reminded, almost inevitably, of his farsighted and dire prediction made at Sparta: "Let us not be excited by the hope that the war will be quickly ended if we ravage their land; I fear rather that we shall leave it to our sons" (1.81.6). Here in 7.19.1 is Archidamus' own son repeating his father's act and starting a new war.

But at the same time that we note the similarities between the two statements, we also become aware of the crucial differences in the actual acts: Archidamus, who seriously doubted Sparta's legal and moral right to declare the "first war" (1.85.2), as well as her ability to win it (1.80-81), had made every conceivable effort to avoid it (2.12 and 2.18); finally, when all his attempts to make Athens give up without a fight failed, he began the invasion in the middle of summer. He ravaged the land of Attica hoping to bring out the Athenians (2.19-20). When that failed, he eventually went home (2.23.3).

Archidamus' son led an altogether different kind of invasion. Confident of success for the moral and military reasons stated in 7.18, he entered Attica at the earliest break of spring. First he ravaged the plain, then he fortified Decelea. Thucydides heightens the contrast a few chapters later: "For before the invasions were brief. . . . But now, occupying the land continuously, . . . with Agis, King of the Lacedaemonians, present and prosecuting the war relentlessly, the Athenians suffered a great deal of harm" (27.4).

A new kind of war had begun, far more devastating than the first. This one was nearly total. Thucydides emphasizes the

47

contrast between the two wars in the next chapter (28.3). What especially harmed the Athenians was that they had to face two wars. The φιλονικία into which they fell was unbelievable.[48] Thucydides again returns to the beginning of the whole war: the παράλογος was all the greater since at the beginning of the war some thought the Athenians would hold out a year, two years, maybe three; but, already worn out by the war, they had undertaken an expedition to Sicily, seventeen years after the first invasion of Attica, and they took on besides a war no less serious than the former one from the Peloponnese.

It does not appear that commentators have properly understood the last part of 28.3. The two phrases ἦλθον ἐς Σικελίαν and πόλεμον οὐδὲν ἐλάσσω should not refer to the same event. There are several indications that they designate two different subjects: (1) Thucydides uses καί to separate them, rather than a subordinating participial phrase; (2) the verb προσανείλοντο must mean "they took on besides, or in addition"; (3) An examination of 6.1.1, which is often cited as a parallel to this passage, reveals the differences, not the similarities in the two expressions: "The same winter the Athenians . . . and they did not know that they were taking upon themselves a war not much inferior to the one against the Peloponnesians."

There are four basic differences between the two passages. (1) In 6.1.1 the Athenians decide to go to Sicily ignorant of the size of the island and unaware that they were taking on (ἀνῃροῦντο) a war somewhat smaller than the one against the Peloponnesians; in 7.28.3 they go to Sicily and "take on in addition [προσ-] a war no smaller than the one which occurred before out of the Pelopponnese." These two clauses must refer to different events. (2) The Sicilian war was inferior by a little to the "first Peloponnesian War"; the "second Peloponnesian War was every bit the equal of the first." (3) Note also the difference in the prepositional phrases at the ends of the two sentences. Chapter 6.1.1 ends with "the war πρὸς Πελοποννησίους," an expression contrasting that war with the expedition "to Sicily," ἐπὶ Σικελίαν. Chapter 7.28.3 ends with "the former

[43] See Dover, *Comm.* on 7.28.3.

48

war out of the Peloponnese" (τοῦ πρότερον ὑπάρχοντος ἐκ
Πελοποννήσου), an expression contrasting that war with the
"new or present war out of the Peloponnese." (4) In addition,
and this is the critical and forgotten element, the whole point
of 28.3 is that "what most harmed the Athenians was the fact
that they had two wars simultaneously" (ἅμα). We must remember the temporal context of 7.28—it is 413, after the occupation of Decelea, and Thucydides is discussing the debilitat-
ing effects of that occupation upon the Athenians and their
incredible resilience in the face of it. The great παράλογος consists of the Athenians' taking on two wars at once, when no
one expected them to withstand Peloponnesian invasions more
than three years. The climax of the argument comes in the last
part of the long and complex sentence with the mention of
both wars. The amazing aspect of the φιλονικία into which
the Athenians had now fallen was that they had two wars, one
only a little inferior to the "first Peloponnesian War," the other
every bit its equal. This point serves to substantiate the Spartans' expectations in 7.18.2: "what especially gave the Spartans
confidence was that they thought the Athenians would have
a double war."

All these considerations taken together constitute an explicit
comparison of the two parts of Thucydides' *History*, the first
war and the second war, which was itself a double war. It is,
of course, not so much a comparison as a contrast. The second
war was far greater than the first. In addition, the Spartans entered it in a far more confident frame of mind, with a far better strategy, and with the "legal" and moral advantages on
their side. The Athenians, on the other hand, were faced with
overwhelming odds. They had, as Thucydides makes clear,
brought this situation upon themselves. Their expedition to
Sicily, undertaken in ignorance and greed, had brought not
just one war upon them, but two. The invasion of Sicily led
directly and inevitably to the invasion of Attica and the occupation of Decelea, just as Thucydides makes Nicias predict
(6.10.2 and especially 6.10.4: εἰ δίχα ἡμῶν τὴν δύναμιν λά-
βοιεν ["If they should catch our forces divided"]).[44] Thucyd-

[44] For the correctness of all Nicias' predictions in his speech at Ath-

ides is thus not only conscious of the contrasts between the two wars; he expressly identifies them.

STRUCTURE: IMPLICIT CONTRAST

We have seen that Thucydides on several occasions explicitly contrasts the first and second ten-year wars, what we term the Archidamian and Decelean wars. It will be the contention of this work that implicit contrasts between the two wars, expressed by the structure in which they are written, pervade the entire *History*. What precisely do we mean by historiographical structure?

Three elements comprise the structure of an historical work: selection, emphasis, and juxtaposition. Selection is the inclusion or exclusion of events by the historian; emphasis is the form in which the included events are expressed; juxtaposition is the order in which the included events are composed. Together, selection, emphasis, and juxtaposition determine the structure of the historian's work. A study of the structure, in turn, reveals the historian's principles of selection, emphasis, and juxtaposition. The three categories, of course, overlap. They constitute, however, a convenient system for the analysis of the structure of an historical work.

We have only recently begun to appreciate how carefully Thucydides selects his facts and to understand the principles according to which he makes his selection. Kitto's Sather Lectures contain many salutary warnings on this subject. Thucydides uses extremely rigorous criteria in selecting ἔργα for inclusion in his work. At the same time, what he chooses to exclude is often of equally great importance. The following assertion of Karl Reinhardt is as good a description as any of the significance of omissions in Thucydides:

> Es gibt, wie mir scheint, keinen Historiker, ja überhaupt nicht viele Schriftsteller, bei denen das Nicht-Gesagte nicht

---

ens at the beginning of Book VI, see H.-P. Stahl, "Speeches and Course of Events in Books Six and Seven of Thucydides," in *The Speeches of Thucydides*, ed. P.A. Stadter (Chapel Hill 1973).

nur etwa jenseits des Gesagten läge, sondern so zum Greifen dicht, so spürbar in das Werk hineinreichte, so dass man immer wieder sich gezwungen sieht, das, was gesagt wird, aus dem Nicht-Gesagten zu ergänzen.[45]

We shall need, therefore, to pay very close attention to selection in both its aspects of inclusion and exclusion when examining the structure of Thucydides' work.

Emphasis is, of course, also a double-edged historiographical tool. After he has selected his facts, the historian must still decide what relative weights to give them. He can stress or downplay a particular episode. His decisions will determine the form in which each event is composed. In the simplest case, such a decision might involve whether to give a brief report of a particular battle or whether to write a full description of it. The choice is, of course, governed by the significance the historian assigns to the event relative to the other events he has selected for inclusion. The question is, however, rarely so simple and straightforward, especially for the historian who aims at being more than a compiler. A major historiographical issue for Thucydides throughout his entire composition was whether or not a particular episode merited dramatic portrayal. Dramatic presentation in Thucydides takes many forms, of which the following are the most important: detailed and highly-charged narrative (the plague, Corcyraean stasis, Mycalessus); anecdotal dialogue (the Ambracian disaster in 3.113); formal dialogue (the Melian conference, the dialogue between Plataeans and Archidamus in 2.71-74); indirect dialogue (the Athenian-Boeotian debate over Delium reported in 4.97-99,[46] the Spartan prisoner and his questioner in 4.40.2, which is also anecdotal);[47]

---

[45] K. Reinhardt, "Thukydides und Machiavelli," *Vermächtnis der Antike*, ed. Carl Becker (Göttingen 1966) 202. "There is, it seems to me, no historian, indeed, there exist few authors, in whom what is not said not only lies beyond what is said, but extends so palpably, so perceptibly into the work, that one finds himself again and again forced to supplement what is said with what is not said."

[46] For the importance of this dialogue see Strasburger, "Thukydides und die politische Selbstdarstellung der Athener," *Wege*, 525.

[47] See Edmunds, *Chance and Intelligence*, 102 ff.

an entire speech (Pericles' first speech, the Funeral Oration, the Mytilenean speech at Olympia, Spartan speech at Athens asking for peace); paired speeches (passim); a conference consisting of several speeches (at Sparta 1.68-86, at Syracuse 6.33-41). All of these forms are means of artistically emphasizing a particular event or episode.

It is also possible, and here we enter less familiar territory, to stress by deemphasis or underplaying. This technique we term irony, a tool whose importance in Thucydidean composition we are only beginning to recognize.[48]

Irony can also be produced by juxtaposition, the third element in historiographical structure. Here we are back on familiar ground. Kitto has given us, in several examples, an acute analysis of Thucydides' use of juxtaposition to attain dramatic effect, and other scholars have long recognized such outstanding cases as the Funeral Oration-plague and Melian dialogue-Sicilian expedition pairs. Perhaps Strasburger describes this technique most cogently when he speaks of Thucydides' "geübten Technik, durch literarische Komposition geschichtliche Sinndeutung ohne Wörte sichtbar zu machen."[49] Here the emphasis is properly laid on the intent of careful juxtaposition: to extract and present historical meaning without explicitly saying what that meaning is. Careful juxtaposition is the most subtle aspect of Thucydides' art of composition and, therefore, the most difficult to study and appreciate. It is also the most dangerous because the tendency toward overinterpretation is most prevalent. What appears to be created by intentional juxtaposition may be governed only by historical sequence. Dover makes this distinction forcibly in his recent survey of Thucydidean scholarship: "That he described the fate of Melos just before he came to the Athenian plans for Sicily was dictated by the order in which events happened, not by any choice of his;

[48] See H. Flashar, *Der Epitaphios des Perikles*, Sitzungsberichte der Heidelberger Akademie, Phil.-hist. Klasse, 1. Abhandlung (Heidelberg 1969).

[49] H. Strasburger, *Die Wesensbestimmung*, 73: "skilled technique of making, without explicit words, historical interpretations apparent through literary composition."

that he treated the occasion as deserving a six-page debate, but not, apparently, as deserving fuller indication of the reasons why Athens at that moment thought Melos worth a campaign, reflects his choice."[50]

In studying the structure of Thucydides' *History*, we should also be aware of a principle of Thucydidean style that has been amply documented at the sentence level. G. Wille states this principle as follows: "Formale Analogien können sachliche Unterschiede verdecken, während sachliche Analogien in formalen Variationen verborgen werden."[51] While tension between form and content was frequently assayed by Greek authors, Thucydides was the most constant and successful in its pursuit. Ros' study of *Variatio*[52] provides an abundance of evidence for this aspect of Thucydidean style, and Wille has confirmed its significance in his close analysis of 1.22, the complex statement on methodology. It is possible, I believe, to show that this stylistic principle holds true not only for the smallest unit of composition, the syntax of the sentence, but also for the largest, the structure of the work as a whole. Thucydides was fond of the unexpected ($\pi\alpha\rho\acute{\alpha}\lambda o\gamma o\nu$) and the ironic, as Stahl has amply demonstrated.[53] One of the most effective ways of evoking irony is the use of formal analogies to mark real differences. It will be our contention that Thucydides frequently contrasts events, leadership, and opportunities taken or missed in the two wars of his *History* by couching them in identical structure or form. The reader finds himself making implicit comparisons, only to be struck more by the change in conditions or responses than by their similarity. Thucydides was extremely fond of and adept at this technique of producing analogies between events which were similar, but

---

[50] Dover, "Thucydides," in *Greece and Rome*, New Surveys in the Classics No. 7 (Oxford 1973) 41.

[51] G. Wille, *Wege*, 691. "Formal analogies can conceal real differences, while real analogies can be hidden in formal variations of expression."

[52] J. Ros, *Die μεταβολή (variatio) als Stilprinzip des Thukydides* (Paderborn 1938).

[53] H.-P. Stahl, *Thukydides*. For Thucydidean irony and the need for further study of this slippery subject, see F. Wassermann, *TAPA* 87 (1956) 32 n. 9, and W. Liebeschuetz, *JHS* 88 (1968) 73-77.

had different, often opposite outcomes. It is an extraordinarily effective technique for creating in the reader the impression that he has made the comparison and contrast himself and thus that he has formed his own judgment of a particular act or set of acts. A study of examples illustrating this technique reveals Thucydides at his artistic best.

LITERARY COMPOSITION

This last point leads us to a final introductory remark on the subject of the proper interpretation of Thucydides' literary art. The following questions might be put: Do we not open the door to overinterpretation when we seek patterns of interrelationships between widely-separated portions of Thucydides' text? Are we not guilty of anachronism when we assign sophisticated literary technique to Thucydides, an author who composed his *History* in the late fifth century, when book trade and reading public were only just coming into existence? The answer to these and similar questions must, I believe, be a definite and resounding no. Few authors have ever been more acutely conscious of the profound difference between their predecessors and themselves and more fiercely proud of their contributions to their genre; few authors have ever been more arrogantly confident of their literary immortality than Thucydides. What he makes Pericles say about the Athenians' right to disdain their opponents (2.62.3-4) could with equal appropriateness be said of Thucydides' view of his own relationship to his predecessors, whom he disdainfully refers to as logographers: "My work is composed as a possession for all time rather than as a piece to be heard once at a competition" (1.22.4). With these words Thucydides asserted in clear terms his aim: to create a literary work that could be read by each succeeding generation. Thucydides wrote for readers, and intelligent readers at that.[54]

The significance of this last fact is only beginning to be

[54] Günther Wille, "Zu Stil und Methode des Thukydides," in *Wege*, 690. See C. R. Beye, *Ancient Greek Literature and Society* (New York 1975) 220-221.

recognized, and it can never be fully appreciated because we cannot write a complete intellectual or even literary history of late fifth-century Athens. But one can say this much. Herodotus, whose work was "published" in the 420s, composed by essentially oral methods. That is, "the text of Herodotus as we have it is a continuous piece of writing which Herodotus set down from beginning to end in the order in which we now have it."[55] In addition, Herodotus' "whole History is, substantially at least, a first draft which was never revised, nor meant to be, because the first draft was always meant to be the final draft." Those are Lattimore's assertions about Herodotus' method of composition and no one has seriously challenged their general argument. Herodotus wrote linearly or, as Lattimore says, in "what might be called a forward, or point to point, or progressive style."[56] This style is, in general, characteristic of oral composers or of composers of written literature who are not far enough along in a literary tradition "to be able to think in terms of writing." There is perhaps some exaggeration in this case, an overemphasis upon the nonliterary nature of Herodotus' work, especially when one considers the compositional artistry of Books VII-IX. But the general point is well taken, and can be supported by other arguments. Herodotus' style is basically conversational or "strung together," λέξις εἰρομένη as Aristotle calls it in *Rhetoric* 3.1409A24. The structure is built on the same principle, as Immerwahr shows: "It is by a simple system of external repetition between semi-autonomous parts of his narrative . . . that Herodotus has created a large unified work." And "Herodotus' style everywhere exhibits the single chain rather than complex interweaving."[57]

Thucydides' work exhibits an entirely different method of composition, both at the sentence level and in the structure of the work as a whole. His style is the λέξις κατεστραμμένη, the "knit together" or periodic style that developed in the late

[55] R. Lattimore, "The Composition of the History of Herodotus," *CP* 53 (1958) 9.

[56] Ibid., 10.

[57] H. Immerwahr, *Form and Thought in Herodotus*, Philological Monographs of the APA 23 (Cleveland 1966) 59.

fifth century and was predominant in the fourth. He cared little for how it sounded. "Per contra, the self-conscious contrast drawn by Thucydides (1.22.4) between his own κτῆμα ἐς αἰεί and the ἀγώνισμα ἐς τὸ παραχρῆμα ἀκούειν of predecessors surely identifies the permanent influence of a MS stylistically composed for readers, as against the more ephemeral effects of a composition designed for recitation at an oral 'competition,' an interpretation strengthened by the previous sentence but one: καὶ ἐς μὲν ἀκρόασιν ἴσως τὸ μὴ μυθῶδες αὐτῶν ἀτερπέστερον φανεῖται."[58] This is true of even the presumably most orally-determined part of Thucydides' work, the speeches, which "sind ja auch, . . . gar nicht so sehr für imaginäre politische Zuhörer als für historiche Leser bestimmt."[59]

In structure too, Thucydides composes according to different principles from those used by Herodotus. The Peloponnesian War is described year by year. Only the events which are "worthy of record" are selected.[60] Emphasis is based upon the quality of the ἔργον, rather than its size.[61] And juxtaposition is dictated neither by what occurs to the memory next, nor by what the story next requires, but by what comparison or contrast Thucydides wants to make clear.[62] Edmunds succinctly defines the difference between the two historians in their treatment of structure: "Herodotus is to some degree subject to his logos, whereas in Thucydides, as the methodological statements clearly show (cf. 3.90.1), a consistent intention has been

---

[58] E. Havelock, *Preface to Plato* (Cambridge, Mass. 1963) 54, n. 8.

[59] Ebener, *Wissenschaftliche Zeitschrift der Universität Halle Wittenberg* 5 (1956) 1086: "are certainly not so much meant for imaginary political listeners as for historical readers."

[60] Contrast Thucydides 3.90.1 and Herodotus 2.3.2.

[61] See H. Immerwahr, "Ergon, history as a monument in Herodotus and Thucydides," *AJP* 81 (1960) 261-90.

[62] See Herodotus 1.23 and many other such digressions in Herodotus' work for memory as a criterion for juxtaposition; Herodotus 1.95.1 offers an example of the author in the grip of his logos. See Thucydides 7.34.5 and 7.36.2, also 4.30.1, for comparisons, and Thucydides 7.71.7 and 4.12.3 for contrasts. For useful comments see Strasburger, *Wesensbestimmung*, 73, n. 7.

imposed upon the narrative."[63] A study of the structure of Thucydides' narrative reveals his control over his material. That control is the basis of Thucydides' art, which is found everywhere in the work:

Bereits in den schlichtesten, scheinbar rein chronikartigen Partien seiner Erzählung arbeitet Thukydides durch die planmässige Gewaltsamkeit der Stoffauswahl im Sinne seiner neuen politischen Geschichtskonzeption mit den Privilegien des Künstlers.[64]

[63] Edmunds, *Chance and Intelligence*, 208. See G. Wille in *Wege*, 695.
[64] H. Strasburger, "Thukydides und die politische Selbstdarstellung der Athener," *Wege*, 519. "Even in the plainest, apparently purely chronological sections of his narrative Thucydides works with the licence of an artist, through the systematic control over the selection of his material, in accordance with his new political conception of history."

57

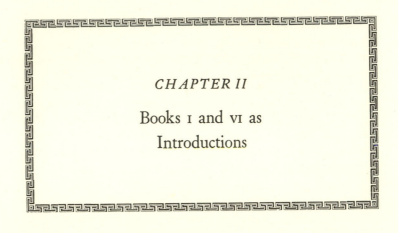

CHAPTER II

Books i and vi as

Introductions

THE FUNCTION OF 6.1-6.93

Thucydides divided his war into three parts: a first war of ten years; an unstable peace of nearly seven years; a second war of ten years. Of these three, the middle element receives the briefest treatment. The first year of the "peace" covers 13 Oxford pages, the second 9, the third 3, the fourth 15, the fifth 2, the sixth 14. Only the seventh, which includes the first year of the Sicilian expedition, is really of "normal Thucydidean length."[1] Indeed, it is quite long by Thucydidean standards, 56 Oxford pages, a fact whose importance we shall discuss shortly. Many scholars have expressed surprise at both the quantity and quality of material in Book V. Some have even gone so far as to argue that it is unfinished because it lacks major speeches and because it contains a number of documents and records in a "raw" state.[2] This view is the product of a failure to distinguish between different kinds of subject. Why should Thucyd-

[1] The war years in Thucydides (years 1-10, 18-21) average approximately 28 Oxford pages: I-29, II-17, III-27, IV-14, V-39, VI-17, VII-32, VIII-39, IX-14, X-14, XVIII-20, XIX-61, XX-35, XXI (unfinished)-38. The peace years, not including the seventh and last year, average 9 Oxford pages.

[2] See especially J. Classen, *Thukydides*, revised by J. Steup (Berlin 1892-1922) Book V, "Vorwort zur dritten Auflage." Hereafter cited as Classen-Steup.

ides devote the same amount and type of attention to a period of peace as he did to the two wars he describes? There is far less military action, especially important military action, to describe in this period. And Thucydides does give careful attention to the two years when significant events did occur: 421/420, when many alliances of political importance were made and 418/417, when the Battle of Mantinea took place, a battle of great military importance, as Thucydides stresses in 75.3. (The sixth year of the peace, 416/415, is also closer to normal length, because it contains the Melian dialogue and the "archaeology" of Sicily.) It should be clear that Thucydides wrote far more briefly and simply about the years 421/420 to 416/415 because he considered those years to be of less consequence than the two periods of "real war." Or, to put the contrast in Thucydidean terms, the difference is between periods of continuous and noncontinuous war. The fighting in the years 421-415 was sporadic compared with the two ten-year periods of intense warfare before and after. A review of the amount and type of material that Thucydides included in different segments of his *History* thus serves to substantiate our argument about the war's component parts. The six years in the middle of the two wars are treated differently from the wars themselves.[3]

But what about the last (almost full) year of peace of 415/414? The narrative of this year is the second longest in Thucydides' *History*. Only the year 413/412, the climax of Athens' Sicilian expedition, receives fuller treatment. But the narrative of 415/414 is not only long, it is also qualitatively one of the most complex in Thucydides' *History*, with six speeches, a long and complicated digression, (53-61), an historical survey (1-5), and one of the most vivid and dramatic descriptions in the entire work (27-32). Thucydides focussed a high degree of his historiographical attention upon this seventh and last year of peace. Why? Part of the answer is, of course, that this was the

[3] For a detailed treatment of the nature of Book V, see H. D. Westlake, "Thucydides and the Uneasy Peace—A Study in Political Incompetence," *CQ* N.S. 21 (1971) 315-325.

first year of Athens' Sicilian campaign, that remarkable and hybristic venture which was to end in such total and incredible defeat. This answer is correct and important, and it is true that Thucydides portrays the Sicilian expedition in a unified and dramatic fashion (he breaks his narrative of it only rarely: 6.7, 6.95; 6.105; 7.9; 7.18-20; 7.27-30, 7.34). But two factors have conspired to make this section of Thucydides' work appear more self-contained than it really is: first, the Hellenistic editor of the *History* set off the account of the campaign in Sicily by creating Books VI and VII, which now impress us as a special part of the work beginning with the introduction to the expedition and concluding with its "total destruction." In fact, neither Book VI nor Book VII begins or ends at a Thucydidean seam, such as the conclusion of a year of the war. Both books begin with passages which are, by Thucydides' own principles of division, quite unmarked. Secondly, Thucydides' description of the second ten-year war is incomplete. We are thus not in a good position to understand the architecture of this part of the *History*. Since Book VIII exists only in the form of a draft and Thucydides was unable to carry his account beyond the fourth year of the second war, our tendency is to see the Sicilian expedition as an artistic unity standing apart from the rest of the *History*.

Yet, according to Thucydides' own stated division of the Peloponnesian War (5.25-26, especially 5.26.3), the war consisted of two ten-year wars. It is true that the second one had two major theatres (7.28.3, and see 7.18.2 and 6.10.4) and that Thucydides can speak of the Sicilian campaign as a war in its own right (see 6.1.1). But in the context of the entire twenty-seven-year war, the Athenian campaign to Sicily becomes part of the second ten-year war. Note, however, that it does so only when the Spartans and their allies become involved in it, that is, when the Spartans decide to send Gylippus to Syracuse (and simultaneously, to renew the war in Greece by fortifying Decelea). Before that time the Athenians were undertaking a "private" venture which did not constitute a war against the Peloponnesians. The Sicilian expedition, as great as it was in itself, was even more significant in its context: it was the turning point in the war seen as a whole, the first step in the decline and fall of the Athenian Empire.[4] Not only did it become a crushing defeat for Athens, but it caused the renewal of the Peloponnesian War. That is, it ended the period of unstable peace and brought on the second ten-year war. Thucydides makes Nicias predict this result of an armada against Syracuse (6.10.1-4) and has Alcibiades draw the vital connection between the war in Sicily and war in the Peloponnese (see 6.91.1-5, especially 6.91.4: "Let no one think that he is taking counsel only for Sicily, but also for the Peloponnese"). It was the latter's speech that convinced the Lacedaemonians to aide the Syracusans and to renew the war in Greece (6.93.1-2).

As we saw, that war began, in Thucydides' view at least, with the Spartan decisions to support Syracuse and to invade and occupy Attica (6.93); since the Sicilian expedition led directly to the Spartan decisions to undertake the second war, the first ninety-three chapters of Book VI are the real introduction and background to the second war. As Thucydides viewed the course of events, the "unstable peace" might have continued for several more years, had not the Athenians decided to invade Sicily. The diplomatic maneuvers that had begun in Greece soon after the signing of the Peace of Nicias did not lead to a renewal of war. Sparta was content to wait and watch and held back from invading Attica and thus starting "open war" again. If Athens had not committed herself so deeply in Sicily, if, in other words, she had listened to Nicias instead of to Alcibiades, it is almost certain that the truce would have been maintained. As a result, 6.1-93 is analogous to Book I, the introduction and background to the first war and, of course, to the entire twenty-seven-year war. This may be the principal reason why the narrative of this year (416/415) is so long and historiographically so complex: it is a parallel section to Book I.

[4] See W. Schadewaldt, *Die Geschichtschreibung des Thukydides* (Berlin 1929) 6-21.

THE STRUCTURE OF BOOKS I AND VI

Of the different segments of the historian's work, the introduction allows the greatest freedom in composition. Once he has begun his subject proper, the historian's composition is dictated to a great degree by the sequence of events he has chosen to describe. This is particularly true for one who, like Thucydides, decides to write annalistically. Once he had made this decision, Thucydides locked himself into a certain kind of writing. He could still select, emphasize, and juxtapose the facts with some degree of freedom, but his area of choice in each case was severely restricted by his annalistic framework. The narrative had to follow the yearly course of events.

Not so with the introduction. Here the historian has almost complete freedom of choice, both in quantity and in quality. He can omit introductory material altogether, he can write a short preface, he can assemble a medium-length introduction that describes the events of the years leading up to his subject, or he can compose a major survey of past history. Qualitatively, the historian has a similar range of choice in his introduction: he can write a simple and direct narrative depicting past events; he can make a careful and detailed analysis of those events; he can inform the reader of his approach to writing history, his historiographical method. This freedom of choice was, for Thucydides, far greater for Book I than for Book VI, since the latter was, in addition to being an introduction to the second war, also a year of the entire twenty-seven-year war. Thucydides was therefore somewhat limited in composing his account of this year by its annalistic framework, though, as we shall see, he manages to overstep those confines when necessary. In composing Book I, on the other hand, Thucydides had almost complete freedom. He could choose virtually any events he wanted, he could emphasize where he wished, he could juxtapose as he desired. Perhaps in this last category of juxtaposition Thucydides had the greatest freedom in his introduction relative to the choice he had in the body of the work itself. He could compose his introduction in any order because there was no need to follow an annalistic pattern. When we look at the structures of Books I and VI, we should therefore be constantly aware of the freedom of choice that Thucydides had in composing these two books, particularly Book I.

When Books I and VI, chapters 1-93 are set before us diagramatically in Figure 1 we are struck by two things: their great similarity of form: their great difference in content. By the formal parallelism the reader is encouraged to compare the two introductions; when he does so, he finds similar situations and opportunities, but different, often diametrically opposed, responses to them. This tension between form and content is, of course, an important element in Thucydidean style. Here, however, it is found at its highest level, in its most remarkable form. Thucydides subtly leads his reader to make comparisons and contrasts that reveal the meaning of the events he describes. The reader is thus made to form ideas that he considers his own, about the historical choices confronted and made by the political leaders and their cities at two crucial mo-

FIGURE 1

Book I	Book VI, 1-93
Introduction and Archaeology of mainland Greece 1-19	Introduction and Archaeology of Sicily 1-5
Methodology and *alethestate prophasis* 20-23	*Alethestate prophasis* 6-7
Corcyraean Question Speeches of Corcyraeans and Corinthians at Athens: should Athens ally with Corcyra? The real question: the coming war with Sparta In a second assembly the Athenians reverse their earlier decision and accept the alliance 24-55	Sicilian Question Speeches of Nicias and Alcibiades at Athens: should Athens support her ally Egesta? The real question: the conquest of Sicily Nicias fails to persuade the Athenians to change their minds 8-26
The problem of Potidaea Troubles in the Athenian Empire 56-66	Preparations for the expedition The incident of the Herms Internal dissension in Athens 27-32

63

FIGURE I (*continued*)

Book I	Book VI, 1-93

Conference at Sparta
Speeches of: Corinthians
                Athenians
                Archidamus
                Spartan ephor
                         67-88
	Conference at Syracuse
	Speeches of: Hermocrates
	                Athenagoras
	                Syracusan general
	                         33-41

The Pentecontaetia
How a unified, aggressive and resilient Athens acquired her empire   89-118
 	
The second conference at Sparta: Speech of the Corinthians
                119-125
	The Athenians in Sicily
	The Athenians are hesitant and militarily ineffective because of dissension among the generals
	                  42-52

Pericles charged by Sparta with blood guilt. Digression on Pausanias and Themistocles, one Spartan, one Athenian 126-139	Alcibiades charged by Athens with sacrilege Digression on Harmodius and Aristogeiton and their effect on Hippias' tyranny 53-61
	The Athenians before Syracuse Nicias fails to follow up his advantage and the Athenians lose their opportunity to end the war quickly with a victory 62-75

	Conference at Camarina
	Speeches of: Hermocrates
	                Euphemus, an
	                Athenian 76-88

Pericles' speech at Athens calling for war against Sparta 140-144	Alcibiades' speech at Sparta calling for war against Athens 89-92
Summary of the speech's effect: *Arche* of the first ten-year war 1.145-2.1	Summary of the speech's effect: *Arche* of the second ten-year war 93

ments in the Peloponnesian War, one before the first ten-year war, the other before the second. The analogies are drawn with care and subtlety and they pervade every episode in these two books. Books I and VI are each written with the other in mind.

THE ARCHAEOLOGIES

Both books begin with a statement about the war that Thucydides is about to describe and a declaration of its greatness. In Book I Thucydides says he expected the war of the Peloponnesians and Athenians to be great and indeed more worthy of récord than all previous wars. In Book VI he says that the Athenians wanted to conquer Sicily, ignorant of its size and the number of its inhabitants and of the fact that they were taking on a war only barely inferior to the one against the Peloponnesians. Here at the very outset Thucydides explicitly compares this new Athenian venture with the first war and finds it nearly equal in magnitude. The reader is thus told to compare two wars. The second sentence in both books begins an explanation and proof of the first: Book I—"For [γάρ] this was the greatest κίνησις"; Book VI—"For [γάρ] the periplous of Sicily." The third sentence then states the difficulty, in each case, of acquiring a reliable picture of the early history of the area involved: Book I—"It was impossible to find out clearly"; Book VI—"The oldest inhabitants are said to be the Cyclopes and Laistrygones, whose race I am unable to identify, and I cannot say where they came from or where they went; let what the poets say and what each person thinks about them be sufficient." The fourth sentence then commences the archaeology proper: Book I—"For what is now called Hellas appears not to have been securely inhabited long ago"; Book VI—"The Sicanians appear to have been its [Sicily's] first inhabitants after them."

The similarity between these two sets of four sentences is too great to be accidental or unconscious. Thucydides has composed them according to the same pattern. First comes the statement of the size of the war (and an explicit comparison in 6.1.1), then the proof. The difficulty of reconstructing the past is registered, and the record of successive inhabitants is then begun with the oldest. In each book an "archaeology" follows, the first of mainland Greece, the second of Sicily. In each Thucydides makes a conscientious and indeed self-conscious attempt to find out the truth about the past. He mentions the evidence of the poets in a way that makes clear his low opinion of their reliability (1.9.4, 1.10.3; 1.21.1; 6.2.1). He uses the argument from likelihood when evidence fails (1.4; 1.9.4; 1.10.4; 6.4). He refers with evident pride to his own efforts as attempts to find the truth (1.20-21; 6.2.2). Each archaeology is a record of the successive generations of inhabitation, with the emphasis on the rise of powerful states.

There are, of course, differences between the archaeologies. The first is far more analytical. By that we mean that in Book I Thucydides was concerned with how civilization, particularly power, developed in the course of generations from weak, constantly changing towns to settled, secure cities. In Book VI there is no such concern because there is no need for it. The first archaeology had outlined the probable course of development, not simply for Greece, but generally for mankind. Thus in Book VI there is no need for extended analysis of the benefits that money, walls, stability, and ships confer in creating *dynamis*. Nor is there a need to speak again of the relative insignificance of the Trojan War. Instead, the primary concern of the second archaeology is to familiarize Greeks with the size of Sicily and the number of its cities. Chapter 2 describes the island's barbarian settlements,[5] 3, 4, and 5 register the Greek foundations, which are surprisingly and impressively numerous. Thucydides adds to this impression by his plain, repetitive style of recording the centuries of Greek colonization. By the end of chapter 5 we are not only aware of the Athenian miscalculation of the size and strength of Sicily, we are appalled by it. This is surely the reaction Thucydides meant us to have. Thus, while the first archaeology was designed to show us the relative insignificance of early Greece, the second was composed to impress upon us the surprising size and power of contemporary Sicily.

Both archaeologies are thus concerned, though in different ways, with a question of size and power. But there is another, often overlooked, parallelism. Each archaeology has its exemplar. In the first it is Athens which stands out: "But the

---

[5] Note how Thucydides was interested in the naming of Sicily (6.2.2 and 6.2.4) just as he was in the naming of Greece (1.3.2).

same people always inhabited Attica . . . and, becoming citizens immediately from antiquity they made the city greater still in the number of inhabitants" (1.2.5-6). It is Athens which best exhibits Thucydides' course of progress from barbarity to civilization. Her history reveals most clearly the successive benefits of stability, increase in population, walls, ships, commerce, income, reserves, which eventually lead to thalassocracy, the apex of civilized power. The case of Athens is thus a paradigm for historical development from migratory barbarity to settled, stable civilization. In the same way Syracuse stands out from the mass of cities in the second archaeology: "And in the following year Archias . . . founded Syracuse, first driving the Sicels out of the island in which now. . . . And later, when the outer part was enclosed by a wall it became populous [*polyanthropos*]" (6.3.2). Again here are mentioned walls and high concentration of population, the elements necessary for power. And, like Athens, Syracuse extended her influence by sending off excess population to colonize other areas (see 6.5.2-3). Syracuse, it is clear, is the Athens of Sicily, at least potentially. She has the prerequisites for *dynamis*. Not only does Thucydides compose archaeologies at the beginning of both introductions, but he composes archaeologies that begin identically, make similar, indeed parallel points, and often in the same language.

THE ALETHESTATE PROPHASIS

Chapters 20 and 21 of the first book are a discussion of the methodology used in the archaeology. Chapter 22 describes the methodology used in the rest of the work. There was no reason for Thucydides to repeat these remarks in Book VI. In 1.23 Thucydides returns, after his historical and methodological digressions, to his subject, the Peloponnesian War. The first three sections, which again apply to the whole work, emphasize its great length and the unparalleled suffering it caused. In sections 4 to 6 Thucydides states its causes. There is no need here to discuss this famous passage at great length.[6] Let us in-

[6] See Hunter R. Rawlings III, *A Semantic Study of Prophasis to 400 B.C.*, Hermes Einzelschrift, vol. 33 (Wiesbaden 1975).

stead note the remarkable parallelism between this statement of causes in 1.23.5-6 and the similar assertion in 6.6.1. Section 1.23.5-6 begins: "And as to why they broke the peace, I wrote first the *aitiai* and the *diaphorai*, so that no one will ever seek the background out of which so great a war arose among the Greeks. But as for the truest *prophasis*, though the least apparent in talk, I believe that the Athenians, becoming powerful and causing fear in the Lacedaemonians, forced them into war." Section 6.6.1 begins: "So many races of Greeks and barbarians inhabited Sicily, and the Athenians were eager to send an expedition against it in spite of its size; they desired to rule all of it [that is the truest *prophasis*], but at the same time they wanted [speciously] to aid their kinsmen and the allies acquired before."[7]

It is difficult to overemphasize the significance of this parallelism of language. The phrase *alethestate prophasis*, striking enough to the Greek ear, occurs only twice in extant Greek literature, in these two passages. In each case Thucydides uses it to distinguish between openly-avowed wishes or charges and the real cause. This distinction, crucial to Thucydides' view of causality, is made to apply to both wars, the Peloponnesian and the Sicilian. Moreover, since the Sicilian expedition leads directly to the Spartan decision to reenter the war with Athens and since Alcibiades' picture of Athenian ambitions to rule Sicily and the whole Mediterranean is an important factor in that Spartan decision, the *alethestate prophasis* of the Sicilian expedition is also the truest cause of the second ten-year war between Athens and Sparta. The truest reason for the first war is the growth of Athenian power and the consequent fear it caused in the Spartans; the truest reason for the second war is the Athenians' desire to spread their empire to Sicily, the Mediterranean, and eventually the Peloponnese, and the consequent decision by the Spartans to stop the process in Sicily before it went too far to be stopped. That Thucydides meant the reader to be reminded in Book VI of the passage in Book

[7] See A. W. Gomme, A. Andrewes, and K. J. Dover, *A Historical Commentary on Thucydides* (Oxford 1945-1970) on 6.6.1 regarding πρo- versus πρos-. Hereafter cited as *Comm.*

I seems quite likely. With the phrase *alethestate prophasis* he is, as it were, holding up a sign for the reader saying "Recall, if you will, the real reason for the outbreak of the first ten-year war. Compare the causes of the two wars."[8] Immediately after the archaeologies, Thucydides wrote in both Books I and VI statements of the truest cause of the wars. He not only composed the two books with parallel structures, but he used identical language to stress the similar features in the two cases.

This use of a striking phrase a second time should alert the conscientious reader to the importance of what follows in chapter 6 of Book VI. The Athenians are confronted with a choice in Sicily remarkably similar to the decision they had to make in 433. An embassy has come from the Segestans asking for support from Athens for Segesta's war against Selinus and Syracuse. The envoys' chief argument (κεφάλαιον in 6.2) is that if the Athenians allow Syracuse to continue to strip Athens of allies in Sicily and gain total control of the island, there is a danger lest that powerful Dorian city join her kinsmen in the Peloponnese and put an end to Athenian power. It would therefore be wise for the Athenians to join their Sicilian allies in opposing Syracuse now, and in Sicily. Is this not a similar argument to that which Corcyra presented to the Athenians in 433? In that year envoys came from the Corcyraeans to ask Athens for help in their war with Corinth, which was raising forces in the Peloponnese and the rest of Greece (1.31.1). The envoys' primary argument (βραχυτάτῳ . . . κεφαλαίῳ in 1.36.3) is that there are three Greek cities with substantial fleets, Athens, Corinth, and Corcyra; if the Athenians allow the Corinthians to gain control of Corcyra and her fleet, then Athens will have to fight against a formidable sea power when the war with the Peloponnesians breaks out, as it inevitably and soon will because of Lacedaemonian fear and Corinthian hatred of Athens (1.33.3). It is therefore best for the Athenians and Corcyraeans to make an alliance now in order to form plans against the Peloponnesians rather than wait to defeat the plans they might form first. Thucydides tells

[8] See K. von Fritz, *Die Griechische Geschichtsschreibung* (Berlin 1967) 1:724-725. Hereafter cited as *Gr. Ges.*

us (1.44.2) that it was this argument which persuaded the Athenians to accept the request for alliance.

The Athenians are given nearly identical choices by Corcyra and Segesta. In each case the city making the offer really wants Athenian help in a war of its own making, indeed, a war in which the Athenians have had little interest. But in order to obtain Athenian assistance each "freely" offers its money and assistance to Athens for a war which, it argues, will come to Athens whether she accepts the offer of alliance or not.[9] The situations are quite similar. But the careful reader, alerted to the parallelism between the two cases by the similarity of structure and language with which Thucydides composes them, will note also several important differences, which are also subtly brought out by Thucydides' historiographical treatment. In order to make clear to the reader the similarities between the two situations but the differences in the Athenian responses to them, the historian reported certain speeches delivered in Athens in both Books I and VI. Why he selected the ones he did, and how he drew comparison and contrast simultaneously, we shall see shortly.

THE TWO ATHENIAN ASSEMBLIES

Before comparing the first pair of speeches in Book I with their counterpart in Book VI, it is useful to examine briefly all the speeches of Books I and VI, in order to appreciate the degree to which Thucydides selected them for purposes of comparison. A glance at Figure 2 reveals how closely the speeches in Book VI reflect those of Book I in number, speaker, occasion, and subject.

Even this cursory survey should suggest that Books I and VI, chapters 1-93 were planned as a pair. Thucydides has chosen to report parallel sets of speeches at parallel places in the narrative.[10] This evidence corroborates that of the archaeologies and

[9] Neither offer is fulfilled. The Corcyraean fleet is never of any use to the Athenians because of Corcyra's devastating civil war. The promised Segestan money did not exist.

[10] See O. Regenbogen, *Kleine Schriften* (Munich 1961) 221; and Stahl, "Speeches and Course of Events in Books Six and Seven of Thu-

FIGURE 2

I			VI	
Corcyraeans	(32-36)		Nicias	(9-14)
Corinthians	(37-43)	ATHENS	Alcibiades	(16-28)
			Nicias	(20-23)
Corinthians	(68-71)		Hermocrates	(33-34)
Athenians	(73-78)		Athenagoras	(36-40)
Archidamus	(80-85)	SPARTA SYRACUSE	Syracusan	
Spartan ephor	(86)		general	(41)
Corinthians	(120-124)	SPARTA CAMARINA	Hermocrates	(76-80)
			Euphemus	(82-87)
Pericles	(140-144)	ATHENS SPARTA	Alcibiades	(89-92)

the two statements of *alethestate prophasis*. When we turn to a more detailed analysis of the speeches themselves, we do so with a broadened perspective, in fact with a double vision which the historian has provided for us. We read Books I and VI together.

The Corcyraeans begin with a defense of their conduct (ἐπιτήδευμα in 32.3). Their previous policy of staying away from entangling alliances (ἀπραγμοσύνη in 32.5) which seemed to be σωφροσύνη (32.4), appears now to be ignorance and weakness (32.4). It is necessary to look for allies against the menace of Corinth. Such an alliance, freely offered without danger and expense (ἄνευ κινδύνων καὶ δαπάνης in 33.2), will be beneficial to Athens too, because in her inevitable and fast-approaching war with Sparta and Corinth she will need the Corcyraean fleet (33.3, 36.1). Worry about breaking the peace is misplaced. Athens' real concern should be with preparing against her enemies before they prepare against her (33.4). He who makes the fewest changes as concessions to the enemy is the one who comes out most safely (ἀσφαλέστατος in 34.2).

The Corinthians begin with an attack upon Corcyra's past conduct. Her apparent sophrosyne was really a specious attempt to carry on an unjust policy in private (37.2-4). Now she is asking Athens to join her in iniquity (39). It would be

cydides" in *The Speeches in Thucydides*, ed. Philip A. Stadter (Chapel Hill 1973) 77.

wrong and unlawful for Athens to accept this request for an alliance (40-41). Let the young learn from their elders (42.1). You Athenians should above all not listen to all this talk of a coming war with which the Corcyraeans are trying to frighten you (ᾧ φοβοῦντες ὑμᾶς Κερκυραῖοι), since that lies in the uncertain (ἐν ἀφανεῖ) future (42.2).

In Book VI the arguments are similar but their reference is different. So is the order of the speeches. Alcibiades begins with a defense of his own conduct (ἐπιτηδεύμασιν in 15.4). The personal extravagance that has caused envy and hatred in Athens has actually been beneficial to the city. After all, he was able, because of his reputation and skill, to gather, without great danger and expense to Athens (ἄνευ μεγάλου ὑμῖν κινδύνου καὶ δαπάνης in 16.6) the most powerful Peloponnesian cities together in a coalition to force Sparta to risk all on a single battle. Worry about Sicily is unnecessary; the cities on the island are politically and militarily inefficient and weak (17). Athens' real business is to continue the policy responsible for her acquiring an empire in the first place, that of intervening, wherever and whenever possible. Athens must attack others before they attack her; otherwise there is a danger lest she be ruled by others rather than ruling them (18.1-3). Do not let Nicias' ἀπραγμοσύνη turn you away from your real nature. A city that is not *apragmon* would swiftly be destroyed by a change to a policy of *apragmosyne*; by the same token those men live most safely (ἀσφαλέστατα) who act politically according to their own nature and custom, even if they are not the best (18.7).

Nicias begins by alluding to the weakness of the argument that it is better for Athens to preserve what she has than to risk even that for the sake of what is unseen and in the future (περὶ τῶν ἀφανῶν καὶ μελλόντων in 9.3). It is dangerous to leave so many enemies behind in Greece while setting off on a far-flung and difficult expedition (10). Leave the Sicilians alone. The Segestans are trying to frighten us (ἡμᾶς ἐκφοβοῦσιν) with the prospect of a Syracusan empire in Sicily. That holds no threat compared with the Spartans, who are constantly looking for an opportunity to redeem their lost *arete* (11), and with the young warmongers here in the assembly who want commands only for their own private advantage (12). You elders should not be ashamed to vote against a war which holds the greatest dangers for the city (13.1).[11] The best citizen is he who always consults for the good of the city, even when such a position appears unpopular (14).

The speeches make similar points in similar, sometimes identical language. Corcyra and Alcibiades push Athens toward a major war. Corinth and Nicias try to prevent it. But in comparing these speeches, we must keep in mind Thucydides' principle of selection. In Book I he gives the speeches of both delegations to Athens, Corcyraeans and Corinthians. He then tells us (1.44.1) that the Athenians held two assemblies and that in the first they accepted the Corinthian arguments against allying with Corcyra.[12] But in a second assembly they changed their minds and decided to form a defensive alliance with the Corcyraeans, according to which each side would help the other if it were attacked. Historians would dearly love to have a report of the Athenians' debates in these two assemblies: who spoke on which side? why? why did opinions change in favor of the *epimachia*? what was Pericles' position?[13] Thucydides could have answered these questions, either in a short narrative report or through speeches. He chose not to. Instead, he thought it more important to give us the Corcyraean and Corinthian speeches.

In Book VI he made the opposite choice. He describes in one paragraph (6.6.2) the first Segestan embassy to Athens in winter 416/415 and reports the second Segestan embassy the following summer in two sentences (6.8.1-2). It was at this assembly that the Athenians voted to send sixty ships to Sicily "to help the Segestans, to restore the Leontines and to carry out

[11] Compare Nicias' speech with Archidamus' in Book I, especially 6.13.1 with 1.80.1. Both speak against war, are then chosen to lead it, and fail to achieve objects because they virtually sabotage their expeditions. See V. Hunter, *Thucydides: The Artful Reporter* (Toronto 1973) 127-130.

[12] Did they hold a vote? Probably not; see Gomme, *Comm.* on 1.44.1.

[13] See D. Kagan, *The Outbreak of the Peloponnesian War* (Ithaca, N. Y. 1969) 237.

actions in Sicily to the best advantage of the Athenians." He elects to give us the full speeches delivered by Nicias and Alcibiades at another assembly held five days later. He even appends another speech by Nicias that failed utterly to achieve its object. Indeed, it had an effect directly contrary to what Nicias intended (24.2). His last attempt to turn the Athenians away from the expedition by a recitation of the immense preparations necessary for success only served to whet their appetites more. Preparations began immediately amid an atmosphere of passion and excitement (ἔρως in 24.3, ἐπιθυμία in 24.4). The emphasis is totally different, indeed it is reversed. In Book I Thucydides underplays the political split, clearly serious, which the decision caused in Athens. In Book VI he goes out of his way to emphasize not only the uninformed and greedy passion characterizing the Athenian decision, but the dissension that it caused in the generalship itself between the extravagant and ambitious Alcibiades and the cautious and conservative Nicias. It is necessary to stress that this was a matter of historiographical decision. Thucydides could have done the reverse. Why did he make the choices he did?

Thucydides wanted to contrast the Athens of 415 with the Athens of 433. The latter was, in Thucydides' view, a great and unified city under the wise and strong guidance of a capable leader. We are not allowed even a glimpse of political debate or controversy in the assembly. A decision is made, then changed. We are not told the reason, only the result. An excellent compromise is reached, *epimachia* with Corcyra. Her powerful fleet is added to Athens' own, but no breach of the peace is committed. The Athenians have added a potentially useful ally for the coming war with the Peloponnesians but have done nothing, at least technically, to provoke that war. This perspective is maintained throughout Book I. We learn only of Athenian actions, never of Athenian policy making. The Athenians almost always act as a unified, purposeful power: in the war against Potidaea; in the speech at Sparta; in the Pentacontaetia against everyone.[14] The introduction to the first

[14] This last is the most remarkable case, historiographically speaking. There is not a word of internal Athenian politics during the period

war ends with another Athenian assembly, this one held to give a final answer to Sparta on war and peace (139.3). At this one too speeches were delivered on both sides (139.4) of a critical issue, but we are given only one, that of Pericles himself. Again there is no interest in Athenian political debate. It was, from Thucydides' point of view, unimportant. There is only cool and dispassionate logic, a calculating assessment of the odds presented by the threatened war with Sparta. Athens is portrayed in Book I, and indeed in most of the first war as a unified state of singular power and purpose. She is, as the Corinthians say, "swift to plan and swift to carry out what she has planned" (70.2). This is because under Pericles Athens was "more the rule of the first citizen than a democracy" (2.65.9).

In 415 the situation was different. Athens was a changed city. We can hardly recognize her. There were two reasons for the change: Athens' political leadership was split among men more on a level with one another, each vying for control. To win control, these men appealed to the masses, the demos, for support, and thus were led by the demos rather than leaders of it. The results were devastating:

> From which many other mistakes were made, as would be expected in a city that was great and held an empire, and particularly the Sicilian expedition, which was not so much an error in the enemies whom it attacked, as much as the fact that those who sent it out did not later take sufficient measures for those who had gone out, but became occupied with private disputes about the leadership of the demos and blunted military effectiveness and for the first time brought political dissension in the city. (2.65.11)

The problem became manifest after Pericles' death, but catastrophic only in 415. That was when Athens' military capability was first affected and her political unity was first broken. What better way to introduce these themes than a full-scale presentation of the bitter debate in the Athenian assembly of

---

479-433 B.C. There is, in fact, hardly a name, except those of the leaders of expeditions.

415? This is Thucydides' first warning to the reader that the
second ten-year war will be different from the first. Similar
opportunities arose, but different responses followed. This time
there was no *epimachia*, but rather a massive invasion of Sicily,
the most ambitious in Greek history (6.31.1), undertaken amid
greed, ignorance, and divided leadership. Thucydides never
lets us forget the last. He gives us not only the debate at the
assembly in chapters 8-26, but also the dissension among the
generals (6.47-49), the incident of the Herms, the sacrilege of
Alcibiades, the panic in the city, even a long digression on that
earlier example of internal breakdown in Athens, the tyrannicide and its effects. Thucydides' interest in Book VI is in Athenian division. He takes every opportunity to note it, describe
it, analyze it, dramatize it, in short, to emphasize it because he
felt that it was the crucial factor in the second ten-year war. It
resulted in a political coup in 411 that produced nearly fatal
division, and political dissolution in 405, when divided leadership gave the final victory to Sparta. In the second ten-year war
Athenian internal politics not only impinged upon the war,
they dictated it. This is the reason for Thucydides' historiographical choices of speeches at the assemblies in Books I and
VI. The reader is properly informed of the difference in political leadership, carefully prepared for what will follow. As
von Fritz, who adumbrates these same points in his *Griechische Geschichtsschreibung*, tellingly remarks,

> Die Geschichte der Expedition gegen Melos und die Vor-
> geschichte der sizilischen Expedition weisen also starke kom-
> positorische Zusammenhänge mit der Vorgeschichte des
> Archidamischen Krieges auf, aber so, dass gerade durch die
> Analogien in der Komposition der Vorgeschichte des sizi-
> lischen Unternehmens und des Archidamischen Krieges die
> Unterschiede der Politik, die zu dem einen und zu dem
> andern Ereignis führten, besonders deutlich in Erscheinung
> treten.[15]

[15] von Fritz, *Gr. Ges.*, 725-731. "The history of the expedition against
Melos and the prelude to the Sicilian Expedition thus exhibit strong
compositional connections with the prelude to the Archidamian War,

POTIDAEA; THE HERMOCOPIDAE

In Book I Thucydides concludes his account of the first *aitia* of the war (55.2) with the description of the Battle of Sybota. He then proceeds to narrate the second *aitia* involving the revolt of Potidaea and the escalation of Athenian-Corinthian hostilities. This account is a full and detailed description of the difficulties Athens faced in dealing with an ally in revolt, especially one which was a colony of her enemies, was located on the Greek mainland, and was close to a power hostile to Athens. Potidaea derived a special advantage from each of these facts: she had strong sympathy in the Peloponnese, especially from Corinth; she could be reached by land from the Peloponnese; she had a natural ally in Perdiccas, King of Macedon. All three advantages were exploited in the revolt, which taxed Athens severely, in time, manpower, and money (1.65.2, 2.58, 2.70.2). Thucydides thus had ample reason to describe the revolt in detail. But there is another aspect of his historiographical treatment requiring attention, attention which it has not heretofore received.

Thucydides takes great care in portraying the leader of the forces that came to Potidaea's aid. The Corinthian Aristeus came at the head of 1600 hoplites and 400 light-armed troops. Some were mercenaries from the Peloponnese (τῶν ἄλλων Πελοποννησίων μισθῷ πείσαντες; 1.60.1), the rest were Corinthian volunteers, most of them willing participants in the expedition because of friendship with Aristeus, who had always been closely tied to the Potidaeans. Throughout the account Thucydides enables us to follow Aristeus' thoughts and actions with some precision. The allies (Peloponnesians, Potidaeans, Chalcideans, Bottiaeans, and Perdiccas, who had also sent to Lacedaemon and Corinth for help against Athens; 57.4) elect him general over their whole infantry. In 62.3 we are given his plan of battle. In 62.6 we are told of the victory

---

in such a way, however, that through the analogies in composition between the prelude of the Sicilian undertaking and that of the Archidamian War the differences in the politics which led to the two events are brought to light with particular clarity" (p. 731).

of the troops on his wing over the Athenians. In 63.1 we follow his consequent dilemma, whether to try to save Olynthus or Potidaea. He chooses the latter and succeeds under great stress. When reinforcements arrive from Athens and complete the encirclement of Potidaea, he is again faced with a difficult problem, described for us in detail: how to obtain assistance from the Peloponnese. His plan to help 500 persons escape in order to make the food supply last longer does not persuade the populace, in spite of his willingness to stay behind himself. He therefore effects his own escape and, remaining among the Chalcidians, continues to carry on the war against Athens, with notable success. This success is all the more remarkable since his repeated attempts to attract help from the Peloponnese were apparently unsuccessful (65.2). The Athenians were so severely harmed by his activities at Potidaea and in Thrace that when he was caught, a few years later, together with other ambassadors from the Peloponnese on their way to the Persian king, they put the whole embassy to death the same day they were brought to Athens, without trial and in spite of their request to speak in their own defense (2.67). They were afraid that Aristeus would escape and cause them more trouble.

Thucydides thought Aristeus important not simply because of his own actions, but because of the example he set. He was the precursor of the general responsible for Sparta's recovery from the shock and loss of confidence caused by Pylos. Moreover, Brasidas' expedition to Thrace is a replica of Aristeus'! He came to precisely the same area with a nearly identical army in both size and composition: 700 helot "volunteers," 1000 mercenaries from the Peloponnese (τοὺς δ᾽ ἄλλους ἐκ τῆς Πελοποννήσου μισθῷ πείσας, 4.80.5; see 4.78.1). These 1700 hoplites were almost exactly the equal of Aristeus' 1600 hoplites and 400 light-armed soldiers. Brasidas too was invited by Athenian subjects who had revolted and by Perdiccas (4.79.2). He too tried unsuccessfully to relieve Potidaea (4.135.1). He also failed, despite several attempts, to obtain reinforcements from the Peloponnese (4.108.6-7). Above all, Brasidas, like Aristeus, succeeded in causing Athens enormous difficulties in the Thraceward region with little more than his wits, his courage, and his bravado. Both men had precious little help from their governments at home in the Peloponnese and no regular citizen troops, but they made up for those deficiencies with intelligence and personal ability.

For these reasons Thucydides felt it useful to portray the actions and thoughts of Aristeus at some length in his account of the Potidaean revolt. His expedition was, after all, a sign of things to come in the first ten-year war, indeed, a precursor of the campaign which, more than any other, was responsible for ending that war. This account in 1.56-66 is thus an historiographical model for later events in the first war.

In the same way Thucydides gives us in Book VI a detailed exposition of the incident that so rudely marred Athenian preparations for the Sicilian expedition. After the assembly voted to give the generals control over the size of the forces and the planning of the voyage (26.1), the preparations begin. Thucydides reminds us of the position Athens is now in: "the city had recently recovered from the plague and the continuous war, both in terms of number of soldiers and financially, because of the period of truce, so that everything was more easily provided" (26.2). Again the same distinction is made between parts of the war that Thucydides first made in 5.25-26, this time at the beginning of Athenian preparations for the expedition which would cause the breaking of the truce and the beginning of a second continuous war. Even while preparations were being made an event occurred that seemed to forbode ill: most of the stone Hermae in the city were secretly mutilated. No one could identify the culprits, but rumormongers implicated Alcibiades, in this and other such desecrations. His political enemies fed the rumors with talk of an intended coup against the democracy, citing his undemocratic, excessive style of living. Competition for political leadership now seriously marred the preparations. Politics began to blunt military capability, the theme of Thucydides' second war. Indeed, this war was decided by Athenian political dissension. The Sicilian expedition failed because of it (2.65.11),[16] the final battle of the war was

[16] See W. Thompson, "Thucydides II, 65, 11," *Historia* 20 (1971) 141-151.

lost because of it.[17] Thucydides' detailed description of the opposition that Alcibiades faced amid political enemies, informers, rumors, and gossip serves as a prologue to many such cases in the next ten years, all of which contributed to Athens' downfall. Just as the narrative of the Potidaean revolt revealed the nature of the problems Athens would have to face in the northern region of her empire, so the narrative of the defacing of the Herms shows us the essence of the internal dissension that so sorely beset Athens in the second war. The great expedition to Sicily left under a cloud in spite of its immense size and splendor, which made it the greatest undertaking of any Greek city up to that time, greater even than the expedition to Epidaurus under Pericles, and the same one to Potidaea under Hagnon (31.2).

THE CONFERENCES AT SPARTA AND SYRACUSE

After Thucydides has in Books I and VI given the reader a sample of debate in the assembly and followed that debate with an account of consequent Athenian actions, he takes him to a conference in the city of Athens' future enemy, Sparta in Book I (67-88), Syracuse in Book VI (33-41). By selecting several speeches delivered at these two conferences for presentation, Thucydides enables us to form an impression of the character (*tropos*) of Athens' opponent in the coming war. Thus he continues his introductory portrait of the two sides on the eve of the two wars, Athens and Sparta in 433/432, Athens and Syracuse in 416/415. But we find once again in the parallel structures more of a contrast than a comparison. Just as the Athens of 415 differs from the Athens of 432, so Syracuse is nearly the opposite of Sparta. Later in his work Thucydides made this point explicitly: "Not in this instance alone were the Lacedaemonians the most convenient of all enemies for the

[17] It appears virtually certain that the Athenian fleet at Aegospotami was betrayed to Lysander by at least some, if not all, of its commanders. See Xenophon, *Hellenica* 2.1.32, Lysias 2.58, 14.38, Pausanias 4.17.2, 10.9.5, Socrates *ad Philipp. Or.* 5.70 and George Grote, *A History of Greece*, 12 vols. (London 1869) 8:11-12.

Athenians, but in many other cases as well. For they were completely different in character (*tropos*), the one swift, the other
slow, the one daring, the other not, and the Athenians particularly benefited in their naval empire. The Syracusans
showed this: for, being especially close in character to the
Athenians, they were their most able opponents" (8.96.5). The
Spartans are the opposites of the Athenians, the Syracusans are
ὁμοιότροποι.[18] Such is the picture Thucydides draws in his
two conferences. His selection of speeches elicits comparisons
and contrasts. The only speech without a counterpart is the
Athenian speech in Book I (73-78). This speech, however,
finds an almost exact parallel in the Athenian Euphemus'
speech at Camarina in Book VI (82-86), and I shall withhold
it from discussion until we reach that point.

The Corinthians speak first in Book I, Hermocrates in Book
VI. Both speeches begin with the theme of trust and ignorance:
"Your trust, Lacedaemonians, in your own political and social
institutions makes you, if we may say so, distrustful of others;
as a result you are moderate at home, but rather ignorant when
it comes to foreign affairs" (1.68.1); and "Perhaps I, like some
of the others, shall appear to you to make untrustworthy remarks about the truth of the expedition; I am aware that those
who say or announce things which seem to be untrustworthy
not only fail to persuade, but also appear to be ignorant"
(6.33.1). The triplets Τὸ πιστὸν ... ἀπιστοτέρους ... ἀμαθία,
Ἄπιστα ... τὰ μὴ πιστὰ ... ἄφρονες parallel one another.
The Corinthians assail the Spartans for their failure to heed
repeated warnings from their allies that Athens is seriously
harming and threatening them. Though they have legitimate
complaints against Athens, the allies have been consistently
neglected (ἀμελούμενοι) by the Spartans. It is already late in
the day, they affirm, time to see, not whether they are wronged,
but how they can defend themselves (καθ' ὅτι ἀμυνούμεθα;
69.2). Hermocrates chides the Syracusans in similar language:
"The Athenians come against you with a great army and
fleet, intending to conquer you and thereby all of Sicily. Since
they will soon be here see how you can best defend yourselves

[18] See also 7.55.2.

81

[ὅτῳ τρόπῳ κάλλιστα ἀμυνεῖσθε αὐτούς]. Do not be caught defenseless, do not, in your distrust, be guilty of neglect" (μή τε ἀπιστήσαντες . . . ἀμελήσετε; 6.33.2-3). Both speeches begin with an appeal for trust first, then immediate defensive action.

The Corinthians intensify their attack upon Spartan βρα-δύτης: "We both know that the Persian came from the ends of the earth to the Peloponnese before you put up any opposition, and now you overlook Athenian aggression right next door" (1.69.5). They then add, the barbarian failed, for the most part, because of his own problems (τὸν βάρβαρον αὐτὸν περὶ αὐτῷ τὰ πλείω σφαλέντα), and we have succeeded in the past against the Athenians primarily because of their errors too. Hermocrates makes the same point. Do not fear the size of the Athenian forces. Few great expeditions, Greek or barbarian, which went far from home have succeeded. And if they fail (ἤν . . . σφαλῶσι) because of a lack of provisions in alien land, they leave a reputation to those whom they attacked, even if they failed, for the most part, because of their own problems (κἂν περὶ σφίσιν αὐτοῖς τὰ πλείω πταίσωσιν). This indeed happened to these same Athenians when, against all expectations, the Persian failed (τοῦ Μήδου παρὰ λόγον πολλὰ σφαλέντος). Hermocrates here echoes the Corinthians' point and then generalizes it to include all great armies that undertake long expeditions.

The Corinthians, after their brilliant portrayal of the differences in national temper and character beween Athens and Sparta (70) go on to castigate Sparta's well-known ἡσυχία (71.1 and 71.3); in the same way Hermocrates, introducing a plan for meeting the Athenian fleet with offensive action, deprecates the Syracusans' "customary quiet" (τὸ ξύνηθες ἥσυχον in 34.4).[19] Each concludes with an appeal for an end to habitual delay and hesitation in the form of an immediate attack against Athens the aggressor. Corinthians: "Let your βραδύτης end here; help the Potidaeans and others now, as you promised, by invading Attica immediately" (71.4). After outlining his plan of attack, Hermocrates exhorts the Syracusans: "I could wish to persuade you to show this kind of courage; but if not,

[19] Quiet only, however, in foreign affairs: See 6.38.3.

prepare immediately in other ways for the war. . . . The Athenians attack us, indeed are already on the way and all but here —that I know" (34.9). The first speeches at both conferences are thus calls to action against Athens the aggressor.

The speeches delivered by leaders of the two cities to which these appeals are made—Archidamus the Spartan in Book I and Athenagoras the Syracusan in Book VI—serve to acquaint us more closely with the nature of these two opponents of Athens. Thucydides selects carefully. One of his purposes is to contrast Sparta and Syracuse: "And Archidamus their king came forward, a man who seemed to be both wise and moderate, and he spoke as follows" (1.79.2); then in Book VI, "And Athenagoras came forward, a man who was *prostates* of the demos and at that time most persuasive with the masses, and he spoke as follows" (6.35.2). The two men could not be more ideally suited to represent their cities: the wise and moderate Spartan king who praises Spartan slowness and hesitation as wise moderation, which has made the city free and respected through all time; the witch-hunting Syracusan demagogue who embodies the worst characteristics of the volatile Syracusan democracy, which has been so frequently interrupted by factional strife and unjust tyranny (38.3). Through these two mouthpieces Thucydides draws his contrast. Indeed, Athenagoras' speech seems to be reported for this purpose alone. His advice, such as it is, is not taken, and he is not heard from again in Thucydides' history, or anywhere else for that matter. His speech is recorded only for the light it sheds upon Syracusan political and social conditions.

Each begins with an assessment of his own city's adequacy for a war with Athens. Archidamus is pessimistic: "On what basis could we, unprepared as we are, start a war against men who live far away, are most experienced on the sea and are superbly prepared in all other respects too [τοῖς ἄλλοις ἅπασιν ἄριστα ἐξήρτυνται], in private and public wealth, in ships, horses, heavy infantry and sheer numbers better off than any other single Greek state, and who in addition have many tribute-paying allies" (1.80.3). Athenagoras seems to have this very sentence in mind when he makes his own appraisal: "And

83

if, as is said, the Athenians do come, I believe that Sicily is better able than the Peloponnese to defeat them to the extent that it is better prepared in all respects" (ὅσῳ κατὰ πάντα ἄμει-νον ἐξήρτυται; 6.37.1). He goes on to register Syracusan superiority to the invasion force in horses, in hoplites and "in other resources" (τὴν τε ἄλλην παρασκευήν). Here is an explicit comparison between Peloponnesian and Sicilian resources, made in similar terms and language. The Sicilians are, in Athenagoras' mind, clearly superior. For this reason he wonders whether or not it is "likely that they [the Athenians] would leave behind the war which is not yet firmly settled there and come willingly to another comparable war in Sicily" (36.4).

After his initial assessment of the military odds each speaker turns to consider the political situation in his own city. Here we see two entirely different sets of political institutions, one characterized by sophrosyne, εὔκοσμον, εὐβουλία, and ἐλευθερία, the other by stasis, tyranny, division between old and young, democrats and oligarchs. Sparta is an old and stable oligarchy, as Thucydides had told us in the first archaeology (1.18.1). She derives her strength from this very stability (δι᾽ αὐτὸ δυνάμε-νοι). Syracuse, as Thucydides tells us in the second archaeology (6.3.2) is next to the sea, has defensive walls and is heavily populated. She is governed, as Athenagoras tells us, by a democracy (39.1-2). All of these characteristics make her a second Athens, or at least a potential second Athens. There are dangers in a volatile and unstable democracy, dangers which Nicias will nearly exploit to Athens' advantage (7.48.2 and especially 7.49.1). The crux is politics. Who will emerge as the city's leader, the rabble rouser Athenagoras or the intelligent and resourceful Hermocrates, the new Cleon or the new Pericles? This is the issue that will determine the fate of Syracuse and, for that matter, the fate of Athens.

Thucydides concludes his two conferences with short speeches, the first by "one of the ephors," of Sparta, Sthenelaidas, the second by "one of the generals" of Syracuse. Sthenelaidas wastes no words: "If we are wise [ἢν σωφρονῶμεν] we will not allow our allies to be injured" (1.86.2). He goes on to say that others have money, ships, and horses, we have brave allies. This issue should not be settled with law and words, but with arms. Vote, worthily of Sparta, for war. The Syracusan general is more calm and far more circumspect: "It is not wise [οὐ σῶφρον] to speak or to hear slanders, but rather to see to what has been reported, so that each individual and the city as a whole will be well prepared to meet the invader. Even if the reports are not true, there is no harm in a general muster of horses and infantry and the other apparatus of war. We shall report to you on what we find out further from our envoys and scouts" (6.41.2-4). Thus the conferences are concluded in different moods, the Spartans bullied by the belligerent ephor into voting for war, the Syracusans, saved for the present from another political split by the moderate general, cautiously planning their own defense in case the invasion does in fact come. Through the presentation of speeches in these two assemblies Thucydides has given us an intimate portrait of the future opponents of Athens. We the readers have been adequately prepared to appreciate the issues on which the upcoming struggles will turn.

ATHENS IN ACTION: PENTECONTAETIA AND SICILIAN VENTURE

After presenting their opponents, Thucydides returns to the Athenians. In Book I he writes a long excursus on the fifty years of Athenian history between the Persian and Peloponnesian Wars. In Book VI he describes the passage of the Athenian fleet across the Adriatic and its first actions in Italy and Sicily. It is important first to notice in Book I what Thucydides has not done. He has chosen not to move directly from the Spartan assembly to the conference of all the allies called by the Spartans (1.87.4) in order to make plans in common for the coming war. He has instead decided to insert a digression on Athenian history between the two conferences, in part in order to engage in a bit of historical writing for its own sake.[20] Thucydides tells us, twice, why he wrote the Pentecontaetia:

[20] Gomme (*Comm.* on 118.2) seems to me to be misleading on this point.

"For the Athenians went, *in such a way*, to the circumstances in which their power grew" (my italics; 89.1). Then, a few chapters later, "I write this section and make this digression for this reason: since this period of history was left out by my predecessors. . . . At the same time this digression contains an explanation of the way in which the Athenians established their empire" (97.2).[21] In both these statements, one made to explain his inclusion of the events of 479-478, the other his inclusion of the actions of 478-433, Thucydides emphasizes that his purpose is to explain how Athens became powerful.[22] Both statements depend on 1.88: "The Spartans voted that the peace was broken and they must go to war not so much because they were persuaded by the words of the allies as because they feared lest the Athenians would become stronger, seeing many parts of Greece already subject to them." Thucydides wants to show the reader, in an excursus of bare and brief narrative, how Athens reached a position in which the Spartans believed she posed a serious threat to their hegemony. The best way to explain this process was to exhibit those traits (*tropoi*), as Pericles says, "by which we built the power of the city" (2.41.2), to describe, as the Corinthians do, "just what sort of people the Athenians are" (1.70.1). This is the purpose of chapters 89-118 of Book I.

These chapters display the Athenians in constant and vigorous activity. Indeed, this is their major characteristic: "If someone summed them up by saying they were born to take no rest themselves nor to allow anyone else to do so, he would be correct" (1.70.9). Thucydides rarely pauses in his narrative. He moves directly from one campaign to the next (Πρῶτον μὲν . . . ἔπειτα . . . πόλεμος ἐγένετο . . . μετὰ ταῦτα; 1.98.1,2,3,4). His account is designed to give the reader an overwhelming impression of Athenian energy and ambition. We begin to appreciate why the Spartans fear those restless men: their τολμηρόν ("daring") and νεωτεροποιία ("revolutionary character") (102.3) are dreadful. When their fleet and army are engaged

---

[21] In 97.2 the first statement is the excuse, the second the reason for the digression.

[22] See Rawlings, *A Semantic Study of* Prophasis, 88.

elsewhere, their *presbytatoi* and *neotatoi* ("oldest and youngest men") engage and rout the invading Corinthians (1.105-106). The Athenians make no distinctions between Greeks and barbarians, whom they invade with equal daring. But most of their campaigns are directed against Greeks. Indeed, Thucydides focuses most of his attention in the Pentecontaetia upon Athenian attacks against the Hellenes. The famous (later, at least) campaigns under Cimon against the Persians receive comparatively little narrative.[23] It is Athenian treatment of Ionian allies that most interests the historian. He pauses in chapter 99 to give the reasons for their frequent and unsuccessful revolts; he devotes three chapters (115-117) to the Samian revolt. The only campaign against the barbarians that Thucydides emphasizes is the Egyptian expedition (104, 109-110). It was large and far-flung, and it involved many different kinds of warfare (109.1). The Persian king tried to secure the aid of the Lacedaemonians, who were asked to invade Attica in order to force the Athenians to leave Egypt. When that failed, he sent a large army under a Persian commander to Egypt by land. Soon the besiegers became the besieged. The Persians enclosed the Athenians in an island fortress for eighteen months. The Athenians had overextended themselves. The first contingent of 200 ships was crushed after six years of fighting, and a relief force of 50 ships was annihilated.

Thucydides' narrative of the Sicilian expedition in 6.42-52 reveals a different Athens from that portrayed in the Pentecontaetia. The expeditionary force is large and impressive enough (43-44), but its leaders are depressed (ἐν ἀθυμίᾳ in 46.2) because the promised money and military support in Sicily are not forthcoming and the Athenians have been tricked: the Segestans do not possess the money they had claimed, the Rhegians are unwilling to take part in the war they had espoused.[24] They also are divided because the generals cannot

[23] See Rawlings, "Thucydides on the Purpose of the Delian League," *Phoenix* 31 (1977) 1-8.

[24] Thucydides gives a full account (46.3-5) of the Segestans' treachery. He is interested in showing why their "sudden" lack of money was so unaccountable (ἀλογώτερα) to Alcibiades and Lamachus.

87

agree on basic strategy. Thucydides finds this division so significant that he stops to give in detail the opinions of Nicias, Alcibiades, and Lamachus. Their indirect speeches (47-49) emphasize the disunity and weakness in command from which the Athenians will suffer during their entire stay in Sicily. Thucydides puts these fatal flaws on display here at the very outset of operations. Nicias, in consonance with his original opposition to the expedition, wants to give the Sicilians a show of Athens' power before returning home "without risking the city's resources" (6.47). For all intents and purposes his plan is to abort the campaign. Alcibiades favors a strategy of gathering allies from all over Sicily for assaults upon Syracuse and Selinus. Lamachus prefers an immediate attack upon Syracuse while the city still dreads Athenian power and is unprepared for a sudden invasion. Alcibiades' plan, really a compromise between the other two, wins the debate when Lamachus gives it his vote. Our impression of Athenian leadership is nonetheless one of serious divisiveness. That is clearly what Thucydides wanted us to feel when he gave so much attention, almost for the first time in his *History*, to differences among Athenian generals on the strategy which an expeditionary force should employ.[25]

This impression is strengthened by what follows. Thucydides reports the arrival in Sicily of the Salaminia, which has come to bring Alcibiades back to Athens to face trial for *asebeia*. Political competition in Athens has now begun to impinge upon military effectiveness in the field. The long digression that follows in chapters 53-61 reveals, as we shall see, Thucydides' desire to make this point as strongly as possible. The contrast with the Athens of the Pentecontaetia is striking. The remarkable energy and effectiveness of that Athens are replaced by the hesitation and self-doubt of this one. The summer is spent touring the coast of Sicily so ineffectually that Syracusan fear of the invader turns to disdain (63.2) and eventually to contempt and overconfidence (64). Indeed, the overconfidence almost proves to be fatal when the Athenians seize

[25] The only previous occasion is the disagreement among the generals about fortifying Pylos. See 4.3.2-4.3.3.

a convenient place for battle near Syracuse while the Syracusan army is on the road to Catane to engage the Athenians. When the Syracusans return to their city to face the Athenians, they are defeated in a hoplite battle. But the Athenians do not follow up their victory because the enemy's superiority in cavalry seems too great and because the winter seems too far along to conduct operations from an ill-supplied camp (71.1-2). Their great opportunity to encircle Syracuse before it realized its need for assistance had been lost, in part because of delay and indecision. Thucydides will later say so.[26] No longer do the

[26] See 7.42.3. This difficult and controversial passage (see Dover, *Comm.* on 7.42) has occasioned problems of interpretation that are far too complex to discuss in detail here (see most recently E. Christian Kopff, "Thucydides 7.42.3: an Unrecognized Fragment of Philistus" *GRBS* 17 [1976] 23-30, and its aftermath, *GRBS* 17 [1976] 217-221). Suffice it to say that I believe that 7.42 refers directly to 6.71 and thus that Demothenes (and Thucydides, to some degree at least) criticized Nicias' failure to take advantage of his victory in the harbor to press hard upon Syracuse (this is the meaning of προσέκειτο ταῖς Συρακούσαις, a phrase of great importance). In fact the Athenians did not attack the city of Syracuse at all after their victory next to the harbor. There is, then, no inconsistency in referring the words ὡς οὐκ εὐθὺς προσέκειτο ταῖς Συρακούσαις to the situation described in 6.71.2. There seems to be distortion in the attribution to Nicias of a decision apparently made by both Nicias and Lamachus. But it is important to recall that in his own account Thucydides clearly makes Nicias the leader of the Athenian army at the harbor (see his speech to the soldiers in 6.68 and especially the words Ὁ μὲν Νικίας τοιαῦτα παρακελευσάμενος ἐπῆγε τὸ στρατόπεδον εὐθύς ["Nicias, having encouraged them with these words, immediately led the army forward"] in 6.69.1). Lamachus is never mentioned in the whole account of this campaign. In addition, Demosthenes, whose opinion Thucydides is referring to in 7.42, would naturally think of Nicias as the general responsible for the decision since he was now discussing strategy with him near the very spot where the Athenians won their victory in the winter of 415 and since the other general present at that victory was now dead. The other apparent problem with this interpretation is that "It necessitates reference of ἀφικόμενος to the landing in the harbour, not to the Athenians' arrival in Sicily" (Dover, *Comm.* 4: 420). But here too the fact that Demothenes is now standing near the place where the Athenians won the victory in winter, 415 makes the statement relatively unambiguous, especially when we realize that the subject of ἀφικόμενος is Nicias, not the three generals who came to Sicily together in the summer of 415 (to whose arrival some think the phrase refers—

Athenians fit the description the Corinthians give them in 1.70.2 ("they are revolutionary, and swift to conceive and to accomplish in deed whatever they resolve"), and which they so well exemplify in the Pentecontaetia. Their most zealous and, according to Thucydides, effective commander is removed from the army because of political intrigues. Lamachus takes a back seat to Nicias, who appears to be solely in charge of the army from this point onwards. Nicias is, of course, an unenterprising commander. Under him, the Athenian force loses its initiative and, before long, its effectiveness. The contrast with the Athens of the Pentecontaetia is complete. The narrative of the Sicilian expedition contains an explanation of the way in which the empire of the Athenians was lost.

THE DIGRESSIONS

In both Books I and VI Thucydides writes digressions on earlier Athenian history (1.126-138; 6.54-59). These digressions are occasioned by contemporary concerns with religious outrages. In Book I Thucydides reports that the Athenians and Spartans each demanded that the other drive out a curse (or curses) dating back to earlier times. Thucydides describes, twice in some detail, once briefly, the events that caused the curses. In the last case (the curse of the Bronze House) he composes a long excursus on the personal histories of "Pausanias the Lacedaemonian and Themistocles the Athenian, the most famous Greeks of their time" (1.138.6). In Book VI Thucydides interrupts his narrative of the recall of Alcibiades to face charges of impiety with a remarkable account of the tyrannicide of 514 B.C. This excursus is notable for its great interest in personal detail, its use of documentary evidence, including inscriptions, and particularly for its rather polemical tone. It is no wonder that scholars have been puzzled by Thucydides' inclusion of these lengthy and somewhat loosely connected di-

---

see Dover, *Comm.* 4: 420 [ii]). That Thucydides was himself in some doubt about the advisability of leaving Syracuse after the victory in the harbor may well be indicated by his use of ἐδόκει in 6.71.2: "it did not yet *seem* possible to carry on the war from there" (my italics).

gressions in an otherwise tightly-knit narrative that shuns extraneous material.[27] Why compose such "Herodotean digressions" in the first place, and secondly, why insert them in these particular places? If we approach these problems from the perspective we have been using, namely that of the structure of the work, solutions might present themselves.

Books I and VI are, as we have argued, introductions to the two great phases of the Peloponnesian War. As such, they present the issues and decisions that led, in each case, to the outbreak of hostilities. But Thucydides was also concerned in these sections to give his readers an analysis of the character of the coming struggle. In Book I his major focus was on the Athens-Sparta dualism. The archaeology ends by stressing it (18-19); the Corcyraeans and Corinthians mention it in their speeches at Athens; it is the subject of the conference at Sparta, where the Corinthians raise it to a philosophical level; the Athenians discuss it; Archidamus fears it; Sthenelaidas revels in it.[28] The Pentecontaetia constantly refers to it. It is clearly the major theme of the first war. Time after time, Thucydides juxtaposes Athens with Sparta, in large and small episodes, narrative and speeches, action and thought.[29] The structure of the first four books is dictated by this overriding concern with showing Athens and Sparta pitted against each other. This war ends in stalemate.

In Book VI Thucydides introduces the issue that will dominate the second war. Actually, he had already broached it in 2.65 by his uncharacteristically explicit declaration of the reason for Athens' downfall: internal dissension. The controlling

[27] We are speaking here primarily of the Pausanias-Themistocles part of the digression. The Cylon affair is probably introduced for the light it sheds on Pericles (see 1.127). The one-sentence mention of the "curse from Taenarum" is not a digression. It is particularly important to note that the narrative of Themistocles' later career has no bearing on the occasion for the digression, viz., the curses.

[28] See 77.6, 78; 80.3-81; 86.3.

[29] Note how throughout Books II and III, in particular, Thucydides constantly juxtaposes Athenian and Spartan episodes: 2.7.2 vs. 7.3; 9.2-3 vs. 9.4; 10-12 vs. 13-17; 18-20 vs. 21-22; 23 vs. 24; 70 vs. 71-78; 86.6-87 vs. 88-89; 3.1-19 vs. 20-24; 29-33.1 vs. 33.2-34; 37-50 vs. 52-68.

factor in the second war is Athenian political division, dissension, and finally dissolution. The political split in Athens determines the outcome of the Decelean War; when the Athenians "finally fell victim to their own internal disorders and failed in themselves" (2.65.12), Sparta took the victory, by default. By 404, there was no more Athens to fight. In Book V, Thucydides adumbrates this theme, in VI he announces it. The Nicias-Alcibiades debate at Athens introduces it, the historian's own remark in 15.3-4 states it explicitly, the incident of the Hermocopidae dramatizes it, the debate at Syracuse mirrors it,[30] and the narrative of Athenian dissension and impotence in Sicily illustrates it. In Book VII Thucydides constantly shows how political differences blunted the Athenian effort in Sicily. In Book VIII these differences lead to stasis and become the major subject of the narrative. We can surmise that the trial of the eight generals in 406 and the intrigues of the demagogue Cleophon would have dominated the end of the *History*, not to mention the suspicious actions of the Athenian generals at Aegospotami in 405.

With these perspectives on the two wars, hence on the introduction to the two wars in Books I and VI, we can readily comprehend the function that Thucydides designed his digressions to serve. We can do no better than to turn, for clear statements of their function, to the analyses of Eduard Schwartz and Wolfgang Schadewaldt.[31] In spite of their almost obsessive concern with the composition question, or perhaps because of it, these two scholars gave extraordinarily sensitive readings to the work of Thucydides. Their intuitive understanding of the purpose of these two digressions has not, however, made a great impact upon later Thucydidean scholarship.[32] The reason

[30] The two debates are meant, at least in part, to compare Athenian and Syracusan democracies.

[31] E. Schwartz, *Das Geschichtswerk des Thukydides* (Bonn 1919) 158-162, on 1.126-1.138; W. Schadewaldt, *Geschichtschreibung*, 84-95, on 6.53-59.

[32] For explicit denials of Schwartz's view see Lippold, *RhM* n.s. 108 (1965) 337; and for similarly explicit denials of Schadewaldt's view, see Dover, *Comm.* 4: 328-329, and H.-P. Stahl, *Thukydides Die Stellung des Menschen im geschichtlichen Prozess* (Munich 1966) 7.

is precisely that their understanding was intuitive and was not based on a solid groundwork of argument and proof. This can, I think, now be provided from the structural criteria we have established for Books I and VI and from other structural criteria developed for the Pausanias-Themistocles episode by H. Konishi.[33]

Schwartz begins his discussion of the digression in Book I with its last sentence: "Thus ended the affairs of Pausanias the Lacedaemonian and Themistocles the Athenian, the most illustrious of the Greeks of their era" (1.138.6). He remarks that Pausanias and Themistocles have already been contrasted, if not in an expressed parallel, nonetheless clearly enough, in the Athenian speech at Sparta (74.1, 77.6). He then continues: "Der fundamentale Gegensatz zwischen Athen und Sparta, der die gesamte Retraktation der ersten beiden Bücher beherrscht, ist auf das Schicksal zweier Individuen übertragen, die beide von dem staatlichen Ganzen, das sie einst führten, abgelöst, sich mit dem hellenischen Erbfeind, den sie selbst besiegt haben, einlassen und nun, als auf sich gestellte Einzelpersönlichkeiten, zeigen was sie von Spartaner- oder Athenertum noch bewahren."[34] Schwartz goes on to note the numerous contrasts drawn by Thucydides between the "first men of their time": at every step their careers illustrate the characteristic *tropoi* of Athens and Sparta.[35] This series of contrasts is planned with great care. Konishi has recently shown just how precisely the episodes are contrasted.[36] Through a careful struc-

---

[33] H. Konishi, "Thucydides' Method in the Episodes of Pausanias and Themistocles," *AJP* 91 (1970) 52-69.

[34] Schwartz, *Geschichtswerk* 158. "The fundamental opposition between Athens and Sparta, which dominates the entire revision of the first two books, is transferred to the fate of two individuals, both of whom are removed from the states which they once led, are taken in by the traditional Greek enemy, whom they have themselves defeated, and now, as individual personalities put on their own mettle, show what they still preserve of Spartan or Athenian character." I would only emend "revision of the first two books" to "theme of the first four books."

[35] See J. Finley, *Thucydides* (Ann Arbor 1963) 139.

[36] H. Konishi, "Thucydides' Method . . ." *AJP* 91 (1970) especially 61-62.

tural comparison he succeeds in demonstrating that "the episodes of Pausanias and Themistocles . . . are contrasted with each other so formally and mechanically that the difficulties of chronology and authenticity of information in these episodes seem to have been caused to a great extent by Thucydides' own conscious manipulation of evidence to attain his purpose."[37] These two episodes are thus shown to be almost pure historiographical *exempla* or *paradeigmata*. There is little interest in establishing fact. There is almost no connection with the original occasion for the digression, that is, the curses. In particular the Themistocles episode is totally unrelated to this occasion, which is really not an occasion but an excuse. All of Thucydides' attention is devoted to providing historical analogy. The reader is furnished with two *typoi*, a powerful but inept and misguided Spartan, a brilliant and able Athenian. The narratives are artificially manipulated to furnish point-by-point comparison and contrast.

But this is not all. As Schwartz perceives, there is another parallelism in the two cases:

> Pausanias, in spite of the serious charges of the allies, gets off essentially scot-free and can, although without an official command, return to the scene of his schemes. When he behaves very badly indeed, he is recalled, but remains for a short time under arrest and quietly awaits his trial; not once do his plots with the helots seriously endanger him: it is not Spartan practice to put to death a Spartiate without incontrovertible proof. (132.5) First the treachery of his trusted servant and finally the trap laid by the ephors lead to catastrophe; and even then his corpse escapes the usual punishment of the high traitor, since the Delphic Oracle procures for him a tomb and two statues. Quite the contrary in the Athenians' case. They expel their brilliant statesman on the basis of hearsay evidence and give a full hearing to the Spartan accusations; without examining the accusations, they join with the Spartans in a repulsive execution squad which hunts down the defenseless fugitive from asylum to asylum.

[37] Ibid., 52.

Even burial in his homeland is denied him; only secretly can his bones be interred: the contrast with Pausanias is set in such sharp relief that it cannot be missed.[38]

Here we have the second aspect of the theme of Athens-Sparta dualism. Athens produces, it is true, a superior type of leader, indeed citizen, to that produced in Sparta; but Athenian democracy treats its leaders shabbily, even disastrously, compared to the way Spartan oligarchy handles its leaders. This point also becomes an important theme in Thucydides' work. On several occasions he stops his narrative in order to decry the insane demands that Athenian democracy put upon its leaders.[39] Thucydides was in a position to know. He had suffered exile for twenty years for what he considered to be competent, indeed, capable leadership.[40] On the other hand, Thucydides several times stops to remark on Spartan political stability. Note especially the cause-effect relationship that he draws in 1.18.1: "For a little more than 400 years down to the end of this war the Lacedaemonians used the same *politeia*, and because of that they are powerful and regulate affairs in other cities" (καὶ δι' αὐτὸ δυνάμενοι καὶ τὰ ἐν ταῖς ἄλλαις πόλεσι καθί-στασαν). Archidamus makes the same point in his speech at Sparta praising Spartan *tropoi* (especially 1.84). This theme too, the contrast in Athenian and Spartan treatment of leaders, thus pervades the entire *History*. The issue on which the war will depend is a two-fold one: can Athens avoid betraying her great advantages in leaders and national *tropoi* through political instability and envy of her own leaders; and can Sparta overcome the disastrous impression which her leaders frequently make (1.77.6) upon the rest of Greece through her great stability and cautious handling of political problems? Thucydides presages this two-pronged issue in his paradigmatic historical digressions on the careers of Pausanias and Themistocles.

These arguments lead to a further consideration. It is true that the theme of Athenian-Spartan dualism dominates Thu-

[38] E. Schwartz, *Geschichtswerk*, 160-161.
[39] See 2.70.4, 4.65.3-4.65.4, 7.48.3-7.48.4.
[40] See 4.102-4.108.

cydides' narrative of the first war. But the additional theme of the two states' handling of their leaders extends to the history of the second war and indeed becomes most important toward the end of that war. That is why we should accept Schwartz's brilliant suggestion that the Pausanias-Themistocles digression is a paradigm, an historical model, not only for Athenian and Spartan leaders in general, but also specifically for the careers of Alcibiades and Lysander.[41] Not only do these latter figures repeat, to a remarkable degree, the careers of Pausanias and Themistocles, but their treatment at the hands of their respective states mirrors the treatment that their two predecessors received. There are many such points of comparison. First, the two Athenians Themistocles and Alcibiades were both leading men of their time, were both implicated in supposed crimes, were both recalled to Athens to face trial, escaped their would-be guards, found refuge first in Greece and then in Persia, used merchantmen for one of their escapades, promised a Persian king that they would help him conquer Greece, found great favor in the Persian court, died in Asia as exiles. More importantly from Thucydides' standpoint, both were brilliant men who could adapt to any circumstance. This is surely Thucydides' emphasis in his treatment of Themistocles, as Méautis points out.[42] He could deal with any situation because he was κράτιστος . . . αὐτοσχεδιάζειν τὰ δέοντα ("most capable of improvising whatever is required"; 1.138.3). This was precisely Alcibiades' genius as well. Not only do the historical facts of the two men's lives conform, but far more importantly, Thucydides' historiographical emphasis makes the parallelism even clearer.[43]

There is thus good implicit evidence that Thucydides had Alcibiades' career in mind when he wrote the excursus on Themistocles. But there is another piece of evidence that can be adduced to help clinch the case and to clarify Thucydides' intention in writing this excursus on Themistocles. Thucydides

[41] E. Schwartz, Geschichtswerk, 161-162.
[42] See G. Méautis, L'Ant. cl. 20 (1951) 297-304; also M. F. McGregor, Phoenix 19 (1965) 27.
[43] Contrast Herodotus' treatment of Themistocles (especially 8.57).

concluded his excursus in 1.138.6 with the remark, "Thus ended the affairs of Pausanias the Lacedaemonian and Themistocles the Athenian," λαμπροτάτους γενομένους τῶν καθ᾽ ἑαυτοὺς Ἑλλήνων ("the most illustrious of the Greeks of their
time"). In his speech at Athens in 416, Alcibiades defends himself against Nicias' charge (6.12.2) that he was privately glori-
fying (ἐλλαμπρύνεσθαι) and enriching himself at the city's
expense and risk. Alcibiades (16.3) argues that

> whatever splendor I have exhibited [ὅσα . . . λαμπρύνομαι]
> in the city in providing choruses or otherwise, is envied by
> the citizens, but appears as strength to foreigners. And this
> is no useless folly. . . . What I know is that persons of this
> kind and all others who have attained to some distinction
> [ὅσοι ἔν τινος λαμπρότητι προέσχον], though they may be
> unpopular during their lifetime in their relations with their
> fellow-men and especially with their equals, leave to posterity
> the desire of claiming connection with them even without
> any ground, and are vaunted by the country to which they
> belonged, not as strangers or ill-doers, but as fellow country-
> men and heroes (Crawley translation, slightly modified).

It seems probable that Alcibiades is here referring to the case
of Themistocles. The words λαμπρότητι προέσχον, ἐν μὲν τῷ
καθ᾽ αὑτοὺς βίῳ λυπηροὺς ὄντας ("were particularly illustrious, though in their own lifetime they were objects of envy")
recall the λαμπροτάτους γενομένους τῶν καθ᾽ ἑαυτοὺς Ἑλλήνων of 1.138.6. But note the bitterness of tone in the words
"and are vaunted by the country to which they belonged, not
as strangers or ill-doers, but as fellow-countrymen and heroes."
This is Thucydides speaking, as well as Alcibiades, and he is
speaking specifically of Themistocles. The Athenians use Themistocles' name as if he were their hero. Thucydides makes
them do so in 1.74.1. There, in their proud reference to their
leading role in the Persian wars the Athenians lay claim to
Themistocles' leadership and particularly to his great wisdom
(ξυνετώτατον).

It was precisely that wisdom that Thucydides adumbrated in
the archaeology, illustrated in the Pentecontaetia (1.90-93), and

explicitly described in the excursus (1.138.3). The Athenians threw it away and then unashamedly claimed it as their own. That is Thucydides' point, made clearly and bitterly in 6.16.5. When he goes on in section 6 to have Alcibiades say "such men I emulate" (ὧν ἐγὼ ὀρεγόμενος), the comparison is complete. Thucydides makes Alcibiades emulate Themistocles.[44] The irony is that the Athenian democracy of 415 will also follow the example of its predecessor in the 470s. It will reject Alcibiades' talents. Thucydides makes it quite clear where he stands on this issue in 2.65.11 and 6.15.3-4. A man who had no peers in conducting public business, particularly Athens' war effort, is lost because of the demos' envy and fear of tyranny. (What that fear was worth, and what is caused by it, we shall soon see; that is the subject of Thucydides' digression in 6.53-59.) Thucydides thus draws together the careers of Themistocles ·and Alcibiades to make a crucial point about Athenian history: Athenian democracy abused its greatest leaders and thus lost their abilities. Even worse, in pursuing these men all over the world it frequently drove them to use those talents against Athens. Themistocles, according to Thucydides, was relatively ineffective in this venture, perhaps even apathetic. The Athenians were not so fortunate in the case of Alcibiades. That is the motivation for Thucydides' inclusion of the excursus on Themistocles.

It seems quite likely, then, that the digression on Themistocles is written in order to provide an historical paradigm for the problem of Athenian leaders and their treatment at the hands of the Athenian democracy, and specifically for the career of Alcibiades. The remarks that Thucydides gives Alcibiades support this case.[45] But once this is proven a further

[44] Remarkably enough, we have other ancient evidence suggesting that Alcibiades did in fact consciously emulate Themistocles. See the Socratic dialogue of Aeschines of Sphettus, quoted in Aelius Aristeides' Oration 46, and preserved fragmentarily in *The Oxyrhynchus Papyri*, ed. by B. P. Grenfell and A. S. Hunt (London 1898-) 13: 1608. The same rivalry is attributed to Cleon: see Aristophanes, *Knights* 811-813, 817-819.

[45] *Pace* P. J. Rhodes, *Historia* 19 (1970) 399, n. 91. It does not seem helpful to explain the different tone of the digression on the grounds

consequence follows. The digression on Pausanias, formally and mechanically contrasted with that on Themistocles, must serve the same function for Spartan history generally, and for Lysander specifically. At the very end of the fifth century B.C. the two "most illustrious Greeks of their time" were certainly Alcibiades the Athenian and Lysander the Spartan. Furthermore, though Thucydides was unable to compose his account of Lysander and we cannot, therefore, draw connections between his handling of the two men, we do know from other sources that Lysander's life parallels that of Pausanias to the same degree that Alcibiades' parallels that of Themistocles. Like Pausanias, Lysander won the final victory of a great war, received extravagant honors throughout Greece as a result, dedicated offerings at Delphi in his own name, began soon to act arrogantly and ambitiously, angered Greek opinion by his private and public insolence, was said to be planning to establish himself as tyrant of Greece, was recalled to Sparta by the ephors, who sent a herald bearing a skytale to bring him back, underwent a trial before the ephors who found damning evidence in a letter but for the time being did not feel confident enough to punish a man who at that time held great honor, and schemed to overthrow the Spartan government.[46] How much of this last part of Lysander's life Thucydides lived to see is uncertain, but he probably survived long enough to see the pattern of Pausanias repeated in a remarkable way.[47] To a reader in the late fifth or early fourth century Thucydides' digression on Pausanias would immediately bring to mind contemporary events. As in the excursus on Themistocles, the issue would be two-fold. Lysander was repeating the career of Pausanias; the Spartans were imitating in the late fifth century

---

that Thucydides wrote it "as a youth," as Rhodes and F. E. Adcock (*Thucydides and his History* [Cambridge 1963] 23-24) suggest. It is rather an historical paradigm, a *Tendenzschrift*, written to prove a point.

[46] Thucydides 1.131.1, and Plutarch, *Lysander* 19; Thucydides 1.132.1 and Plutarch, *Lysander* 20-21; Thucydides 1.132.4 and Plutarch, *Lysander* 24-25.

[47] It is possible that Thucydides outlived Lysander, who died in 395, but there is no way of telling.

their treatment of Pausanias in the 470s. Again they acted slowly and deliberately in assessing evidence against a much-honored leader whose arrogant behavior was now wrecking the reputation they had just won for liberating Greece. It did not take great foresight to predict, as Thucydides makes the Athenians do in 1.76.4 and 1.77.6, that Spartan supremacy in Greece would soon make the Greeks realize how lenient Athenian hegemony had been. Thus the digression on Pausanias serves as a model for the crucial issue in Spartan history: could Spartan hegemony survive the ill effects that the actions of Spartan leaders had upon Greece? This had been the critical question with Pausanias in the 470s;[48] it was clearly a major issue on men's minds at the end of the fifth century.[49]

These arguments show that Thucydides' digression on Pausanias and Themistocles in Book I, his introduction to the Archidamian War and to the Peloponnesian War as a whole, was designed to provide an historical model for a crucial issue on which those wars would turn. The digression on the tyrannicides, which Thucydides inserts at a similar place in the structure of Book VI, can be shown to perform the same function for the second ten-year war. Schadewaldt argued this case almost fifty years ago but, like Schwartz, he failed to convince later scholars.[50] In particular, Dover and Stahl explicitly deny that Thucydides' aim in including the excursus on the events of 514 was to furnish a parallel case to the events of 415.[51] Their cases appear to be based on two misunderstandings: first, of the true political point that Thucydides is making

[48] See 1.130.2, where Thucydides says "[Pausanias] made himself hard to approach and was so arrogant toward all equally that no one could associate with him. It was not least for this reason that the alliance went over to the Athenians." See also 1.77.6.

[49] Note Thucydides' emphasis upon this theme in 3.32: The irony in the Samians' remarks to Alcidas is heavy: "you are not freeing Greece very well, Alcidas. If you do not stop you will turn more friends into enemies than enemies into friends." Does this not apply *a fortiori* to Lysander's massacre of the Milesians in 404? See Plutarch, *Lysander*, 19. See also 3.93.2 and 5.52.1 for Thucydides' stress upon this point.

[50] W. Schadewaldt, *Geschichtschreibung*, 91-95.

[51] Dover, *Comm.* 4: 328-329; Stahl, *Stellung*, 7.

in the digression; second, of the kind of readers for which Thucydides wrote his work.

We begin with the former. Only Schadewaldt seems to have fully appreciated the polemical tone of the digression and the immediate impulse for its inclusion at this place in Thucydides' narrative. But he appears not to have convinced others. Let us try to understand the nature of this polemic by tracing it from its beginning in the chapter preceding the digression, through its emergence in the digression itself, to its development in the chapters following the digression and finally to its conclusion in Book VIII. Only then can we appreciate the function of the excursus itself.

In 6.53.1 Thucydides reports the arrival in Sicily of the Salaminia, which has "come from Athens in order to fetch Alcibiades for trial on charges which the city brought against him, and to take back those others of the soldiers who were charged with him for profaning the mysteries, and some for the affairs of the Herms." The next sentence explains ($\gamma \acute{a} \rho$) why:

> For the Athenians, after the expedition sailed away, continued the vigorous search for the perpetrators of the crimes involving the mysteries and the Herms, and, not testing the informers, but in their suspicion accepting all testimony, arrested and imprisoned the *very best of the citizens* on the evidence of *lower class rogues,* thinking it better to investigate the matter and find it out than to let some accused person *of the better class* escape unquestioned because of the *lower class baseness* of an informer (my italics).

The italicized words ($\pi o \nu \eta \rho \hat{\omega} \nu \ \dot{a} \nu \theta \rho \acute{\omega} \pi \omega \nu \ \ldots \ \pi \acute{a} \nu \nu \ \chi \rho \eta \sigma \tau o \grave{\upsilon} \varsigma$ $\tau \hat{\omega} \nu \ \pi o \lambda \iota \tau \hat{\omega} \nu \ \ldots \ \pi o \nu \eta \rho \acute{\iota} a \nu \ \ldots \ \tau \iota \nu \grave{a} \ \kappa a \grave{\iota} \ \chi \rho \eta \sigma \tau \grave{o} \nu \ \delta o \kappa o \hat{\upsilon} \nu \tau a$ $\epsilon \hat{\iota} \nu a \iota$) seem not only exaggerated and tendentious, but they are repeated for effect! Athens' highest-born aristocrats were jailed on the testimony of lower-class scoundrels, whose evidence was not even scrutinized. Furthermore, as Thucydides intimates ($\dot{a} \nu \theta \rho \acute{\omega} \pi \omega \nu \ \ldots \ \pi o \lambda \iota \tau \hat{\omega} \nu$), the informers were not even citizens! In his initial discussion of the Hermocopidae in 6.27-28 he had gone out of his way to make this same point.

The Athenians, he says in 27.2, were so concerned with that incident that they passed a decree that allowed anyone who knew of this or any other profanation to inform without fear about it, whether he was citizen, foreigner, or slave. In 28.1 he tells us who came forward: some metics and some slaves; in other words, no citizens. It even appears that Thucydides has here in 28.1 as well as in 53.2, "sacrificed accuracy to indignant rhetoric."[52] It is probable that Teucrus, the metic who informed, did not do so until the expedition had already left. Thucydides has apparently antedated this testimony in his effort to denigrate the informers, who now include members of two of the three possible categories of inhabitants of Athens— the lowest two! Thus "indignant rhetoric" describes Thucydides' handling of the episode in both chapters 28 and 53. He seems to be making an effort to slander the informers, not personally (he never even bothers to name them), but in terms of their social rank, their class. He seems to have been so desirous of creating this impression that he was willing to bend the truth in 28.1 and to overemphasize it in 53.2. Thucydides does not often betray his bitterness in so unguarded a fashion. He has an axe to grind. His next sentence (53.4) sharpens it further. "For the people, knowing by hearsay that the tyranny of Peisistratus and his sons ended by becoming harsh, . . . were always afraid and took everything suspiciously." We know what Thucydides thought of this kind of knowledge from 1.20-21. There Thucydides mentions, in his attack upon those who rely on oral evidence, this very case: "For men accept the hearsay stories of previous generations, even if they are native to them, equally uncritically [ἀβασανίστως] from each other. For example, the lower class of the Athenians thinks . . ." Surely this reminds us of Thucydides' remark on the demos' handling of the affair of the Herms. There too they accepted hearsay evidence without testing it (οὐ δοκιμάζοντες in 6.53.2). Thucydides goes on in 1.20.3 to complain: "so careless [ἀταλαίπωρος] is the search for truth among people generally, and they turn rather to what is at hand." For Thucydides, the demos' handling of the Hermocopidae affair, like that of its

---

[52] Dover, *Comm.* 4: 274.

knowledge of the tyrannicide, is a question of hearsay evidence, untested and unreliable. That is why he lays so much stress on their search (ζήτησιν and εὑρεῖν in 53.2) for the culprits and its failure.[53] But the demos' ignorance of the real nature of the events of 514 is not limited to the position Hipparchus held when he was murdered. Rather, it concerns the whole meaning of that assassination; its intent, its background, and above all, its effects. To explain (γάρ) this, Thucydides writes his excursus.

The first sentence of the excursus, in its surprising choice of words, reveals Thucydides' two reasons for composing it: "For the daring venture of Aristogeiton and Harmodius was attempted because of an erotic liaison; by describing it in greater detail I will reveal that neither others nor the Athenians themselves say anything accurate [ἀκριβές] about their own tyrants nor about what happened" (6.54.1). His first intention is to mock Aristogeiton's and Harmodius' "glorious deed." His second is to make explicit what he implied in the previous sentence: the Athenians' hearsay knowledge is totally incorrect. The next sentence gives an example of the second intention: "For when Peisistratus died as an old man in the tyranny, not Hipparchus, as many think, but Hippias, being the eldest son, took over office."[54] The next one gives us an example of the first intention: γενομένου δὲ Ἁρμοδίου ὥρᾳ ἡλικίας λαμπροῦ Ἀριστογείτων ἀνὴρ τῶν ἀστῶν, μέσος πολίτης, ἐραστὴς ὢν εἶχεν αὐτόν ("Harmodius was splendid in the prime of his youth and Aristogeiton, a man of the commons, an average citizen, became his lover"). Only Schadewaldt seems to have understood the import of the words ἀνὴρ τῶν ἀστῶν, μέσος πολίτης. To him their connotation was so implicitly obvious as to require no elaboration. Others seem to have missed even

---

[53] See the heavy irony in 60.4.

[54] This is only a minor example, one among many popular misconceptions about the tyrants, which Thucydides clears up in the digression. He had already corrected it in 1.20. For this reason Lang seems misguided in trying to make it one of the major points of Thucydides' excursus (see M. Lang, "The Murder of Hipparchus," Historia 3 [1955] 395-407).

their denotation.[55] They can only mean "a man of the commons, an average citizen." They are, it appears, a slur upon the social and political status of Aristogeiton. The sentence should be translated as follows: "Aristogeiton, a man of the commons, an average citizen, being a lover of Harmodius, an aristocrat in the season of youthful beauty, possessed him." That ἀστός can be used in a restricted sense to mean commoner as opposed to aristocrat or nobleman (ὁ ἄριστος) is clear from several instances in Pindar.

Pythian II 82-3   ἀδύνατα δ᾽ ἔπος ἐκβαλεῖν κραταιὸν ἐν
                   ἀγαθοῖς δόλιον ἀστόν ("it is impossible
                   for a deceitful commoner to cast a strong
                   word among noblemen");

Pythian III 70-71 ὃς Συρακόσσαισι νέμει βασιλεὺς
                   πραΰς ἀστοῖς, οὐ φθονέων ἀγαθοῖς, ξεί-
                   νοις δὲ θαυμαστὸς πατήρ ("the King
                   who governs the Syracusans is kind to
                   commoners, unenvious of the noblemen,
                   and a wonderful father to guests").

These passages show that οἱ ἀστοί, when distinguished from οἱ ἄριστοι, are "commoners."[56] The phrase ἀνὴρ τῶν ἀστῶν, added to μέσος πολίτης, should not mean "a citizen." Πολίτης is inclusive of ἀστός.[57] Ἀστός is therefore, used here in the re-

---

[55] J. K. Davies for one. In *Athenian Propertied Families* (Oxford 1971) he fails to adduce this evidence in his (tentative) suggestion (p. 474) that Aristogeiton's family was from an inferior branch of the Gephyraioi. It is not only worth adducing—it is our most important testimony to this fact. A fact it almost certainly must be. Thucydides makes the distinction between Harmodius and Aristogeiton with confidence, almost delight.

[56] See H. G. Liddell and R. Scott, *Greek-English Lexicon*, revised by H. S. Jones (Oxford 1940), hereafter cited as LSJ, *s.v.* ἀστός, "οἱ | ἀστοί the commons, opp. οἱ ἀγαθοί." The example cited from Isocrates (3.21) is worthless, that from Pindar (*Pythian* 3.71) far less helpful than *Pythian* 2.82.

[57] See Aristotle, *Politics*, 1278a34. Ἀστός is distinguished from πολίτης, the former being "one who has civil rights only," πολίτης being "one who has political rights also." Thus when the same person is described with both terms, ἀστός must mean a commoner. See LSJ.

stricted sense, "a commoner." Taken as a whole the phrase is derogatory: "a man of the commons." This was the social slur. Thucydides added insult to injury by appending the political slur μέσος πολίτης. This phrase has no technical meaning, but is intentionally bland and damning: "A citizen of average political influence, neither prominent nor unknown."[58] Considering the fact that Aristogeiton came from the Gephyraioi, "one of the most notable family groupings known to us from independent Athens,"[59] it appears that Thucydides has attempted to belittle his social rank and political status.

Two sentences later Thucydides continues this derogation of Aristogeiton. After telling us that Harmodius rejected an overture from Hipparchus and then informed Aristogeiton of it, Thucydides gives us Aristogeiton's reaction: "And he, in a jealous rage and afraid that Hipparchus would use his power to force Harmodius to accept him, immediately plotted an overthrow of the tyranny, in so far as his rank currently allowed" (ὡς ἀπὸ τῆς ὑπαρχούσης ἀξιώσεως; 6.54.3). The last words add to the indictment against Aristogeiton. From his unimpressive position he, and only he (not Harmodius) planned to end the rule of Athens' tyrants because of sexual grief. In Thucydides' eyes the tyrannicide was not, as fifth-century Athenians believed, an heroic deed planned and carried out by two young, freedom-loving aristocrats. It was an audacious act (τόλμημα), plotted by a commoner crazed with sexual jealousy and fear and perpetrated against one of Athens' greatest and most beneficent families. This last point is developed in detail in the following two sections (54.3-4). Hipparchus, far from using force, as Aristogeiton feared, "wished to do nothing violent, but began to make preparations to insult him [Harmodius] in some inconspicuous way as though it were unrelated to this business." Thucydides explains: "For in no other aspect of its rule was the tyranny harsh against the commons, but it carried out its administration in a way which allowed no reproach. Indeed, these tyrants lived according to

---

[58] See the scholiast, who glosses μέσος with οὔτε ἐπιφανὴς οὔτε ἄδοξος ("neither renowned nor obscure").

[59] See Davies, *Athenian Propertied Families*, 472.

the highest possible standards [ἐπετήδευσαν ἐπὶ πλεῖστον δή] of moral and intellectual excellence."[60] This assertion is just as remarkable in its judgment as those denigrating Aristogeiton. Thucydides begins his digression within a digression with extraordinary praise of the Peisistratids. They are the only persons in his entire work, other than Brasidas, to be given the twin characteristics of high moral and intellectual qualities.[61] The sentence continues: "They taxed the Athenians lightly, adorned their city splendidly, carried on their wars and provided sacrifices for their temples." These are the intended objects of Aristogeiton's assassination plot. The contrast between murderer and victim is sharp: a scoundrel against the finest of gentlemen.

After correcting several other misconceptions about the tyrants (54.6-55.4), Thucydides returns to his narrative. Hipparchus carried out his plan of embarrassing Harmodius. "For, after inviting his sister to take part in a certain procession by bearing a basket, they rejected her, saying they had not invited her in the first place because she was not of sufficiently high rank" (56.1). As Thucydides' words imply, the insult consisted of a social slur against the rank of Harmodius' family.[62] Note the reactions in the following sentence of Harmodius and Aristogeiton: "Harmodius took this insult hard, and Aristogeiton for his sake was now much more provoked (than before)."[63] It is a social insult which is the direct cause of the

[60] For the problem of the subject of this sentence, see Dover, *Comm.* 4: 319. I have adopted what I consider to be the easiest solution. The subject of the sentence goes back to the last words of the previous sentence but one. See J. L. Creed *CQ* n.s. 23 (1973) 222 on the meaning of ἀρετή here. Compare 7.86.5.

[61] See 4.81.2.

[62] Dover is surely right in suggesting that they "alleged she was not ἐν ἀξιώματι," which is Philochorus' phrase (F. Jacoby *Die Fragmente der Griechischen Historiker*, Berlin and Leiden 1923, III B 328 F8) for those virgins qualified to carry baskets in Athenian processions (αἱ ἐν ἀξιώματι παρθένοι), and in thus concluding that "the insult necessarily touched her brother's status" (*Comm.* 4: 334).

[63] Classen-Steup on 6.56.2: "The particle καί shows that the present exasperation of A. is compared with his previous mood (cf. 54.3), not with the rage of Harmodius."

plot's being put into effect. The Peisistratids reviled the status of the Gephyraioi. Aristogeiton, a member of the latter family's inferior branch, took special offense. The tyrannicide, engendered by a lover's jealousy and fear of an aristocratic rival, was provoked by a social insult that further enraged the "commoner" and spurred him to action. In Thucydides' portrayal, the tyrannicide was motivated by personal and class hatred. Is this not also Thucydides' picture of the affair of the Herms?

Thucydides gives the sordid story of the murder in 57-58. The panicked and desperate actions of Harmodius and Aristogeiton in the former chapter are contrasted with the cool and efficient reactions of Hippias in the latter (note especially the contrast between εὐθὺς ἀπερισκέπτως προσπέσοντες in 57.3 and ἀδήλως τῇ ὄψει πλασάμενος in 58.1). The conspirators looked only at the present moment, Hippias looked to the future (58.1). Note also the same contrast in 59.1-2. The "irrational, reckless act" was the result of "immediate fear." Hippias' attention was directed toward the future: πρὸς τὰ ἔξω ἅμα διεσκοπεῖτο, εἴ ποθεν ἀσφάλειάν τινα ὁρῴη μεταβολῆς γενομένης ὑπάρχουσάν οἱ ("The tyranny became harsher after this towards the Athenians. Hippias put many citizens to death and began to look abroad for security in fear of a revolution"; 59.2). When he was overthrown three years later, he had a safe refuge with Darius. Twenty years later he returned with the Medes in their invasion of Marathon. This is the concluding chapter of the digression and it contains Thucydides' statement of the importance of the tyrannicide: it had the reverse effect of what its perpetrators intended. Instead of ending the tyranny they made it harsher; in fact they turned a benevolent, enlightened leader into a paranoiac tyrant who mistreated his subjects and eventually, after his expulsion, led an invasion of the city. That, says Thucydides, is the true meaning of the tyrannicide.[64]

[64] For this reason we should reject one important aspect of Stahl's (*Die Stellung*, 1-11) interpretation of the digression. In his attempt to make the case that Thucydides intended only to show how the demos' ignorance in 415 of the events of 514 led them to fear tyranny and that Thucydides drew no parallel between these two events, Stahl is forced

When Thucydides returns in chapter 60 to his narrative of the affair of the Herms, he once more stresses his two major points: "With these things in mind, and recalling what they knew *by hearsay* about them, the Athenian people were harsh, . . . and they thought that everything done was designed for an oligarchical and tyrannical conspiracy. And since they were outraged by this affair many *very reputable men* were already in prison (my italics)" (6.60.1-2). Here again the double emphasis is upon the demos' ignorance and the high position of the victims. In sections 4-5 Thucydides' feelings are again evident: "And in this business it was unclear whether or not the victims were punished unjustly, but the rest of the city [the demos] for the moment obviously benefited." Thucydides' tone in chapter 60, as in 53, where he began this narrative, is unexpectedly bitter. Athenian aristocrats of the very best families are sacrificed to the fear and ignorance of the lower class.

In chapter 61 Thucydides finally comes back to his starting point, Alcibiades.[65] He too is implicated in a conspiracy against

to argue (pp. 6-7) that the "high point" of the digression comes in 59.1-2 and that the remainder of that chapter is only "a short, summary note." But this is quite misleading, as Schadewaldt (*Geschichtschreibung*, 91) saw: "Secondly, we saw—and this is decisive—that Thucydides in 59.1-2, where he has reached the summary of the critical purpose of the narrative, continues his account still further. The fact that he does not wish simply to bring the account to an end in a few lines is proven by the inclusion of a 'tekmerion' (59.3)." Thucydides did not append sections 3 and 4 to fill out the story; they detail the real effects of the tyrannicide and therefore define its historical meaning. Note also in this connection how Thucydides' remark in 59.4 about Hippias' removal by the Lacedaemonians and the Alcmeonid exiles connects the digression to contemporary Athenian fear of a plot between Alcibiades, an Alcmeonid about to be exiled, and the Lacedaemonians (61.2).

[65] This point is often overlooked. Thucydides' digression(s) really begins in 53.2, and is designed to explain why the Salaminia came to fetch Alcibiades and the other soldiers implicated in the affairs of the Herms and the mysteries. These are the digressions, composed in ring form:

52.2 Athenians in Sicily	A
53.1 Salaminia comes for Al.	B
53.2 For, Athenians made search	C

108

the demos (τῆς ξυνωμοσίας ἐπὶ τῷ δήμῳ) because of his part in the profanation of the mysteries. Thucydides tells us of the demos' belief, again incorrect, as he is careful to inform us, that the appearance of a Lacedaemonian army in the Isthmus at the time of this agitation was connected with Alcibiades' supposed intrigues against the democracy. In addition, his friends in Argos were suspected of plotting to overthrow the democracy at this same time: "From all sides suspicion surrounded Alcibiades. So that, wishing, by bringing him to trial, to kill him, they thus sent the Salaminia" (61.4). Thucydides describes Alcibiades' arrest and his subsequent escape. He ends this account by saying that "Alcibiades, now an exile, not much later crossed in a boat from Thurii to the Peloponnese. And the Athenians passed a sentence of death by default upon him and the ones with him" (61.7). Again, the most capable leader Athens possesses,[66] from the highest social and political class, has been forced to seek refuge among Athens' most dangerous enemies by lower-class scoundrels, acting out of fear and jealousy.[67]

53.3 For the demos knew of tyranny	D
54.1 For the τόλμημα of H and A	E
60.1 the demos remembered	D
60.1 and was harsh and suspicious	C
61.1 and concerning Alcibiades	B
62.1 Athenians in Sicily	A

In sum, there are several digressions within the first digression, which interrupts the narrative of the Athenian campaign in Sicily. That, in turn, is resumed in 62.1. (See K. H. Kinzl's much more elaborate scheme in *Historia* 25 [1976] 480.)

[66] At least in Thucydides' view: see 6.15.4.

[67] See Schadewaldt, *Geschichtschreibung*, 92. On the tyrannicide he writes, "An act of political folly, born in emotion, guided by fear and chance, perpetrated by means of the lower class, produces the change from a beneficent government to a reign of terror, costs the lower class the lives of numerous citizens, leads the ruler to treason and leaves him, in league with the bitter enemy, to set out for the destruction of Athens. That is the historical point which the whole account makes"; on the Herms, "since the legal proceedings of the Hermocopidae and its political aftermath, an act of political folly born in the pathos of the lower class, guided by fear and chance, will cost the lower class (in Sicily and further afield) the lives of numerous citizens, lead the most

But there is worse to come. The demos also acted out of gross ignorance, ignorance of the Hermocopidae and of the real effects of the tyrannicide. Between those two events there is a further parallel bringing together the two points, one political and one historiographical, that Thucydides intends to stress by means of his digression. This parallel is the most critical one of all for Thucydides' conception of history and historiography. The lowly Aristogeiton plotted his overthrow of the tyrants out of a fear that they would use force (βία) against him. That fear, Thucydides makes clear, was unfounded. The tyrants did not employ force in their rule. But when Harmodius and Aristogeiton responded to the tyrants' covert social insult (ἐν τρόπῳ δέ τινι ἀφανεῖ in 54.4) by using force themselves, they forced Hippias, for the first time, to use this same weapon against the Athenians. Thus what had been a tyranny in name and in Aristogeiton's crazed imagination only became a tyranny in fact. But the Athenian demos in 415 ignorantly reversed this process. As Stahl points out, they "confused cause and effect."[68] The demos believed that Aristogeiton and Harmodius killed Hipparchus because the tyranny used violence. Thucydides shows the reverse to be the case. The tyranny used violence because Aristogeiton and Harmodius killed Hipparchus.

But note the events of 415. In that year the lower class feared that Alcibiades and his associates were plotting an oligarchical and tyrannical conspiracy (ξυνωμοσίᾳ ὀλιγαρχικῇ καὶ τυραννικῇ; 6.60.1). The last word is historically superfluous and even inappropriate. But it is historiographically informative. It is Thucydides' way of linking the two episodes, tyrannicide and Hermocopidae. The demos' fear that Alcibiades was intriguing with Sparta and conspiring to overthrow the democracy led it, in ignorance and passion, to put to death those accused Athenian aristocrats whom it caught and to condemn Alcibiades and other aristocrats to death in their absence. Alcibi-

capable and dangerous man, in whom one rightly fears a future tyrant, to treason, to let him work, in league with Sparta, for the destruction of Athens."

[68] Stahl, *Stellung*, 8.

ades, Thucydides makes clear, was not in fact plotting such a conspiracy. The demos only imagined he was. But what did Alcibiades do after many reputable citizens were imprisoned (6.60.2) or put to death (60.4), and he and others were frightened into exile with a price upon their heads (60.4, 61.7)? He intrigued with Sparta and later formed an oligarchical conspiracy! In other words, just as Aristogeiton, by his jealous fear of the tyrants' power and his murder of Hipparchus, drove Hippias to become the tyrant he had not been before, so the demos, by its suspicious fear of Alcibiades' ties with Sparta and his plans to form an oligarchic conspiracy, and by its killing of some Athenian aristocrats, drove Alcibiades to seek refuge in Sparta and to form the conspiracy he had not plotted before! In Thucydides' view, this is the most telling parallel between the two events.

We know that, historically, Alcibiades did go to Sparta and lend his efforts to the defeat of Athens, and we know that he also was instrumental in forming the oligarchical conspiracy that in 411 overthrew the democracy. But how can we be sure that Thucydides had these events in mind when he wrote chapters 53-61? That is, how do we know that he was drawing this parallel historiographically? Stahl and Dover, for two, doubt that Thucydides meant to suggest such similarities.

There are several pieces of evidence that we can adduce in making this case. The first is the simple fact that Thucydides included chapter 59, sections 3 and 4 at all. These sections are unnecessary and superfluous on the assumption that Thucydides simply "succumbed here to the temptation before which all historians and commentators are by their very nature weak, the temptation to correct historical error wherever they find it, regardless of its relevance to their immediate purpose."[69] They serve primarily to recall and stress for the reader the results of the tyrannicide: that Hippias found refuge and allies in Asia and twenty years later returned to aid the Persians in their invasion of Attica. And since Thucydides includes a *tekmerion* in this section, it cannot be dismissed as "ein kurzer,

[69] Dover, *Comm.* 4: 329.

III

summarischer Hinweis," as Stahl would have us believe.[70] In addition, Thucydides concludes the digression on the tyrannicides (59.4) with the same remark as that with which he ends the digression on Alcibiades (61.7): Hippias finds safety in Persia, Alcibiades finds refuge in the Peloponnese. Thus Thucydides emphasizes historiographically the similarity between the results of the two affairs.

Secondly, as we have shown, the two episodes contain the same political bias and tendentiousness. The bitterness revealed in Thucydides' treatment of the Hermocopidae (53.2, 60-61) is matched by that which he betrays in his handling of the tyrannicide (54.2-5, 56-59.1). Thucydides emphasizes the contrast between the ignoble baseness of the perpetrators and the upper-class distinction of the victims of the two crimes.[71] Indeed, he is so concerned to impress the reader with these contrasts that he indulges in uncharacteristic exaggeration (53.2, 54.2) and sarcasm (ὡς ἀπὸ τῆς ὑπαρχούσης ["in so far as his rank currently allowed"] 54.3; ἄσμενος λαβών, ὡς ᾤετο, τὸ σαφὲς ["happily taking, as it thought, the truth"] 60.4) in describing the murderers. He also goes out of his way to stress the rank and quality of the victims (πάνυ χρηστοὺς τῶν πολιτῶν ["quite the best of the citizens"] 53.2; πολλοὶ . . . καὶ ἀξιόλογοι ἄνθρωποι ["many . . . and noteworthy men"] 60.2; compare 54.5-6). Thucydides' political point is clearly the same in both cases: members of the lower or middle classes, acting on personal and private motives and suspicious impulses, murder Athenian aristocrats of the highest quality, thus causing a bitter reaction among members of the upper class that will result in disastrous public consequences for the state as a whole.[72]

Third, Thucydides emphasizes several times that, just as Hippias' tyrannical behavior and his escape to and support of Persia were based upon the murder of his brother and his fear of the Athenians (διὰ φόβον ἤδη μᾶλλον ὢν τῶν τε πολιτῶν ["being now more afraid of the citizens"] 59.2), so Alcibiades' aid to Sparta and his fomenting of the oligarchic revolution

---

[70] Stahl, Stellung, 7.

[71] See W. Schadewaldt, Geschichtschreibung, 88, 93, n. 1.

[72] See 2.65.11 for Thucydides' clearest statement of this point.

were directly related to his suffering (and that of others) at the hands of the demos. The telling word Thucydides uses in describing Alcibiades' political enemies is πονηρία. Thucydides reserves this highly charged political term and the adjective from it exclusively for the opponents of Alcibiades.[73] In 6.53.2, as we saw, he uses both πονηρία and πονηρός to stress the baseness of the informers in the affairs of the mysteries and the Herms. Here the fact that Thucydides contrasts these words with χρηστός in both instances proves their political application, and the fact that they are repeated proves the historian's emphasis, even bias. Then in 6.89.5 he makes Alcibiades, in his explanation to the Spartans of his political stance at Athens, say the following: τῆς δὲ ὑπαρχούσης ἀκολασίας ἐπειρώμεθα μετριώτεροι ἐς τὰ πολιτικὰ εἶναι. ἄλλοι δ᾽ ἦσαν καὶ ἐπὶ τῶν πάλαι καὶ νῦν οἳ ἐπὶ τὰ πονηρότερα ἐξῆγον τὸν ὄχλον.[74] Here again the context assures us that τὰ πονηρότερα refers to political baseness. Toward the end of the speech Alcibiades makes explicit the connection between his exile and his service to Sparta: φυγάς τε γάρ εἰμι τῆς τῶν ἐξελασάντων πονηρίας, καὶ οὐ τῆς ὑμετέρας, ἢν πείθησθέ μοι, ὠφελίας ("I am an exile from the baseness of those who drove me away, and not, if you trust me, from your advantage"; 92.3). That this is Thucydides' own view, as well as Alcibiades', is shown by his use of the term πονηρία. Such actions as the demos' handling of the mysteries and the Herms force Athens' friends to become her enemies. Thus Thucydides clearly ties Alcibiades' service to Sparta, which he considers crucial for the entire war, to the πονηρία of his political enemies.

But this is not all. Thucydides emphasizes the same point in

[73] At least in this meaning.

[74] "We tried to be more moderate in politics than the current licentiousness. But there were others long ago and there are those now who mislead the demos to baser ways." It is just possible that the ἄλλοι . . . ἐπὶ τῶν πάλαι whom Alcibiades refers to include Harmodius and Aristogeiton. If so, then Thucydides allows Alcibiades to refer to the tyrannicide just as he earlier made him (6.16.5) refer to Themistocles (and thus to Thucydides' digression in Book I). In any case, no other persons have been found appropriate for Alcibiades' ἄλλοι. See Dover, *Comm.* 4: 362.

his account of Alcibiades' instigation of the oligarchical conspiracy. In 8.47.2 he describes the origins of this plot:

> For when the Athenian soldiers at Samos saw that he [Alcibiades] had influence with Tissaphernes, and when Alcibiades sent word to the most powerful of them to remind the aristocrats [τοὺς βελτίστους] among them that he wanted to return under an oligarchy and not under the political baseness [πονηρίᾳ] and democracy which threw him out, and when he told them that he would bring over Tissaphernes as their political ally, then the trierarchs and the most powerful of the Athenians at Samos became eager for the dissolution of the democracy.

Note in particular that Thucydides makes Alcibiades prefer not only oligarchy to democracy, but "the best men" to the πονηρία which "threw him out." This historically unnecessary addition reminds us historiographically of Thucydides' own contrast, made twice, in 6.53.2, between οἱ χρηστοί and οἱ πονηροί. Again, the stimulus for Alcibiades' treasonous behavior comes from the πονηρία of the men who forced his exile. When Thucydides tells us in the next chapter that Alcibiades' arguments helped persuade the δυνατώτατοι to form a conspiracy, we have come full circle. The suspicion in the Athenian lower class that Alcibiades was fomenting an "oligarchical and tyrannical conspiracy" (6.60.1) has been realized, but only because of that suspicion and its consequences. Thucydides completes his analysis of this cycle (and his use of the term πονηρία in its political sense) by telling us that among the conspirators' first actions are the murders of two of Alcibiades' enemies, carried out in order to win his approval: "Some of the younger men had banded together, and secretly assassinated one Androcles, the chief leader of the commons, and mainly responsible for the banishment of Alcibiades; Androcles being singled out both because he was a popular leader, and because they sought by his death to recommend themselves to Alcibiades, who was, as they supposed, to be recalled, and to make Tissaphernes their friend" (8.65.2; translation by Crawley) and: "they put to death one Hyperbolus, an Athenian, a pestilent

fellow that had been ostracised, not from fear of his influence
or position, but because he was a rascal and a disgrace to the
city" (8.73.3; translation by Crawley). The very use of the term
πονηρία serves to inform us of Hyperbolus' political relationship to Alcibiades. The negative phrase οὐ διὰ δυνάμεως καὶ
ἀξιώματος φόβον reminds us that Alcibiades, who was feared
for both those reasons (see 6.15.3-4), was involved in the same
ostracism vote as Hyperbolus. In his entire history, Thucydides
applies the word πονηρία in its political sense only to the enemies of Alcibiades. These men are singled out by the use of a
term of extreme opprobrium because Thucydides believed that
they, more than anyone else, were responsible for Athens' defeat in the Peloponnesian War. They not only cost Athens her
best and most effective public leader, but they began the process
of political breakdown that weakened and finally broke Athens' military capability. It is they who are described in 2.65.11-
12 and in 6.15.3-4, Thucydides' two explicit statements of the
cause of Athens' downfall. Thucydides stresses that they came
from the lower class and acted out of private motives. In order
to make those same two points about Aristogeiton Thucydides
wrote his scornful and tendentious digression on the tyrannicide. If, "to discover such similarities . . . we have to adopt a
standpoint far removed from that of the candid reader,"[75] we
should not be unduly alarmed. Thucydides wrote for "those
who will want to examine the clear truth of what happened
and will happen again, according to the human condition, in
a parallel and similar way" (1.22.4).

This brings us to my last point about the digression in Book
VI. Thucydides takes pains to impress his readers with the ignorance and prejudiced credulity exhibited by the Athenian
demos in its investigations of both incidents, the tyrannicide
and the Herms-mysteries. Concerning the former, he says
twice (53.3, 60.1) that the demos' knowledge was based on
hearsay (ἀκοῇ). In 1.20.1, referring to this same event, he had
said that "men receive oral reports of past events, even of their
own past, equally ἀβασανίστως from each other. For example
the πλῆθος of the Athenians think that Hipparchus was killed

[75] Dover, *Comm.* 4: 328-329.

by Harmodius and Aristogeiton while he was tyrant and they do not know. . . ." Here Thucydides is criticizing the demos' reliance upon untested oral evidence. After this example and one other he concludes: "Most people do not search hard for the truth, but turn rather to whatever is at hand" (20.3).

Thucydides' criticism in Book VI of the demos' search for the perpetrators of the defacing of the Herms is based on the same arguments: "For the Athenians, when the expedition departed, made no less the search, . . . and *not testing* the informers" (my italics; 53.2). In chapters 60-61, where he resumes his narrative of this affair, he stresses three times (60.2, 60.4, and 61.1) the demos' ignorance of it, once with bitter sarcasm (60.4). Each time he uses the phrase τὸ σαφές. Thucydides employs this word in this sense of "clear truth" only six times in his entire work. He uses it three times within the space of an Oxford page (60.2-61.1) to refer to the demos' ignorance of the affair of the Herms. The demos thought it had the clear truth of the matter, just as it thought it understood the truth about the tyrants, the tyrannicide and its effects. Indeed, it was this belief in its knowledge of the murder of 514 that led it to act so harshly in the affairs of 415. It thought it saw a parallel between the two events. But, Thucydides says, it was mistaken, or rather, it was correct but for the wrong reason. There was indeed a parallelism but a different one from that which the demos thought it saw. Thucydides believed he knew the real truth of the tyrannicide and its relationship to 415. The account of the tyrannicide was written as a paradigmatic model for the events of 415, designed to bring out the parallelism historiographically. Thucydides' heavy emphasis upon ἀκοῇ and σαφές in 6.53-61 is meant to remind us of his methodological section (20-22) in Book I, where he contrasts his own laborious discovery of truth (22.2-3) with most men's "easy" search for it (ἀταλαίπωρος in 20.3) and acceptance of untested oral tradition (20.1). It certainly appears that Thucydides wrote his digression on the tyrannicide for "those who will want to examine the clear truth of what has happened and will happen again, according to the human condition, in a parallel and similar way" (22.4). In 6.54-59 he provides us with the clear

116

truth of the tyrannicide, as he sees it. But note that the reader must do his part too. He must scrutinize the clear truth in order to understand its general applicability. Thucydides will not draw the parallelisms for him; the reader must do that for himself. As Schadewaldt says: "One easily grasps why Thucydides discloses only his purpose of criticizing the tradition, and leaves that of criticizing the political facts to the understanding of his reader. This silence was made possible for him through the very form of the paradigm, to whose nature, since its first entrance in the Nestor/Phoenix speeches of the Iliad, belonged the anticipation, without explicit statements, of the useful comprehension of the ethical as well as the judgmental implications."[76] By placing the digression on the events of 514 within the digression on the events of 415, Thucydides has made the reader's task far easier.

From these arguments it should be clear that Thucydides wrote his digressions in Book VI for the same reason that he composed the parallel digressions in Book I: in order to provide an historical paradigm for the critical issue of one part of the war.[77] The two cases support one another. They also reveal the difference in outlook in Thucydides' treatment of the two ten-year wars. In the first, he emphasizes historiographically the Athens-Sparta dualism. In the second, his emphasis is upon Athens and her political dissension. The digressions serve to introduce these themes and to give them an historical background and context.

THE THIRD CONFERENCES

Toward the end of each introductory section Thucydides reports a third conference. In Book I it is the so-called second conference at Sparta (119-125); in Book VI it is the debate at Camarina between Hermocrates and the Athenian Euphemus (76-88). In the former conference Thucydides gives us only the

---

[76] W. Schadewaldt, *Geschichtschreibung*, 93.

[77] For Thucydides' use of historical paradigms see V. Hunter, *CJ* 67 (1971) 16 and n. 6, 17-18; Jurgen Gommel, *Rhetorisches Argumentieren bei Thucydides*, Spudasmata, no. 10 (Hildesheim 1966) 26 ff.

speech of the Corinthians, but we shall add to it, for purposes of comparison with Euphemus' speech, the speech of the Athenians at the first conference in Sparta (1.73-78). This speech, as we saw (p. 81) had no counterpart in Thucydides' report of the conference at Syracuse, and we therefore postponed discussion of it until now.

The Corinthians begin their speech with an appeal to all the Peloponnesian allies to recognize the threat posed by Athens:

> There is no need to warn those who have had experience with the Athenians to be on their guard against them. But those of us which are more inland and out of the sea routes should know that, if they do not aid the coastal powers, their exporting and importing of goods to and from the sea·will become more difficult; they should therefore not be negligent in their judgment of these matters, as if they were not relevant to them, but should expect, that if they sacrifice the coastal states, the danger will reach them too [κ᾽ ἂν μέχρι σφῶν τὸ δεινὸν προελθεῖν]; thus their interests are no less at stake now than the others'. . . . Let us also recognize that if these disputes were only between rival neighbors about territory, it would be bearable; but now the Athenians are a match for our whole alliance. Unless, therefore, we all make a united stand together, race by race and city by city, they will easily conquer us, divided as we are. (120.2)

Hermocrates makes the same point in appealing to the Camarinaeans to join Syracuse in her opposition to Athens. He too emphasizes that in the coming war with the Athenians everyone's interests are at stake, not just those who appear to be Athens' objects: "Shall we wait until each city, one by one, is taken, knowing that only in this way can we be conquered? . . . And do we think when a distant Sicilian state is first destroyed that the danger will not come to each of us in turn [ἐς αὐτόν τινα ἥξειν τὸ δεινόν] and that he who is destroyed before that suffers in himself alone?" (77.2). (See 79.3-80.1.) Thus both the Corinthians and Hermocrates argue that the threat Athens poses is a general one, for the whole Peloponnese in the former case, for all of Sicily in the latter. It is therefore in everyone's interests to join in opposing the Athenians, who are a match for all the states together, and vastly superior to each one individually.

For this reason, both argue, we must take united action. "It would be dreadful if [δεινὸν ἂν εἴη εἰ], while the Athenians' allies never stop paying money for their own slavery we should refuse to spend money for vengeance upon enemies and for our own preservation" (1.121.5); and "It is dreadful if [δεινὸν εἰ] the Rhegians suspect his specious pretense and are wise without reason, while you, with good reason on your side, still choose to help your natural enemies, destroying your natural kinsmen" (6.79.2).

This last issue, that of race, is a theme in both speeches. The Corinthians refer to Potidaea, where "Dorians are besieged by Ionians, the reverse of the normal order of things" (124.1). Hermocrates encourages the Camarinaeans to take to heart the *paradeigmata* afforded by Athens' conduct in Greece, where she has enslaved many Greek cities. "Let us show the Athenians," he urges, "that we are not Ionians nor Hellespontines and islanders, who are always slaves, though they change Persian and Greek masters continually, but free Dorians from independent Peloponnese, living in Sicily" (77.1). Each contends that the coming war is to be, in part at least, fought on racial lines (see 6.80.3).

Finally, the two speeches end on the same note. "Consider that the city established as a tyrant in Greece stands against all equally, so that it rules some now, and intends to rule the rest; let us then attack and conquer it, and ourselves live without danger in the future, and let us free the Greeks who are now enslaved" (124.3); and "Examine the issue and choose now either immediate slavery without danger or the prospect of conquering with us and thus escaping disgraceful submission to an Athenian master and avoiding the lasting hostility of Syracuse" (6.80.5). There are thus several points of comparison between these two speeches, both of which serve generally as warnings against Athenian aggression and as pleas for unified opposition.

The speech of the Athenians at Sparta and that of Euphemus at Camarina, as has been recognized before, invite compari-son.[78] There are so many phrases in common in these two speeches that there should be no doubt that Thucydides wrote each with the other in mind. They are both, we might say, Athenian statements of the right to empire and thus contain many standard rhetorical arguments traditional in "die politische Selbstdarstellung der Athener." That Thucydides made these speeches so exactly similar suggests that he wanted the reader to compare them, despite the fact that they do not come in parallel places in the structure of Books I and VI.

Both speakers begin by saying that they have come for other purposes, but are forced by the previous speaker's criticism and slander of Athens to defend her claims that she holds her empire "reasonably." It is therefore "necessary to speak."[79] Each begins his case with arguments taken from earlier history, particularly the Persian Wars, though each rhetorically avers that it is superfluous to speak of τὰ Μηδικά (1.73.2 and 6.83.2). Dover seems mistaken in seeing a contrast between the two speeches in their treatment of the Persian Wars.[80] Though Euphemus "declares that he will not expatiate on the services which Athens gave to Greece in the Persian Wars," he nonetheless has just done so in chapters 82.4 to 83.1. They employ similar rhetorical devices: τεκμήριον δὲ μέγιστον αὐτὸς ἐποίησεν and τὸ μὲν οὖν μέγιστον μαρτύριον αὐτὸς εἶπεν ("he himself gave the greatest piece of evidence"; 1.73.5 and 6.82.2). Their points about Athens' role in the Persian Wars are the same, and are expressed in nearly identical language.[81] Even their generalizations are couched in similar words. Compare πᾶσι δὲ ἀνεπίφθονον τὰ ξυμφέροντα τῶν μεγίστων πέρι κιν-

---

[78] See Dover, *Comm.* 4: 353, Strasburger, "Thukydides und die politische Selbstdarstellung der Athener," *Wege*, 521, n. 59, de Romilly, *Thucydides and Athenian Imperialism*, trans. Philip Thody (Oxford 1963), 242 ff., 250.

[79] See 1.73.1-2 and 6.82.1.

[80] Dover, *Comm.* 4: 354.

[81] See 1.74.1 and 6.83.1, 1.74.2 and 6.82.4, where the same phrases are repeated, nearly word for word. Note also the emphasis upon κινδυνεύω in 1.74.2-3 and in 6.83.2.

δύνων εὖ τίθεσθαι and πᾶσι δὲ ἀνεπίφθονον τὴν προσήκουσαν σωτηρίαν ἐκπορίζεσθαι ("it is no reproach for everyone to see to his own safety"; 1.75.5 and 6.83.2). Compare also 1.75.3 and 76.2 with 6.82.3 and 83.4. They both conclude with pleas that their listeners "not be persuaded by others' slanders" (1.78.1 and 6.87.1).

All these similarities make us read the two speeches together. But when we do compare them closely, we become aware that the similarities are in their rhetorical commonplaces, not in their actual intent. "The Athenians at Sparta were essentially apologetic."[82] They were concerned to show how their power arose naturally because of their fear of Persia and Sparta. Their rule is not unnatural (76.3), but is even more just and moderate than necessary (76.3-77.6). They urge the Spartans to think twice before instigating a long and painful war which can be avoided by negotiation (78). Euphemus' speech, on the other hand, is extraordinarily disingenuous. It appears to be blatantly realistic and frank. As Dover summarizes it: " 'we built up our empire to protect ourselves against our hereditary enemies, the Peloponnesians; we had a right to subdue the Ionians, because they had sailed with Xerxes against us; we have come to Sicily because Syracuse is a threat to our security; and as she is a threat to yours also, you will be wise to make use of us while we are here.' "[83] Indeed, Euphemus goes so far as to argue that "for a tyrant or a city with an empire nothing is unreasonable if expedient, no one a kinsman unless sure; friendship or enmity is always a matter of time and circumstance" (Crawley translation). Thus he argues that the Athenians are in Sicily to look out for their own interests.

According to the "candid" Euphemus Athens' interest is in defending herself against her enemy Syracuse, which poses a threat to her security by supporting the Leontines and her "other friends" in Sicily (84.3). But this is not realism, it is pure deceit. As Strasburger has shown, Thucydides makes it clear that the Athenians have come to Sicily on the pretext of wishing to aid their kinsmen and allies, but actually to conquer the

---

[82] Dover, *Comm.* 4: 353.
[83] Dover, *Comm.* 4: 354.

island (6.6.1).[84] He makes the same point about their motives on several other occasions (6.1.1, 6.90, 7.75.7). Euphemus' speech, while it appears to be realistic and frank, is actually designed to hide the Athenians' real intention from a potential ally, and for good reason. If the Camarinaeans knew it, they would certainly not support Athens' campaign in Sicily.

There is thus an essential and revealing difference between these two formally similar speeches. The Athenians in Book I are on the defensive. They make a genuine plea to Sparta to put away thoughts of war and to settle their differences peacefully by negotiation. In Book VI the Athenians are plainly the aggressors. They must cover up their real aim, the conquest and subjection of Sicily, and proclaim a false one, the support of their kinsmen and friends. The Camarinaeans were not fooled: "They sympathized with the Athenians, except in so far as they believed they were going to enslave Sicily" (6.88.1). The irony is heavy indeed.

THE SPEECHES OF PERICLES AND ALCIBIADES

Book I ends with the speech of Pericles at Athens. The event concluding the narrative of the "six years and ten months of unstable peace" is the speech of Alcibiades at Sparta. It is important first to understand the nature of the historiographical choices that Thucydides made in selecting these two speeches as the end points for his introductions to the two ten-year wars.

At the final Athenian assembly before the diplomatic or political *arche* of the first war many speakers gave their opinions, some for, and some against the war which the Spartans were now clearly threatening. Thucydides chooses to give us only one of those speeches, that of Pericles, "at that time the leading citizen of Athens, the most powerful of the Athenians in both words and deeds" (1.139.4). It is a strong appeal for war (see especially 144.3-4) which, Thucydides says (145), the Athenians voted for and communicated officially to the Spartans, generally and on specific points.

[84] "Thukydides und die politische Selbstdarstellung der Athener," *Wege*, 521.

The last event before the *arche* of the second war is the Spartan ecclesia held in the winter of 415/414. Syracuse has sent an embassy to Corinth and Sparta to ask for help in Sicily. In Sparta, together with the Corinthians and Alcibiades, the ambassadors ask the Spartans "to make war more openly against the Athenians and to send some aid to Sicily" (6.88.8). Their combined efforts succeeded in convincing the Spartans to send ambassadors to the Syracusans to prevent them from coming to terms with the Athenians, but they were still not eager to send actual aid. At that point Alcibiades came forward and gave a speech which "inflamed and stirred the Lacedaemonians" (88.10). At the end of it "the Lacedaemonians, intending before on their own to march against Athens, but still hesitating and holding back, now became much more confident when they learned this information from Alcibiades, for they thought that they had heard it from the man who knew the facts most clearly and truly. As a result, they began giving their attention to the fortification of Decelea and, for the moment, to sending some aid to the Sicilians" (93.1-2). Thucydides goes on to describe the dispatch of Gylippus as archon to the Syracusans. He later (7.18.1) tells us explicitly that the Lacedaemonians at that same assembly had voted to invade Attica. Alcibiades' speech, in Thucydides' presentation, provides the critical impetus for Sparta's decision to renew the war in Greece and to send aid to Sicily.

Thucydides' selection of these two speeches by Pericles and Alcibiades was determined, in part, by his assessment of their extreme importance. But, just as clearly, his historiographical decision was also based on his desire to present parallel speeches at the end of his two introductory sections. The final episode preceding each ten-year war was to be a major policy speech, delivered to the Athenian assembly in Book I, to the Spartan assembly in Book VI. The effect of these two appeals was the same: they convinced their listeners that the time had come to accept a major war with their principal enemies. But again there is an ironic contrast behind the formal parallelism. In Book I Athens' most powerful leader convinces the assembly to accept willingly the "necessity for war" with Sparta and the opportunity it provided to protect the city and "win the greatest honors both publicly and privately" (144.3). In Book VI Athens' most powerful leader (6.15.4), now an exile, convinces the Spartan assembly to renew the war against Athens in order to "tear down the present and prospective power of the Athenians" and to make Sparta's rule of all of Greece safe and secure for the future (92.5). These two speeches prepare us for the different, nearly opposite, conditions in which the two wars begin. In the first the Athenians have all the advantages: the greatest and most far sighted leader, overwhelming superiority in money, ships, and men. In the second, the same advantages have shifted to the Spartans' side. It is now they who have the most effective leader, and he will soon, by his advice and his personal influence and intervention, transfer the advantages to the Spartans. His advice to fortify Decelea (91.6-7) will ruin the Athenians' economic advantage; his advice to send aid to Sicily (91.4) will turn the tide of the war there and lead to a crushing Athenian defeat in which money, ships, and men are destroyed in unprecedented quantities.[85]

But only half of Alcibiades' speech (90-92.1) is devoted to giving advice to Sparta on military matters. The other half (89, 92.2-5) serves to lay the groundwork for Alcibiades' personal assistance to the Spartan state. In these two paragraphs Alcibiades seeks to convince the Spartans that his loyalty to Athens has been broken by the πονηρία of his political enemies

---

[85] It is possible that in making Alcibiades recommend in 415-414 the fortification of Decelea "Thucydides may have incorporated . . . advice which was not in fact given until later." (Dover, *Comm.* on 6.91.6, citing Wilamowitz, *Hermes* 60 [1925] 297 ff. and Schwartz, *Geschichtswerk*, 198 f.) If so, this would support our argument on structure, since Thucydides will have consciously antedated the recommendation in order to have Alcibiades answer Pericles' point about the effect of ἐπιτείχισις. But there is no way of knowing with any certainty. Note how Pericles had tried to deemphasize the military effects of an ἐπιτείχισις in his speech (142.1-4). But he had not foreseen its economic impact, which, Thucydides makes Alcibiades argue (91.6-7), will do the greatest harm to Athens' military efforts. This point will be fully borne out in Thucydides' extended analysis of the effect that the fortification of Decelea had upon Attica (7.27.2-28.4).

there,[86] and that he is now prepared and eager to serve the Spartans in their effort to defeat Athens: "I ask you to use me fearlessly for any mission, no matter how dangerous or difficult, and to remember the old saying, that if I did you great harm as an enemy, I could also do you great service as a friend, in as much as I know Athens' position and only guessed at yours" (92.5). This aspect of Alcibiades' speech is fully as important as his military advice, for it leads to his personal intervention in the war on Sparta's side. Almost single-handedly, according to Thucydides, he will cause the revolt of Athens' Ionian subjects and win the Persian king and his money for Sparta.[87] It is for these reasons that Thucydides gives as much attention in Alcibiades' speech to his explanation of his personal and political attitude as to his military suggestions. His great abilities are removed from Athens and bestowed upon Sparta. Thus the speech of Alcibiades shifts from Athens to Sparta the advantages catalogued in the speech of Pericles. In Thucydides' presentation, Alcibiades' speech not only induces Sparta to renew the Peloponnesian War, it is the crucial turning point in that war. It is the principal reason why the second ten-year war will be so different from the first.[88] Just as Thucydides concluded his introduction to the first war with a portrait of Athens' great statesman[89] and his military and political policy, so he ends his preface to the second war with a picture of Alcibiades, who has left Athens for Sparta and taken his talents and his strategy with him. The second war begins ominously for Athens, propitiously for Sparta.

[86] These, says Alcibiades, are my real enemies, not you Spartans (92.2-3). Thus Pericles' worst fear (144.1) is realized. "I fear more our own mistakes than the plans of our enemies."

[87] See especially 8.11-14 for Thucydides' emphasis upon the vital role that Alcibiades played in the revolt of Chios. Also see my Chapter V, pp. 192-198. For the impact upon the King, see 8.16-17, where Thucydides makes it clear that it was Alcibiades' swift and efficient actions which convinced Persia to make the first treaty with Sparta.

[88] See especially 7.27.2-28.4 and Schadewaldt, *Geschichtschreibung*, 82-83, for the way in which Thucydides develops this line of analysis.

[89] Note especially how Thucydides portrays Pericles' staunch resolve in 140-141.1, and again in 144.1-4. His military advice is framed within these personal sections, just as is the case with Alcibiades' speech.

CHAPTER III

Books II and VII: The First Years of the Wars; Leaders and Problems

Once he has begun his account of the wars proper, Thucydides is far more restricted in the historiographical treatment of his material than he was in the introductory sections. With his strict annalistic method providing the framework, his narrative moves chronologically from one event to the next. Indeed, he even breaks off the account of a particular series of events in order to record what was happening elsewhere at the same time, though this often results in the weakening and even confusion of a particular episode.[1] In addition, the narrative is much more intense. There are fewer pauses, asides and backward glances, fewer digressions. In Book I the archaeology, the methodology, the Pentecontaetia, and the digression on Pausanias and Themistocles all interrupt the flow of the narrative to a significant degree; Book VI has its own archaeology and a major excursus on the tyrannicides. In the narrative of the wars proper Thucydides does not often indulge in digressions, and when he does, they are generally brief and contemporary narratives, not historical paradigms and parallels. Thucydides did not have the freedom in constructing his account of the wars that he did in composing his introduction to them. At least, such was his historiographical decision.

Given this fact, we can hardly expect to find the same formal parallelism between the accounts of the two wars that we found between Books I and VI. Thucydides was too careful

[1] See especially 2.95-101, 7.9, etc.

and honest in his compilation and presentation of the facts to try to make them fit a particular scheme or pattern. He was, first and foremost, a conscientious historian, i.e., inquirer.[2] But this basic outlook does not preclude a lively and serious interest in historical parallels and analogies when they strike the careful observer's mind. As we saw, Thucydides on several occasions draws such analogies explicitly and often has his speakers do the same thing.[3] His very division of the Peloponnesian War into two ten-year wars with a seven-year peace in the middle was designed, to some extent, to produce historical parallelism on a major scale. In this and the succeeding two chapters we argue that he frequently made implicit comparisons and contrasts between the two parts of the war by means of formal, i.e., structural parallelism. As in Books I and VI, so in the rest of his work Thucydides was concerned with pointing out the contrasts between the two ten-year wars, or, more precisely, the differences in men's responses to similar situations and opportunities presented by those wars. In drawing the reader's attention to these differences, he often exhibits a masterful use of irony that is acerbic, sometimes pathetic, but always telling and perceptive.

PERICLES AND NICIAS

By far the most significant parallelism between Book II on the one hand and Book VI, chapters 94-105 plus Book VII on the other is the one Thucydides draws between the figures of Pericles and Nicias. It is true, as some scholars have pointed out, that one political successor to Pericles was Alcibiades.[4] We saw

[2] Here we part company with the modern "school" of Thucydidean scholarship which argues that Thucydides was everything else, a brilliant political scientist, sociologist, etc., but not an historian. See Chapter I, note 1, and Chapter VI.

[3] See note 77, Chapter II on παραδείγματα and see especially 7.71.7 and 4.36.3.

[4] See A. W. Gomme, A. Andrewes, and K. J. Dover, *A Historical Commentary on Thucydides* (Oxford 1945-1970) 4: 246 with references. Hereafter cited as *Comm.* But A. B. West has made a good case that the real political heir of Pericles was Nicias: see "Pericles' Political Heirs," *CP* 19 (1924) 124-146, 201-228.

in the last chapter that Thucydides contrasted these two great leaders at the end of his two introductions, where each delivered a speech that brought on war between Athens and Sparta. But in Book VII Alcibiades temporarily drops out of Thucydides' *History*, while Nicias becomes the focus of attention.[5] This is, of course, to be expected given that Book VII is almost exclusively concerned with the Sicilian campaign, from which Alcibiades has been removed by politics and Lamachus by war, leaving Nicias for a time sole commander of the expedition. But there is a strong element of historiographical choice in the elevation of Nicias in Book VII. Even after the arrival of Demosthenes and Eurymedon in Sicily Nicias receives most of Thucydides' attention. His plans and strategy are given in far more detail, his speeches are recorded while the others' are not, his contingent's march at the end is treated much more dramatically and fully than is Demosthenes', and his fate is carefully reviewed and judged, while the others' are only briefly registered.[6] Nicias is clearly the Athenian leader whom Thucydides wants to emphasize in Book VII.

But even this choice is not surprising, given the fact that Nicias did indeed have the most important position in Athens' campaign in Sicily. He was, it is true, the only general in command there for the entire duration of the expedition, and he does appear to have played the leading role in decision making, especially after Alcibiades' recall and Lamachus' death (see 6.103.3). One might argue, then, that Thucydides' focus upon Nicias in Book VII is based upon the same criteria as his almost exclusive focus upon Pericles in Book II. These two men dominate Books II and VII because to a large degree they determined Athenian policy in 431-429 and 415-413 respectively. There is, however, a far greater parallelism between Thucydides' treatment of these two leaders than one of simple emphasis and focus. In Thucydides' composition of Books II and VII, Pericles and Nicias confront similar situations and give the same formal responses to them. They are, historiographically

[5] There is only one brief mention of Alcibiades in 7.18.1.

[6] Contrast 7.48 with 47.3-4; see 7.61-4 and 77; contrast 7.81.4-82.3 with 82.3-85; contrast 7.86.3-5 with 52.2, and 6.101.6.

speaking, almost identical. But the historical picture that emerges from this constant formal comparison is one showing them to be, historically, complete opposites in almost all respects. They are foils for each other. A cursory review of Pericles in Book II and Nicias in VII suggests analogous treatment. A detailed comparison will then confirm it.

Pericles	Nicias
2.13 indirect speech to the assembly detailing resources for war with Peloponnesians	7.11-15 letter to the assembly detailing resources for war in Sicily
2.35-46 funeral oration	7.61-64, 69.2 speech to soldiers
2.60-64 exhortatory speech after plague	7.77 exhortatory speech after defeat in Great Harbor
2.65 political assessment	7.86 personal assessment

The speeches of Pericles in Book II and Nicias in VII not only correspond in number, but respond, for the most part, to similar situations and problems. Each gives first an indirect speech on the resources that Athens possesses for the coming campaign. Then they deliver a major speech: Pericles, the Funeral Oration, Nicias, the *parakeleusis* to the army before the battle in the Great Harbor. (This speech is followed by an indirect appeal to the πατρικαὶ ἀρεταί, γυναῖκες, παῖδες, and θεοὶ πατρῷοι ["ancestral virtues, wives, children, and native gods"] in 69.2). A great catastrophe immediately follows in each case, the plague in Book II, the final naval defeat in VII. Each leader then responds to the *aporia* which this disaster causes with a speech whose purpose is to raise the people's (or soldiers') failing spirits and to restore order and purpose to their efforts. Shortly afterwards, each man's death is recorded and Thucydides renders a judgment on his life, his public life in Pericles' case, his private life in Nicias'. There is thus strong reason to believe that Thucydides drew his portraits of Pericles and Nicias within similar frames. The pictures that emerge, however, as a close comparison reveals, are quite different from one another.

To begin with, what we already know about the two leaders before Books II and VII suggests that they are in every way opposites. Our first real introduction to Pericles comes in

1.127.3: "For being the most powerful of the men of his time and at the head of the state, he opposed the Lacedaemonians in all matters, and did not let the people give in to them, but drove the Athenians into war."[7] Pericles' speech at the end of Book I fills out this picture of the powerful and forceful leader. He tells the Athenians that "they must realize that it is necessary to go to war," that "from the greatest risks the greatest honors accrue to state and private citizen alike" (144.3) and that "It is therefore right to oppose the enemy in every way and to try to hand down to our descendants an empire no smaller than that which our fathers bequeathed to us" (144.4).

Our first full description of Nicias comes in 5.16. He was "most eager for political power in Athens and for peace and wished, while he was still undefeated and highly respected, to preserve his good fortune, and for the moment to be rid of troubles himself and to end those of his fellow citizens, for the future to hand down a reputation for having in no way harmed his city, thinking that he could achieve this if he took no risks and least offered himself to chance, and that a state of peace provided freedom from risk." Pericles and Nicias are opposites. Thucydides intimates that the difference in their approaches results from strongly contrasting views on two fundamental issues, one epistemological, one moral.

GNOME VERSUS TYCHE

On the question of what man can know and achieve in the world Pericles and Nicias stand at opposite poles: Pericles is the great champion of *gnome*, in its two senses of intelligence and will; Nicias, on the other hand, believes in the overwhelming power of *tyche*, fortune or chance.[8] The result is that one puts his faith in man, the other in fortune or god.[9] There is no

---

[7] He had been mentioned briefly as a general in 1.111.2, 114.1 and 3, 116.1 and 3 and 117.2.

[8] See especially 2.62.5 and 7.61.3.

[9] Pericles subordinates fate to the human (see 1.140.1 and Lowell Edmunds' discussion, in *Chance and Intelligence in Thucydides* [Cambridge, Mass. 1975] 16-17), while Nicias does the reverse (see 6.23.3 ["it is difficult for us, being men, to have good fortune"] and 7.77.1-4).

need to describe in detail the ways in which Thucydides portrays this basic opposition between Pericles and Nicias in Books
II and VII: L. Edmunds has analyzed in great detail Pericles'
and Nicias' positions on *gnome* and *tyche*.[10] It is enough for
our purposes here to examine this antithesis briefly and in
broad outline.

The Thucydidean Pericles is characterized most cogently
and clearly by *gnome* in its twin aspects of reason and resolve.
Thucydides uses this term to describe Pericles directly (2.34.6,
2.65.8) and it appears with great frequency in Pericles' direct
and indirect speeches. The two senses of *gnome* as it is used
by and of Pericles can best be understood by noting the contrast it forms with *orge* on the one hand and *tyche* (or *symphorai*) on the other. Thucydides often opposes Pericles' rationality
and steadfast resolve to the Athenians' passionate temper and
changing moods. The very first sentence of Pericles' first
speech draws this distinction explicitly: "I, Athenians, hold always to the same *gnome*, . . . although I know that men do not
decide to go to war and do so in fact with the same *orge*"
(1.140.1). In 2.22.1 Thucydides tells us that, during the first
Peloponnesian invasion, Pericles refused to call an assembly
or any convocation whatsoever, in order to prevent the Athenians from "making an error by joining battle more with
orge than with *gnome*." After the second Peloponnesian invasion, Thucydides remarks three times on the Athenians' changing, failing or passionate *gnome* (2.59.1, 2 and 2.59.3), and in
the speech that immediately follows, Pericles contrasts the people's weakness with his own resolve (ὑμετέρῳ ἀσθενεῖ τῆς
γνώμης and ἐγὼ μὲν ὁ αὐτός εἰμι in 2.61.2). In his summary
of the speech Thucydides says that "with such words Pericles
tried to release the Athenians from their *orge* against him and
to lead their *gnome* away from their present troubles" (2.65.1).
In his famous judgment of Pericles in the same chapter
(2.65.8-9) he says that by his ἀξίωμα and *gnome* Pericles was
able to control the people to such an extent that he could manipulate their moods, either bringing them down from hybris
to fear, or raising them from fear to confidence.

[10] L. Edmunds, *Chance and Intelligence.*

With this sense of *gnome* Thucydides generally denotes the will or resolve by which Pericles was able to hold the demos' *orge* in check and lead it rather than be led by it. In its other sense, that of intelligence or reason, *gnome* is often contrasted by Pericles with *tyche* or *symphorai*, chance or (mis)fortune. In the opening of his first speech (1.140.1) Pericles uses *gnome* (and *dianoia*) in this sense, and contrasts it with *symphorai* and *tyche*. Men "turn their *gnomai* in relation to their *symphorai*." Then he adds: "It is possible for the *symphorai* of our affairs to proceed no less illogically than the *dianoiai* of man; for this reason, we are accustomed to blame *tyche* for whatever turns out contrary to our calculation (παρὰ λόγον). As Edmunds demonstrates, "To put the case in this way is to make planning primary: through the use of this simile, Pericles describes adversity *in terms of* human planning, which thus becomes the criterion. . . . In this way Pericles trivializes chance, while yet admitting its existence.[11] In the last section of the same speech Pericles praises the former generation of Athenians for defeating the Mede "more by *gnome* than by *tyche*" (1.144.4). Thus Pericles' first speech is framed by two declarations of the contrast between *gnome* and *tyche*, human reason and parahuman chance. In each case, Pericles makes it clear which he prefers to trust.

Pericles makes similar points several times in his last speech. In 2.61.2-3 he warns the Athenians that "things which happen suddenly and unexpectedly and contrary to reason [τὸ αἰφνίδιον καὶ ἀπροσδόκητον καὶ τὸ πλείστῳ παραλόγῳ ξυμβαῖνον] are wont to enslave the *phronema*, which has happened to you especially in the case of the plague." "But you must be willing to withstand the greatest *symphorai*." He urges the Athenians to rely upon *gnome* rather than *elpis*, because its *pronoia* is firmer (2.62.5). Finally, he urges (2.64.6) the Athenians not to let *symphorai* weaken their *gnome* with grief. Pericles believes that human reason and intelligence are paramount, while chance and mischance are of minor significance in the nature of things. This proud humanism is based upon Pericles' belief in *techne* and *episteme* and *empeiria*, especially in sea-

[11] Edmunds, *Chance and Intelligence*, 17.

132

manship, which Athens has brought to near perfection. Through their art, knowledge, and experience, the Athenians can overcome *tyche*.[12] Thus *gnome* in its two senses describes the two great aspects of Pericles' character: his ability to control and lead the people; his belief in the paramount importance of man and his ability to control his fate.

There can be little doubt that Thucydides consciously compares Nicias, Athens' leader at the beginning of the second war, with Pericles in these respects. While Thucydides used *gnome* to characterize Pericles, in both of his direct descriptions of Nicias he uses *tyche* compounds to characterize his aspirations and his fate (διασώσασθαι τὴν εὐτυχίαν ["to preserve his good fortune"] in 5.16.1; and ἐς τοῦτο δυστυχίας ἀφικέσθαι ["to have reached this point of ill fortune"] in 7.86.5). More importantly, it is abundantly clear that Nicias is the foil of Pericles on the issues of control of the demos and man's relationship to *tyche*.

Thucydides makes a point of emphasizing the problems Nicias encountered in controlling the Athenian people. Three times he offers to resign his commands (4.28.1-2, 6.23.3, 7.15.1), the first time because of Cleon's vituperative attack in the assembly, the second because of potential opposition in the assembly, the third time because of sickness of body and of spirit. And three times Thucydides lets Nicias describe in his own words the difficulties he faced as a politician and as a commander. In 6.9.3 Nicias concedes that if he argues to conserve Athens' present strength and not take risks he will appear "weak in relation to your [the assembly's] *tropoi*." Later in the same speech (6.13.1) he admits fear of his political opposition made up of Alcibiades and his supporters. In his letter from Syracuse to Athens Nicias confesses that his worst problem as general is his inability to control his soldiers: "for your *physeis* are difficult to rule" (7.14.2). In 6.24.2 Thucydides says specifically that Nicias' attempt to dissuade the Athenians from sending the expedition to Sicily by cataloguing the enormous quantities of men and material necessary for success

---

[12] See 2.42.4 and Edmunds' discussions of this passage, *Chance and Intelligence*, 61-68, and appendix, 217-225.

backfired and only made the Athenians more eager than ever for the venture—"the opposite befell him."[13]

If Nicias is thus a foil for Pericles in terms of *gnome* or will, he is also Pericles' antithesis in terms of the *gnome-tyche* contrast. For Nicias, intelligence and planning are important, but *tyche* is more so: "I know that it is necessary for us to plan well in many respects, but to have good fortune in even more (and that is difficult for us, being mere men); I wish to sail out having trusted myself to *tyche* as little as possible, having rather based my safety on the best possible preparations" (6.23.3). Even when he states the need for human thought and reason, Nicias acknowledges the greater power of chance. In 7.50.4 Thucydides tells us that Nicias was a little too attached to superstition and such things.

Finally, and most significantly, Nicias bases his exhortations to his soldiers on hope and the chances and reversals of war, those very same forces that Pericles had admonished the Athenians to subordinate to their mind (*phronema* and *dianoia*) and resolve (*gnome*). In 7.61.3 Nicias tells the Athenians to "remember the *paralogoi* of wars, and hope that the force of *tyche* will stand with us." In 7.77 it is only hope of future *eutychia* which is left, hope "from the divine." The man who had tried to "give in as little as possible to chance" has now given himself up entirely to it.

Edmunds' study of *gnome* and *tyche* led him to the following conclusions about Thucydides' portraits of Pericles and Nicias:

> As Pericles was characterized by gnome, so Nicias is characterized by his pious concern with tyche. . . . In his concern with tyche, Nicias has an old-fashioned Spartan character. . . . The debate of Nicias and Alcibiades, with its echoes of Archidamus by the one and of Pericles by the oth-

---

[13] Nicias' offer to resign his command over the question of resources necessary to the expedition suffered the same reversal: "Finally, one of the Athenians came up and called upon Nicias to stop giving excuses and wasting time, but to say here and now in front of everyone what resources the Athenians should vote for him. And he reluctantly said that . . ." (6.25.1-2).

er, reestablished the antitheses expressed by the Corinthians and the leaders of the rival cities at the time of the outbreak of the war. But now the course of events gives these antitheses a bizarre twist. With the defection of Alcibiades to Sparta and Spartan adherence to his advice, the spirit of the Athens that entered the Peloponnesian War now belongs to the enemy.[14]

We shall have more to say about the reversal of the roles of Athens and Sparta later in this chapter, but for now we may be content with Edmunds' description of Thucydides' characterization of Pericles and Nicias in terms of *gnome* and *tyche* respectively.

PUBLIC VERSUS PRIVATE

If Pericles and Nicias differ on what man can do, they also disagree on what he should do. This second antithesis is no less fundamental to the contrast Thucydides draws between their approaches to leadership than the first. Thucydides' famous judgment in 2.65.7-11 on Pericles' death and its effects makes this point most clearly. The great difference between Pericles and his successors was that Pericles led the people, while his successors were led by them. The reason for this difference was that Pericles, because of the great esteem in which he was held by the Athenians, ruled the state freely and confidently; his successors, more on a level with each other, were forced to court the people's favor in order to reach political prominence. This had two effects: they catered to the pleasures of the demos and thus relinquished to it political and military affairs (*ta pragmata*); they were more concerned with their private honor and advantage than with the public interest.[15]

Now it is clear, especially from 2.65.11, that Thucydides, in describing Pericles' successors, is thinking primarily of the

---

[14] Edmunds, *Chance and Intelligence*, 139-140.

[15] Thus, in Thucydides' phrase (65.7), they were led by the demos rather than leading it themselves.

demagogues. They were the ones who helped to propose the Sicilian expedition and then wrecked its chances for success by their selfish political actions that "blunted" the effectiveness of the expeditionary force. There were two ways in which these politicians in the city led the Athenians to "make decisions which were detrimental to those whom they had sent out" to Sicily. First, acting solely on private motives and for personal advantage, they persuaded the demos first to recall Alcibiades, "Athens' most effective military leader," from Sicily and eventually to exile him.[16] These votes, more than any others, caused the failure of the Sicilian expedition. But the impact that the demagogues had upon Nicias, while it was more subtle and therefore less obvious, proved to be far more devastating in the long run.[17] Nicias lived (and made his decisions) in mortal dread of the demos and its leaders. The influence that Nicias' fear of failure and retreat had upon his generalship in Sicily was in large part responsible for the destruction of the Sicilian expedition.

Thus Thucydides certainly had the demagogues foremost in his mind when he wrote 2.65.7 and 2.65.11. But it is also important to recognize that these purely political leaders were not the only ones who put private interests over public welfare. Alcibiades, after all, was as guilty as anyone else, probably more so, of acting out of selfish concerns in proposing and successfully supporting the Sicilian expedition. Note especially Thucydides' own words in 6.15.2: καὶ μάλιστα στρατηγῆσαί . . . τὰ ἴδια . . . χρήμασί . . . δόξῃ ὠφελήσειν ("and especially to have a command . . . private affairs . . .

---

[16] See especially 6.28.2 and 6.15.4.

[17] W. E. Thompson is, as far as I can see, the only scholar who has noted and assessed the importance of the demos' impact upon Nicias' generalship. In an excellent article entitled "Thucydides 2.65.11" (*Historia* 20 [1971] 141-151), Thompson points out the crippling effects of Athenian demagogic politics upon Nicias' military decision making (see especially pp. 141-144) and upon the army's morale. He thus shows how Thucydides' judgment on the reason for the failure of the Sicilian expedition in 2.65.11 is consistent with his narrative in Books VI and VII. The analysis in the following pages elaborates upon Thompson's basic points.

money . . . to benefit in reputation"). These words recall those in 2.65.7, as he certainly meant them to. Alcibiades is, in Thucydides' historiographical portrait, the paradigm of the self-centered politician.[18]

But it was the complex and ambivalent Nicias who attracted Thucydides' closest attention and elicited his sublest portrayal. A peacemonger and reluctant general who had been "fortunate in command," Nicias was concerned primarily with personal reputation and prestige, but he tried hard to make private and public interests coincide, or at least coexist.[19] In the Archidamian War he succeeded moderately well, and at its end achieved his greatest triumph in merging τὰ ἴδια and τὰ δημόσια by arranging the peace that later bore his name. The Sicilian expedition, however, in spite of all his efforts, wrecked his hopes. It was passed over his strenuous opposition. He was chosen as one of its commanders against his will. Campaigns, including the one against Syracuse, were conducted contrary to his advice. He was left in command despite his plea to be relieved. Finally, he was forced to make the choice he had long avoided, that between his own fate and his city's.[20] The process whereby Nicias, who initially equated private and public interests, was condemned by the demos' irresponsible

[18] See especially 6.92.4, a passage in which Alcibiades defines love of country (τὸ φιλόπολι) from a purely personal perspective.

[19] See 4.28.3, 6.8.4, 24.1 (especially εἰ ἀναγκάζοιτο στρατεύεσθαι), 25.1-2, 34.6. This last passage is particularly instructive: even the Syracusans had learned of Nicias' reluctance to lead the expedition. Compare 5.16.1, 6.17.1, 7.77.2.

[20] See 7.48.4 with Dover, Comm. ad loc. Dover's remarks, it should be noted, disclose his own opinion of Nicias' decision, not Thucydides'. The latter was far more sympathetic toward Nicias' plight for two reasons: he was fully aware (and took pains to make his readers fully aware) of the Athenian demos' irresponsible treatment of its generals, even making a special point of their grossly unfair condemnation of Nicias' predecessors in Sicily: Pythodorus, Sophocles, and Eurymedon (4.65.3-4). More importantly, he had suffered a similar condemnation himself and therefore had a personal perspective on the dilemma that Nicias faced. In addition, and this passage is frequently overlooked, in 7.85.1 Nicias offers his own life in return for the salvation of his soldiers. He is no coward, as even 7.48.4 makes clear: he would rather die on the battlefield than in an Athenian prison.

decisions to weigh his personal reputation against the interests of his country is the central tragedy of Book VII.[21] Historiographically, this theme is a mirror image of Thucydides' picture of Periclean leadership in Book II.

It is necessary to keep in mind that these contrasts drawn by Thucydides between Pericles and Nicias are to a great extent historiographical, or literary, in nature rather than purely historical. By this we mean that the antithesis between the highly rational and resolutely public-minded Pericles and the superstitious, ambivalent, and private-oriented Nicias is, to some degree, a Thucydidean creation. It is not to say that these portraits are purely fictitious, that they lack historical basis or background, or even that they are misleading. They represent Thucydides' distillation of the major character traits of these two Athenian leaders. Many scholars have noted the one-sided nature of Thucydides' picture of Pericles. Thucydides emphasizes what Schachermeyr calls "die harten Züge" of the great statesman, while ignoring altogether his milder side.[22] This choice, it might be argued, was dictated by his decision to concentrate only upon those factors that had direct relevance to the war. But, I believe, H. D. Westlake answers this objection sufficiently in his introduction to Thucydides' treatment of Pericles:

> It is true that the career of Pericles belongs mainly to the period before the war began and that he survived its outbreak by only two and a half years (2.65.6). It is also true that he was notoriously reserved and aloof, as is attested by other contemporary authorities. Nevertheless, Thucydides seems to have deliberately chosen to direct the attention of

[21] This is, as we shall see, the true meaning of Thucydides' phrase in 2.65.11: "The people at home made additional decisions [see Gomme, *Comm. ad loc.*] which were detrimental to the interests of those whom they had sent out." E.-A. Bétant, *Lexicon Thucydideum* (Geneva 1843) *s.v.* ἐπιγιγνώσκειν, is certainly wrong to include this instance of the verb under the sense of *cognoscere*; it is rather *statuere* here.

[22] See F. Schachermeyr, "Das Perikles-Bild bei Thucydides," *Forschungen und Betrachtungen zur Griechischen und Römischen Geschichte* (Vienna 1974) 228-252. See also J. Vogt, "Das Bild des Perikles bei Thuk.," *Hist. Zeit.* 182 (1956) 17 ff.

his readers only to certain characteristics of Pericles: the far-sighted creator of a strategy which could and should have won the war, the persuasive orator who was almost always able to sway the assembly, the resolute leader of an irresolute populace, the idealist who championed the Athenian way of life. This choice has certainly been influenced by the criterion of relevance to the war; throughout his work Thucydides has interpreted very narrowly his duty as a historian of the war, and he normally excludes purely biographical detail and anecdote. There is, however, abundant, if not always wholly reliable, evidence from other sources to show that in his treatment of Pericles he has omitted much that must have been known to him and is by no means entirely irrelevant to the history of the war. His purpose is not so much to provide a general account of the part played by Pericles in the first stages of the war and its antecedents and to show how influential he was; it is rather to select, for the instruction of the reader, the principal issues of this period and to demonstrate the wisdom of Pericles in dealing with each of them.[23]

This is, I think, the correct approach to Thucydides' "Periklesbild." We must remember what Thucydides has chosen not to give us. Pericles never debates anyone in the *History*. All his speeches stand alone. And yet we know that there was substantial opposition to him in Athens, opposition to his political views, his call for the war, his strategy for the war, and his refusal to give up the war even after the plague. We are not allowed to see this opposition, even though it was, by Thucydides' own account, serious and widespread.

The same is true in reverse for Thucydides' portrait of Nicias. From Thucydides' narrative we would never guess that Nicias had any supporters at Athens other than a few old men too afraid to argue or even vote. And yet we know that Nicias was a very popular politician who enjoyed the favor of large numbers of Athenians from all classes.[24] In addition, Thucyd-

[23] *Individuals in Thucydides* (Cambridge 1968) 23-24.
[24] See Plutarch, *Nicias* 2.

ides selects for dramatization several occasions on which Nicias was embarrassed or worsted in the assembly: chapters
4.28, 5.45-46, and 6.25 all recount incidents in which Nicias is
publicly humiliated or at least disconcerted. Thucydides
chooses, uncharacteristically, to report them in anecdotal form
in order to emphasize Nicias' troubles.

Von Fritz has summarized most cogently the reason for the
one-sidedness of Thucydides' portraits of Pericles and Nicias.

> In Thucydides, by contrast, the common practice of present-
> ing only the results of his research and, by so doing, of re-
> serving for himself the selection of what is presented, in
> order to be able to distribute light and dark in such a way
> as to bring into full light what is, in his opinion, truly sig-
> nificant, has caused several of the most scientific modern
> historians, like Beloch and De Sanctis, to attribute to him a
> conscious misleading of his reader. In reality, as I hope to
> have shown, such distortion exists neither in the case of
> Pericles, as Beloch believed, nor in the case of Nicias, as De
> Sanctis sought to prove. Rather, in both cases it is actually
> what is historically significant that is presented.[25]

It is important to recognize that Thucydides' portraits of
Pericles and Nicias are not only one-sided in and of themselves, but that they are meant to oppose each other. The extent to which Pericles' and Nicias' speeches and actions in the
History look to one another becomes clear from a close analysis of Books II and VII.

THE INDIRECT SPEECH AND THE LETTER: 2.13 AND 7.11-15

Pericles' enumeration of Athenian resources in 2.13 is really a
continuation of the central part of his speech at the end of
Book I. As Thucydides says in 13.2, "he gave them the same
advice about their present affairs as before." In 1.141.2-144.1
Pericles had outlined the advantages that Athens had for the
coming war with Sparta. In brief, his points are these. The

[25] K. Von Fritz, *Die Griechische Geschichtsschreibung* (Berlin 1967)
792 (my translation).

Peloponnesians are conservative farmers, readier to use their bodies than their money upon war, which is always better carried on with monetary resources than with forceful attacks; besides, since they do not have a unified common command, but rather vote equally on matters of war, they cannot accomplish quickly what needs to be done; indeed, often nothing is done (141.2-7). Neither ἐπιτείχισις nor their navy is to be feared. It would be very difficult for them to build a rival city to ours in wartime, and a garrison, while it might cause some damage to the land, will not be sufficient to blockade us, since we have access to the sea.[26] In naval matters they are far behind us in *techne* and *empeiria*, and they cannot catch up because we shall prevent them from practicing by blockading them with superior fleets (142). They might try to lure our foreign sailors away with promises of higher pay, but they will not be tempted because our naval superiority is too great for them to be enticed by a few days' higher wages to join what is clearly the inferior side. The Peloponnesians can never really harm us by land because it is the sea that provides us with all we need (143). Thus I have confidence that we shall succeed so long as we do not try to extend our empire during the war and do not take unnescessary risks; I fear our own mistakes more than the enemy's plans (144.1). In 2.13 Pericles repeats these points (section 2) and catalogues Athenian financial (sections 3-5) and military (sections 6-8) resources.

Nicias' letter informs the Athenians of the difficulties which the army faces at Syracuse in the winter of 414/413. A review of these difficulties reveals that the Athenian force in Sicily confronts precisely those problems that Pericles said the Peloponnesians would face in their war against Athens. The situation in 414/413 is exactly the reverse of the one in 431. Nicias' letter is a recitation of the same points made by Pericles, but from the opposite perspective. The advantages which Athens had in the first war have passed to Syracuse in the second.

A review of Nicias' letter in 7.11, point by point, makes this clear. At first we had the upper hand against the Syracusans in several battles and we built the walls within which we now

26 See pp. 142-144.

live. But when Gylippus came with an army from the Peloponnese and defeated us in a second battle, we were pressed by the multitude of his cavalry and javelin-throwers to retire behind our walls. Now we have ceased our effort to encircle Syracuse with walls and are quiet because the superior size of the opposing army prevents us from using all of our men for building—many have to guard our own walls. The enemy has built a cross-wall against ours, so that it is no longer possible to encircle them, unless, with a larger force, we should be able to take their cross-wall. Indeed, it has turned out that we, who seem to be besieging others, are ourselves now besieged, at least on land.

These words make it clear that the Athenians in Sicily confront precisely what Pericles had said the Peloponnesians would encounter if they tried to build a major military base in Attica. In fact, the words actually clarify two problematical statements in Pericles' speech, as a close look at 1.142.2-3 reveals: καὶ μὴν οὐδ᾽ ἡ ἐπιτείχισις οὐδὲ τὸ ναυτικὸν αὐτῶν ἄξιον φοβηθῆναι. τὴν μὲν γὰρ χαλεπὸν καὶ ἐν εἰρήνῃ πόλιν ἀντίπαλον κατασκευάσασθαι, ἦ που δὴ ἐν πολεμίᾳ τε καὶ οὐχ ἧσσον ἐκείνοις ἡμῶν ἀντεπιτετειχισμένων ("And indeed neither fortification nor their fleet is worthy of fear. For it is difficult to construct a rival city in peacetime; certainly it will be very difficult in an enemy's territory and with us no less a counter fortification against them"). Gomme's *Commentary* on this passage explains the nature of the two problems. First he comments, "is it likely that Perikles would discuss so unlikely an event as the Peloponnesians sending out so large a force, and a permanent force, that it could be described as 'founding a city,' in war-time and in Attica or anywhere within the Athenian empire (ἐν πολεμίᾳ)? It would be a quite fantastic scheme. Remember that, by this interpretation, πόλις ἀντίπαλος is expressly opposed to φρούριον; it is not vague."[27] Gomme finds this interpretation so improbable historically that he emends the sentence to read ⟨πρὸς⟩ πόλιν ἀντίπαλον, in order to eliminate the possibility of a rival city's being built against Athens. He thus denies the idea that one of the forms

[27] Gomme, *Comm.* 1:458.

of ἐπιτείχισις, ("fortification"), in addition to a φρούριον ("garrison"), can be an actual πόλις ἀντίπαλος ("rival city"). As he then points out, "There is the further difficulty of οὐχ ἧσσον . . . ἀντεπιτετειχισμένων." What does this phrase mean? Gomme concludes, with Shilleto, that it must refer to the fact that Athens would be a "counter-ἐπιτείχισμα" to the rival city, or garrison, as he prefers. But even here the sense is somewhat obscure and hypothetical, just as is the phrase πόλις ἀντίπαλος.

Both of these hypothetical examples are illustrated in Nicias' description of the Athenian position at Syracuse. The army has built a major encampment next to Syracuse. It is, for all practical purposes, a rival city. It is referred to as such on several occasions. First, Nicias in 6.23.2 warns the Athenians that "you must realize that we are going to found a city among strangers and enemies." Second, Athenagoras in 6.37.2 tells the Syracusan assembly that "if they [the Athenians] come bringing with them another city as large as Syracuse and settle down and conduct war from our frontier, I do not see how they could avoid complete destruction." And third, in 6.63.3 the Syracusans, confident in their cavalry, taunt the Athenians at Catane and ask them "whether they had not really come to settle with the Syracusans in a foreign country rather than to resettle the Leontines in their own." All these passages show that the Athenians had come to Syracuse with precisely the strategy that Pericles says the Spartans might bring to Attica, that of founding a rival city in wartime. If the Athenians could actually carry it out as far away as Sicily, why could the Peloponnesians not be imagined to plan it in Attica? There is no need for Gomme's emendation: it would actually obscure an important parallelism.

But what of the second problem, that of the meaning of ἀντεπιτετειχισμένων? That too becomes clear from Nicias' letter. The city against which the new "rival city" is established has a great advantage over it. Since it has greater numbers and resources at its disposal, it will become a superior ἀντιτείχισμα to the ἐπιτείχισις: This is precisely what happened at Syracuse. As Nicias explains, the Syracusans through superior numbers have forced the Athenians behind their walls, where they must "spend" many of their hoplites on guard duty. This, in turn, prevents them from continuing their own encircling wall. The enemy, meanwhile, can continue building its counter-wall and eventually nearly encircle the besiegers, who have now become the besieged. This process is foreseen by Pericles in his speech to the Athenians, and dramatically represented in the verb ἀντεπιτειχίζομαι. Thucydides' description of the Athenians' retreat from their encampment in 7.75.5 clinches this argument: οὐδὲν γὰρ ἄλλο ἢ πόλει ἐκπεπολιορκημένῃ ἐῴκεσαν ὑποφευγούσῃ, καὶ ταύτῃ οὐ σμικρᾷ ("they resembled nothing so much as a successfully besieged town put to flight, and not a small one at that").[28] Pericles' prediction comes true, but against the Athenians! The πόλις ἀντίπαλος has been successfully besieged by the ἀντιτείχισμα. Chapter 11 of Nicias' letter serves not only as an exemplum of Pericles' hypothetical case in 1.142.2-3, but as an explanation and elucidation of it. This is its historiographical function.

Nicias' next point (7.12.1-2) is that Gylippus is gathering forces from all over Sicily for the defense of Syracuse. But even worse, he has succeeded in acquiring so great a force, both on land and on sea, that the Syracusans are planning a combined attack upon the Athenian walls and fleet. It is Gylippus who, by his personal, political and military intervention, has accomplished all of this. It was he who had brought over many of the Sicels, together with the Himeraeans and Selinuntines, because he "seemed to have come from Lacedaemon with great zeal" (7.1.4). It was he who encouraged the Syracusans to fight a second battle at the walls and led them to victory by his intelligent use of cavalry and darters (7.5-6). It was he who now sent to the rest of Sicily for more land and sea forces and to Lacedaemon and Corinth for another army and in general, carried the fight against the Athenians (7.7). In these operations Gylippus was fulfilling exactly the functions that Alcibiades had foreseen when he advised the Spar-

[28] See also Nicias' warning later in his letter (14.3) that, if the Athenians are cut off from their only remaining supply bases, Naxos and Catane, they will lose the war without a fight, ἐκπολιορκηθέντων ἡμῶν.

tans to send a "Spartan man as commander in order that he might compose those allies present and compel the unwilling ones to come" (6.91.4).

Again this represents a reversal of the conditions that Pericles had described in his speech at Athens. He had painted a picture of divided Peloponnesian leadership, weakened by the fact that the allies were ἰσόψηφοι and οὐχ ὁμόφυλοι (1.141.6). Because of these problems and their lack of a single βουλευτήριον, the Peloponnesians were wont to accomplish nothing (ἐξ ὧν φιλεῖ μηδὲν ἐπιτελὲς γίγνεσθαι). But the independence of Gylippus has solved these problems. Like Brasidas before him, Gylippus is far away from the shackles normally imposed by the Spartan state upon its generals. Also like Brasidas, he is not a king and therefore is not troubled with watchful and jealous ephors. He is in almost total command of the forces gathered at Syracuse.[29]

Furthermore, those forces do not suffer from the conservative apathy that Pericles says will hamper the Peloponnesians, who are prevented from access to the sea and are αὐτουργοί. The Sicilians are a naval people and are economically closer to Athens than to the Peloponnesians. As Nicias says elsewhere, they are παρεσκευασμέναι τοῖς πᾶσιν ὁμοιοτρόπως μάλιστα τῇ ἡμετέρᾳ δυνάμει ("equipped in all respects exactly like our own force"; 6.20.3). Thucydides makes the same point himself in 7.55.2: "These were the only cities that they [the Athenians] had yet encountered, similar to their own in character [ὁμοιοτρόποις], under democracies like themselves, which had ships and horses, and were of considerable magnitude." Thus Nicias faces in Gylippus and the Sicilians an enemy with the opposite characteristics of those that Pericles describes in the Peloponnesians in 141.2-7.

In 12.3-5 Nicias explains the third major difficulty he faces at Syracuse, the most shocking, as he knows, to the Athenians at

[29] It is true that the Syracusans have their own generals, but they seem, at least in Thucydides' account, always to defer to Gylippus on matters of strategy and even of tactics. And note Thucydides' (Hermocrates') words in 6.72.4: The Syracusans in their early battles against the Athenians suffered from too many commanders.

home. The Athenian fleet is no longer superior to the Syracusan. There are several reasons for the loss of this, the most critical of Athens' initial advantages: the Athenians' ships are rotting; their crews are deserting; the enemy can practice maneuvers, attack when they want and lay their ships in drydock, while the Athenians can do none of these things. These are the very problems that Pericles predicts (142.6-143.2) the Peloponnesians will encounter in a war against Athens. Note how closely Pericles' speech and Nicias' letter correspond on these points.

In 1.142.6-9 Pericles says that knowledge of the sea does not come easily and asks how farmers can acquire it, especially if they are blockaded by Athenian ships in greater numbers, and thus prevented from practicing. If they were blockaded by only a few ships, he notes, they might take heart in numbers and risk an engagement, but shut off by many ships they will be quiet, and from lack of practice they will become less skillful and thus more timid. Seamanship is a matter of art, and will not admit of being taken up only when the opportunity arises.

In 7.12-13.1 Nicias comments that it is not possible for the Athenians to draw up and dry their ships and career them, because the enemy is always a threat to attack in equal or even greater numbers. They can be seen practicing, and the ability to attack and to dry out their ships lies more with them than with the Athenians. For they are not blockading others. The Athenians could scarcely do these things even if they had an abundance of ships and were not forced, as they now are, to use them for guarding the enemy. For if they relaxed their watch even a little, they would have no provisions; they are already difficult enough to bring in past their city.

Note what has occurred. Since the enemy can dry its ships and the Athenians cannot, the Athenians' superiority in number of seaworthy ships has been lost to the Syracusans. The Athenians are indeed blockading the enemy, as Pericles predicted, but they do not have enough ships to guard their own supply lines and to prevent the opposing fleet from practicing

maneuvers. The result is that the blockading fleet cannot practice, while the blockaded one can! This is precisely the reverse
of the situation envisioned by Pericles. The reason is that the
superiority in numbers, which he believed would always rest
with the Athenians, has passed to the enemy. Since, as Pericles
says, seamanship is a matter of *techne*, which depends upon
constant practice, we know, with Nicias, that it will not be
long before the Sicilian fleet is a match for the Athenian one
even in the art of seamanship.[30]

In 1.143.1-2 Pericles says that if they should take money
from Olympia or Delphi and try to seduce our foreign sailors
with higher pay, it would be dreadful if we did not have our
own citizens and metics to put on board our ships. But in fact
we have this potential open to us, and what is more, we have
steersmen among our citizens and more and better rowers than
the rest of Greece combined. And to say nothing of the danger
of such a step, none of our foreign sailors would consent to
become an exile from his country and to join the enemy with
his inferior position for the sake of a few days' higher pay.

In 7.13.2-14.2 Nicias reports that the losses which our crews
have suffered and still continue to suffer stem from the following causes: our long expeditions for fuel cause some to be cut
off; our slaves, now that we have lost our superiority, desert;
the allied crewmen go over to the enemy or lose themselves in
the vast expanse of Sicily. As a result we are losing our peak
efficiency and cannot replace it since we have no source from
which to recruit our crews, which the enemy can do from

---

[30] This process can be clearly traced. See 7.21.3, 34, 36, and especially
37.1: Τοιαῦτα οἱ Συρακόσιοι πρὸς τὴν ἑαυτῶν ἐπιστήμην τε καὶ δύναμιν
ἐπινοήσαντες ("In such ways the Syracusans improved their own skill
and strength"). Compare what the Corinthians say about the Athenians in 1.71.3: "It is the law as in art, so in politics, that improvements
ever prevail; and though fixed usages may be best for undisturbed com-
munities, constant necessities of action must be accompanied by the
constant improvement of methods. Thus it happens that the vast experience of Athens has carried her further than you on the path of in-
novation" (Crawley translation). In Book VII it is the Sicilians who
"improve," the Athenians who "stand still."

many quarters. We are compelled to depend upon the men we brought with us both for supplying the crews in service and for making good our losses.

Note again how the problems that Nicias catalogues correspond, point by point, to the assertions of Pericles. Pericles had listed three deterrents to foreign sailors' deserting to the enemy: it was dangerous; it involved exile from one's city; it meant going over to a vastly inferior navy, an unacceptable risk for a few days' higher pay. It is clear from Nicias' account that the effectiveness of these deterrents had been severely reduced in Sicily. The fact that desertion was generally considered dangerous helps to clarify difficult points in Nicias' letter, in particular the distinctions that he makes between the methods of escape used by the ξένοι ἀναγκαστοί and the other *xenoi* in 13.2.[31] The two problems for the deserter were escaping from the army and finding a safe haven once he had deserted. Since the Athenian force had now lost its superiority to its adversaries (ἐς ἀντίπαλα καθεστήκαμεν; 13.2), even the slaves could now desert, apparently without difficulty. But, more importantly, Sicily offered many safe refuges for deserters. Gylippus had recently made numerous cities in Sicily allies of the Syracusans, therefore enemies of the Athenians. These cities thus furnished refuges for Athenian deserters, whether they were slaves, *xenoi anagkastoi*, or volunteer foreigners come to Sicily for profit.[32] Thus the first deterrent to desertion, fear, had lost its impact. As for the second deterrent, exile, that too had little force in Sicily, since the island was so far from the homes of these sailors that they were, for all practical purposes, already exiles with little chance of returning safely home without a victory, which now appeared more and more remote. This in turn brings us to the third deterrent. Since the Athenian fleet was no longer superior to the Syracusan (a fact which Nicias has just mentioned in 12), foreign sailors did not consider service in the enemy fleet to be μετὰ τῆς ἥσσονος . . . ἐλπίδος ("with less hope"). Indeed, those who had come

---

[31] See Dover, *Comm.* 4: 388-389 for a discussion of these problems.

[32] See my article in *CP* 73 (1978) 134-136, " 'Giving Desertion as a pretext': Thuc. 7.13.2."

to Sicily excited by the prospect of high pay now considered the risk of fighting with the Athenians to be too great. The lure of great pay had ceased to exist, at least on the Athenian side. As Grote remarks, "the Athenian service had now become irksome, unprofitable, and dangerous—while the easiest manner of getting away from it was, to pass over as a deserter to Syracuse."[33] This is the reverse of the situation envisioned by Pericles in 1.143.2, where he argued that the lure of a few days' high pay (μεγαλὸς μισθός) would not overcome the foreign sailor's confidence in Athenian naval superiority.

The same is true of the replacement of lost sailors. Pericles had said that if the Athenians could not replace foreign sailors with citizens and metics, "it would be dreadful" (143.1). But Nicias complains (7.13.2) that Athenian sailors are being captured by enemy cavalry because they must go further and further for foraging, and (14.2) that he has no means of filling the gaps left by the loss of sailors in all categories, while the enemy can replace their losses from all sides.[34] Hence, what Pericles had predicted would be an Athenian capability (νῦν δὲ τόδε . . . ὑπάρχει; 1.143.1) now belongs to the enemy (ὁ τοῖς πολεμίοις πολλαχόθεν ὑπάρχει; 7.14.2).

There are other reversals as well. Pericles had pointed to two other great assets enjoyed by the Athenians in the event of war: money and allies. War is a matter of money (1.141.5, 2.13.2) and since the Peloponnesians can provide it only slowly they will be hampered by great delays—but opportunities in war do not wait (142.1). The Athenians, on the other hand, have enormous financial reserves and revenues (2.13.2). Much of this money comes from the allies, Athens' great source of strength (1.143.5), who must therefore be held tightly in check (2.13.2). The rest consists of the sacred buildings, offerings, statues, and spoils on the Acropolis and elsewhere in the city. For Nicias, money and allies are both major problems. The only allied cities he can count on for resources, Naxos and Catane, are incapable (ἀδύνατοι) of making up his losses in

[33] George Grote, *History of Greece*, 12 vols. (London 1869) 7: 117, n. 1.

[34] See Dover, *Comm. ad loc.* on the meaning of τῶν ναυτῶν in 13.2.

crews (14.2), and he needs a great deal of money (15.1).[35] This is because the "allies" of Athens in Sicily had treacherously promised money that had never existed (6.6.2-3), had provided almost nothing (6.46.1-5), and the other cities on whom Athens was counting as allies had not joined her side: "All of Sicily has joined together" against the Athenians (15.1).[36] Athens' opponent is reaping the advantages of allied aid in the form of soldiers and naval *paraskeue* (7.12.1). And the "opportunities of war" which do not wait, now favor the enemy because the Syracusans can bring in supplies δι᾽ ὀλίγου, while the Athenians must depend upon far-away Attica as a base (15.2).

Pericles had also said that war was won by *gnome* (2.13.2) "firm resolve," in addition to money, and he therefore "encouraged the Athenians to take heart" (θαρσεῖν . . . ἐκέλευε) in their great financial resources (13.3).[37] Nicias' letter reveals a general and his troops who have lost their will to fight. Nicias himself is sick (15.1-2) and dispirited (11.4, 14.2 and 4, 15.2, especially ὥσπερ καὶ πρότερον), the army's morale is so low that everyone who can desert does so at the first opportunity.[38] If, as Pericles says, war is a matter of resolve and money, the Athenians in Sicily are in serious trouble.

[35] Even Naxos and Catane are a threat to go over to the enemy if the Athenian position continues to deteriorate and no aid is sent from Athens (14.3).

[36] Nicias had predicted the financial difficulties: see 6.22. He had also foreseen that only Naxos and Catane could be counted on as allies (6.20.3). Even Rhegium and Camarina, which had seemed certain to be useful allies, had afforded little or nothing in the way of support (6.44.3-4, 46.2, 6.88.1-2).

[37] *Gnome* can, of course, denote "intelligence" as well as "will." The word is ambivalent, as many scholars have shown. See Edmunds, *Chance and Intelligence*, 12, n. 11 for a list of studies. Edmunds (p. 37) translates *gnome* in 2.13.2 as "intelligence" but it is, I think, more likely that Pericles was using the word in its sense of "resolve," just as he does twice in 1.140.1, at the beginning of the speech which, Thucydides says, Pericles is, for the most part, repeating in 2.13 (see 13.2). And note how he picks up the relationship between "resolve" and money in the next sentence: θαρσεῖν τε ἐκέλευε . . . ταλάντων etc., and again in 13.6: χρήμασι μὲν οὖν οὕτως ἐθάρσυνεν αὐτούς.

[38] Contrast Nicias' ὅτ᾽ ἐρρώμην ("when I was strong") with Thucydides' characterization of the Corinthians' and Lacedaemonians' current

In short, Nicias finds himself facing precisely the same problems that Pericles had predicted the Peloponnesians would confront against Athens. What has gone wrong? The answer to this question is also found in Pericles' speech. There he had made two other strategic points of great importance in 1.143.3-144.1. To paraphrase: we are free of those defects from which the enemy will suffer and we have other advantages as well. We have every expectation of success if you are willing not to try to enlarge your empire while you are at war and if you avoid self-imposed dangers. In sending the expedition to Sicily, the Athenians had, of course, neglected both of Pericles' warnings. Nicias had in 415 opposed the expedition on exactly those grounds: "For I say you are inviting enemies" (6.10.1); "so that it is proper to consider some of these very points and not to think it right to risk a city in danger and to grasp after another empire before we have secured the one we have" (6.10.5).[39] The Athenians had sent a force to Sicily in spite of this warning. The result was predictable: they had suffered from just those defects from which Pericles had said they, as opposed to the Peloponnesians, were free. And when they followed the opposite strategy, they brought upon themselves the opposite results. This last point is precisely what Nicias'

---

confidence in the next two paragraphs (πολλῷ μᾶλλον ἐπέρρωντο in 17.3, μάλιστα . . . τις ῥώμη in 18.2). See Thompson's remarks ("Thucydides II, 65, 11," *Historia* 20 [1971] 144-149) on the Athenians' low morale in Sicily, the first traces of which appear in Nicias' letter (p. 148), and on the reasons for it.

[39] That Thucydides agreed with Nicias' point is clear from many indications, especially 5.26.2, and 2.65.11, an often misinterpreted passage. Thucydides does not say that it was not a mistake to send the expedition, but that that mistake was not so great as the later mishandling of it. He still believed it to be a monstrous error of judgment in the first place: See 6.1.1, especially ὅτι οὐ πολλῷ τινὶ ὑποδεέστερον πόλεμον. It is, of course, the height of irony that it is Nicias himself who will suffer from the very problems he had foreseen and warned against. That is a major element of his tragedy. See Strasburger's fine phrase (*Thukydides. Wege der Forschung*, ed. H. Herter [Darmstadt 1968] 515, n. 47): "die hermeneutische Bedeutung der Gestalt des Nikias." Compare the figure of Archidamus in the first war, Nicias' parallel. He too opposed a war he did not think his country could win, and then had to lead it into that war.

letter is meant to convey to the Athenians about the army's position at Syracuse. Note what Thucydides says in his own words, about the Athenians' failure to follow Pericles' advice (2.65.7): "He said they would succeed if they were conservative and paid careful attention to their fleet and neither tried to add to their empire in wartime nor endangered the city. But they did precisely the opposite of all these things."[40] Nicias' letter corresponds to Pericles' speeches at every point.

But if we look at this parallelism from the other side, we are immediately struck by the following realization: all of Pericles' hypothetical points apply far more aptly to the second war (though in reverse) than to the first. *Epiteichisis*, in both its forms, *polis antipalos* and *phrourion*, is practiced in the second war, not in the first. The inability of a fleet to practice because of blockade is never mentioned in Books I-V, only in Book VII. Desertion of foreign sailors occurs in Sicily, not before. Athens' great monetary resources come into play only in the second war when the situation becomes desperate. In fact, we found that several of Pericles' predictions were so

[40] Gomme, *Comm.* on 2.65.7, is certainly correct when he says (pp. 191-192): "If, on the other hand, the historian is in the main thinking of the great Sicilian expedition (as I feel sure he was), then his expression is misleading; for this would mean that (in the main) Perikles' policy was followed during the whole of the Archidamian war, and his death in 429, ... was not therefore as significant as Thucydides says." Thucydides' expression is indeed misleading, but we can, I think, understand the source of the ambiguity. Thucydides no doubt believed that several Athenian campaigns planned and conducted after Pericles' death in the Archidamian War were, to some degree, contrary to Periclean strategic advice (see Gomme, *Comm.* 2: 191, especially on Aetolia and Delion, and compare the bitterness of 3.98.4 and 4.97.2-99 respectively). But this, the first war, was still conducted on basically Periclean principles. The first full-scale expedition, conceived and carried out on principles directly contrary to Periclean strategy was the Sicilian venture, which introduced (and dictated the course of) the second war. See especially 6.1.1, 6.1, 12.2, 24.3-4. We are not forced, as Gomme (pp. 195-196) argues, to conclude that Thucydides' judgment in 2.65.11 was written at a different time from the narrative in Books VI and VII. It is, on the contrary, in essential agreement with that narrative. See W. Thompson, *Historia* 20 (1971) 141-151, for an excellent argument of this case, and compare p. 136 here.

hypothetical that they could not be fully understood until we adduced actual examples of them from Nicias' letter, examples which actually explicated points in Pericles' speech. Pericles' speech, in other words, is written from the point of view of the facts described in Nicias' letter. And what is more, Thucydides almost tells us so. After he has alluded to the possible errors of trying to increase the empire while at war and taking on self-imposed dangers, Pericles adds: "For I fear our own mistakes more than the enemy's plans; but these things will be clarified in another speech when the events require them" (1.144.1-2). Note that Thucydides does not have Pericles say "I shall clarify these things in another speech when the events require them" but "these things will be clarified in another speech when the events require them." These words do not look forward, as has often been stated, to 2.13, where Pericles mentions nothing of Athens' own mistakes, nor to either of Pericles' other speeches, but to Nicias' letter.[41] It is only after

---

[41] See Gomme, *Comm.* on 1.144.2, where he refers to Steup, "who points out that καὶ ἐν ἄλλῳ λόγῳ implies that these points have been mentioned here, but not at length, whereas the financial and military details of ii.13 have not been mentioned at all." This is certainly correct: 2.13 has nothing to do with ἐκεῖνα, which must refer, as Steup saw (*Thukydideische Studien* [Freiburg 1886] see especially supplement to vol. I, 457-458), to the ἁμαρτίαι, not to the πολλὰ καὶ ἄλλα ἐς ἐλπίδα. Both the καί before ἐν ἄλλῳ λόγῳ and the ἅμα τοῖς ἔργοις prove this point (ἅμα τοῖς ἔργοις looks to ἅμα πολεμοῦντες). It is perhaps easier to try to make a case that the promise is fulfilled in Pericles' last speech (2.60-64, especially 61-62), but it would be no less incorrect. There (61) Pericles says that the Athenians are wrong to find fault with his strategy. But, as to "the exertions of war, if you fear they are great and that we might not survive, you know the reasons by which I have often demonstrated to you the groundlessness of your apprehension" (62.1-2). It might be argued that we are now ἅμα τοῖς ἔργοις, that δηλώσω . . . καὶ τόδε is a fulfillment of Pericles' promise and that οὔτ' ἐγὼ ἐν τοῖς πρὶν λόγοις looks back specifically to 1.144.1. But this argument would fail for the same reason the previous one did: it would take ἐκεῖνα in 1.144.2 to refer only to πολλὰ καὶ ἄλλα ἐς ἐλπίδα and not to the two ἁμαρτίαι. For, far from warning the Athenians against the errors of extending their empire and taking on self-imposed dangers, Pericles in 62.2 goes on to inform them that they can extend their sway indefinitely by sea if they wish. This is no warning against overexpansion, but an exhortation to further con-

the Sicilian expedition has been undertaken that the *erga* resulting from Athens' errors require a *logos* and that is just what Thucydides meant Nicias' words to give us. Thucydides has made the connection of Pericles' αἱ οἰκεῖαι ἡμῶν ἁμαρτίαι to Sicily quite explicit in 2.65.11. It seems probable that when Thucydides wrote 1.144.1 he was thinking of Sicily and thus that when he wrote ἀλλ' ἐκεῖνα δηλωθήσεται he was adumbrating the letter of Nicias.[42]

PERICLES' AND NICIAS' LAST SPEECHES

Pericles' Funeral Oration and policy speech stand out among the *logoi* in Thucydides' history. The funeral speech in particular is unique, both for the occasion on which it was delivered and for its great length and didactic quality. It is quite clear that Thucydides meant it to stand out. Yet, in spite of these facts, Thucydides did not intend that either of these speeches should be read by itself, out of the context in which it stands. Several recent treatments have helped us understand the function of these speeches within Thucydides' history.[43] Our task is similar but simpler: to show how Nicias' last remarks in Book VII respond, in part, to these two great speeches of Pericles in Book II.

---

quest. Thucydides draws the distinction between these two Periclean techniques of leadership quite explicitly and carefully in 2.65.9: "whenever he saw them unseasonably and insolently elated, he would with a word reduce them to alarm; on the other hand, if they fell victims to a panic, he could at once restore them to confidence" (Crawley translation). The warning in 1.144.1-2 is an example of the former, the exhortation in 2.62.1-2 an instance of the latter.

[42] The scholiast has noted almost precisely these points. He explains ἀρχήν τε μὴ ἐπικτᾶσθαι ("not to add to the empire") with αἰνίττεται Σικελίαν καὶ Ἰταλίαν, ἧς ἐπεθύμουν κρατῆσαι ("he means Sicily and Italy, which they desired to conquer") and ἐκεῖνα ("those things") with τὰ περὶ Σικελίας ("the places in Sicily").

[43] H. Flashar, *Der Epitaphios des Perikles* (Heidelberg 1969) Sitzungsberichte der Heidelberger Akademie, Phil.-hist. Klasse, 1. Abhandlung; G. Kakridis, *Der Thukydideische Epitaphios. Ein stilistischer Kommentar*, Zetemata 26 (Munich 1961); W. Plenio, "Die letzte Rede des Perikles," Unpublished dissertation (Kiel 1954).

Nicias' penultimate speech is his *parakeleusis* to his army on the eve of the final battle in the Great Harbor at Syracuse. This exhortation is paired with the speech delivered by Gylippus and the Syracusan general to their soldiers. These two speeches are, as we shall see, designed to stand against the very similar pair of speeches delivered by Phormio and the Spartan admirals in 2.87-89. There is no analogue to the Funeral Oration. But Thucydides does make Nicias echo Pericles' public lament for the dead with a private and indirect appeal to the living. The contrast is ironic and striking.

After the pair of speeches in Book VII (61-68) and a summary (69.1) Thucydides appends a paragraph composed of a single extraordinarily long sentence detailing Nicias' further thoughts and actions before the climactic battle in the Great Harbor.[44] This sentence, written in an uncharacteristically paratactic style,[45] suits Nicias' distraught mood superbly well (the translation tries to catch something of the pathos of the Greek):

> Nicias, overcome by the present situation and seeing what kind of danger it was and how near it already was, and that they were just on the point of going on board, and thinking, as men are wont to do in great crises, that in action everything is still undone and that in words not enough has yet been said, again called each one of the ships' captains, and addressing him by his father's name and his own name and his tribe's name, asking him not to betray his own talents, if he had some particular high quality, and not to diminish his family's reputation for bravery, if his ancestors were renowned, and recalling for them their country's unparalleled liberty and the unfettered freedom open to all within it to live the life they wanted, and said other things which men at such a critical moment say if they make no attempt to avoid the appearance of old-fashioned platitudes, and which

[44] The sentence (69.2) is sixteen lines long, or half a page in the *OCT*, certainly one of the longest sentences, possibly the longest, in the entire text.
[45] There are no fewer than 18 "ands" in the sentence, of either the καί or τε . . . καί variety.

serve in much the same form for all occasions, concerning their wives, their children and their ancestral gods, but, considering them beneficial in the present crisis, appeal to them nevertheless.

Several phrases remind the reader of Pericles' funeral speech. The "great contests" reminds us of Pericles' claim that there is more at stake in the Athenians' contests than in others' (2.42.1); the appeals "not to fall short of one's talents" and "not to ἀφανίζειν τὰς πατρικὰς ἀρετάς" remind one of several of Pericles' remarks, especially 36.1, 41.1-3, 42.2-3; Nicias' call to the πατρίδος τε τῆς ἐλευθερωτάτης . . . καὶ τῆς ἐν αὐτῇ ἀνεπιτάκτου πᾶσιν ἐς τὴν δίαιταν ἐξουσίας brings to mind several Periclean phrases, especially τὴν χώραν . . . ἐλευθέραν in 36.1, ἐλευθέρως δὲ τά τε πρὸς τὸ κοινὸν πολιτεύομεν in 37.2, and ἀνειμένως διαιτώμενοι in 39.1; ἐν τῷ τοιούτῳ ἤδη τοῦ καιροῦ recalls δι' ἐλαχίστου καιροῦ in 42.4; finally, appeals to wives, children, and ancestral gods are the stuff of funeral orations, and the final word in the immense sentence, ἐπιβοῶνται, is used of appeals to the graves of ancestors (see 3.67.2) and, in the active, of laments at funerals.[46]

While Nicias' speech is thus full of allusions to the Funeral Oration, a closer look reveals a series of ironic reversals and contrasts. Pericles had addressed the Athenians publicly and formally from the raised speaker's platform in a state ceremony, conducted in "the most beautiful suburb of the city." Nicias speaks with each captain privately and individually on the eve of a desperate last attempt to break out of a miserable position in enemy territory. Pericles appeals primarily to the Athenians as citizens, Nicias to his soldiers as members of families. Pericles avoids the commonplace, whether it be the praise of the citizens' fathers (36.4), their children (45.1), or their wives (45.2); he ignores the gods altogether. Nicias, on the other hand, speaks in an old-fashioned manner about precisely these subjects. We know that these were traditional, mandatory *topoi* of Athenian funeral orations. By alluding

[46] See H. G. Liddell and R. Scott, *Greek-English Lexicon*, revised by H. S. Jones (Oxford 1940), *s.v.* ἐπιβοάω.

to them at all, even if only to say that he will treat them briefly, Pericles admits as much (see especially εἰ . . . με δεῖ καὶ
γυναικείας τι ἀρετῆς . . . μνησθῆναι [if . . . I must make some
mention of female virtue]).[47] In this sense, Nicias' speech is
more properly a funeral oration in the traditional sense than
is Pericles', which contains an unusually long and detailed
section on Athenian *tropoi* and *politeia*. Chapters 37-41 are
very probably atypical, possibly unique, in the long series of
public eulogies delivered under the Athenian democracy.

When we see Nicias' speech as a type of funeral oration,
we become aware of another irony. It is the only burial that
these men will receive. Some of them will die in the battle in
the harbor: their corpses will not even be requested by the
panic-stricken Athenians after the battle (72.2). Others will be
left at the camp when the army begins its retreat, their corpses
unburied (75.3). Still others will die at the Assinarus, where
"many corpses lie upon each other in the river" (85.1). The
rest will die in the quarries at Syracuse and their corpses will
be "piled together on top of one another" (87.2). Thucydides
makes a special point of informing the reader that the corpses
of each category of soldiers were left unburied. We are reminded of what Thucydides tells us the Athenians did with
their corpses during the plague (2.50.1 and 52.4), the disaster
striking Athens immediately following Pericles' Funeral Oration. Is it coincidence that Thucydides takes such pains to tell
the reader that during the catastrophe in Sicily, following Nicias' "funeral oration," the same events occurred?[48]

After the two great catastrophes, the plague in Book II and
the defeat in the great harbor in Book VII, Thucydides gives
us the final speeches of Pericles and Nicias respectively. Each

---

[47] See H. Strasburger, "Thukydides und die politische Selbstdarstellung der Athener," *Wege*, 498-530 for these *topoi*.

[48] Note Dionysius' criticism (*On Thucydides* 352, trans. W. Kendrick
Pritchett [Berkeley, Los Angeles, London, 1975]) of Thucydides' decision not to give us a funeral oration for the Athenians who died in
Sicily, while providing a lofty, formal speech for the "ten or fifteen
horsemen" who died in the first year of the war. Jacoby (*JHS* 64
[1944] 57, n. 92) approved of this strange judgment, which fails to
appreciate Thucydides' historiographical point.

deals with the crisis in his own way, Pericles with an appeal to *gnome* and Athenian power, Nicias with a call for *elpis* and favor from the gods. Thucydides emphasizes the difference in their approaches by giving to Nicias several phrases that recall stylistically Periclean figures of speech, but which prove to be quite their opposite in terms of content. Again, Thucydides uses structural parallelism to create or emphasize real antitheses. As Wille notes, "Formal analogies can conceal actual differences."[49]

While Thucydides' introductions to the two speeches are similar, they stress the differences in the two leaders' methods: In 2.59.3 he tells us that when Pericles saw that the citizens were exasperated at their present situation and that they were reacting in the way in which he expected, he called an assembly (he was still general), to restore their confidence, to lead their angry minds to a calmer state and to make them less afraid. In 7.76 Thucydides says that when Nicias saw the army's loss of spirit occasioned by its great vicissitudes, he passed through the ranks and tried to restore their confidence as best he could in the present situation and he encouraged them, raising his voice in earnestness more and more as he went among them, and, wishing to be of some help, he shouted to as many as possible. Again we see the contrast between the calm, logical, controlling leader who addresses the people formally and publicly and the compassionate and concerned general who speaks, indeed shouts to his soldiers as he passes among their ranks. One attempts to manipulate his audience by superior intelligence and psychology, the other to console his fellow soldiers with sympathetic and personal encouragement.

The speeches begin with similar language, but with antithetical approaches. Pericles says, "I expected your anger against me [I am aware of your accusations] and I called this assembly for this purpose, in order that I might remind you of certain things and blame [μέμφωμαι] you for being unjustly angry with me and giving into your misfortunes" (ξυμφο-ραῖς; 2.60.1). Nicias says, "Even in the present situation, Athe-

[49] Wille, *Wege*, 691.

nians and allies, it is necessary to have hope (some have been saved from positions even more critical than this one) and not to blame [καταμέμφεσθαι] yourselves too much, either for your misfortunes [ξυμφοραῖς] or for your present unmerited sufferings" (7.77.1). Pericles berates his audience for its anger and lack of resolve, Nicias sympathizes with his men's self-deprecation and loss of morale. Pericles is in control (I know what you are saying); Nicias offers genuine, but weak consolations (some have escaped from even worse situations than ours).

This antithesis is developed in the following personal appeal that each speaker makes. Pericles complains that "in me you are angry with a man who, I believe, is second to none in knowing what must be done and in convincing others of it, and who loves his city and cannot be bribed" (2.60.5). Nicias' appeal is pathetic: "And yet I appear to be second to none of you, either in bodily vigor (but look—see how I am afflicted by this disease), or in good fortune both in my private life and in other respects too, but now I am trapped in the same crisis as the poorest among you" (7.77.2). Nicias' "second to none of you" recalls Pericles' phrase, but when we compare the two, what a contrast emerges! Pericles describes himself in political and intellectual terms, Nicias from the personal and moral perspective. One emphasizes his positive qualifications as leader, the other the startling reversals in his fortune. Pericles goes on to portray himself as the man best suited to run the affairs of the city. Nicias speaks of his private life: "And yet with respect to the gods I have devoted myself to the observance of many religious practices, and with respect to men, I have behaved justly and inoffensively." Here is the final and central Thucydidean contrast between Pericles and Nicias in their own words, their own assessments of their lives and works (compare 2.60.5-7 and 7.77.2).

Pericles stands for the city, Nicias for the individual. Having dealt with the past, the two speakers go on to the future. Pericles bases his program, his policy, on resolve (*gnome*), which a great city such as Athens deserves from its citizens (2.61). Nicias offers to his fellow-soldiers hope (*elpis*), hope in the future good will of the gods, who have favored the enemy enough, and should now favor the Athenians.

Thucydides makes Nicias recall Periclean phrases in the remainder of his speech too. To Pericles' great proclamation of Athenian dominance of the sea Nicias responds with a pathetic claim that his dejected and panicked army is still a major force. At 62.2 Pericles says "You think that you rule only the allies but I say to you that of the two usable parts of the world, land and sea, you are complete masters of one in its entirety, not only to the extent that you now control it, but to whatever extent you want to control it. There is no one, king or any other people of those currently alive, who can prevent you from sailing against him with your fleet in its present power." To this arrogant boast Nicias "replies": "Look at yourselves, how you are setting off with a strong and large hoplite force mustered together; do not be too dispirited but consider that you yourselves are immediately a city wherever you encamp, and not one of the cities in Sicily could easily repulse you if you attacked it, or force you to retire if you besieged it" (77.4). The irony in this comparison certainly seems intentional. Thucydides heightens this irony when he makes Nicias conclude: "Know the whole truth, my fellow soldiers; it is necessary for you to be brave men, because if you are cowards, there is no refuge nearby where you can be saved. . . . If you succeed in escaping you will raise again the great power of the city from its fallen state. For men are the city, not walls and ships empty of men" (7.77.7). These words recall Pericles' exhortation in 64.3: "Know that this city has the greatest name among all men because it has not given in to misfortunes, but has spent the most bodies and toils in war, and has acquired the greatest power until now, of which a memory will be left eternally among later generations, even if we should at some time go under (for all things are wont to decay, by their very nature)." Again Thucydides has made Pericles and Nicias speak to one another across a great expanse of time and space. Pericles looks forward to Nicias, Nicias back to Pericles. It appears probable that each of these two speeches was composed with the other in mind. The frequent and close verbal similarities between them were created consciously and carefully in order to make the reader compare them. Pericles and Nicias faced devastating disasters at similar points in the first and second wars respectively. One reacted with the strength of his *gnome*, the other with the hope of his *eutychia*.

Anyone who seeks the source of Thucydides' knowledge of Nicias' last speech need not look beyond the text. Nicias gave no speech. He went among the soldiers offering personal encouragement. Thucydides distills "what, as it seemed to him, he would have said" (1.22.1), from his own analysis of Nicias' personality and above all, from his own conception of the relationship between Nicias and Pericles. The basic difference in their approaches to crisis is no doubt historical; the almost perfect antithesis between their speeches is certainly historiographical, that is, Thucydidean. This antithesis lies at the heart of Thucydides' conception of the dominant issue of the two wars: the Athenian character versus the Spartan.

The combatants in the two wars and their tropoi

The change in Athenian leadership from Periclean *gnome* at the beginning of the first war to Nician *tyche* at the beginning of the second leads to a startling reversal in the roles played by the combatants in these two wars. Edmunds has sketched the terms of this change and we can begin by quoting his words:

> With the defection of Alcibiades to Sparta and Spartan adherence to his advice, the spirit of the Athens that entered the Peloponnesian War now belongs to the enemy. There is also the fact that Syracuse is, despite its being a Dorian city, a latter-day Athens in crucial respects. The death of Lamachus leaves the Spartan Nicias in sole command of the force in Sicily, and by the time the more characteristically Athenian Demosthenes arrives, the Athenians have lost their advantage.[50]

[50] Edmunds, *Chance and Intelligence*, 140.

Perhaps the best means of illustrating and confirming this thesis of the thematic structure of *History* is to trace Thucydides' careful and detailed analysis of the gradual reversal of roles through Book VII and to contrast this historiographical picture with its analogue in Book II. We shall conclude this comparison by discussing the culminating expression of these developments, the paired speeches of the Lacedaemonian admirals and Phormio in Book II and of the Syracusan admirals and Nicias in Book VII. We begin with a brief review of the positions of Athens and Syracuse in Book VI in order to explain the nature of the change that takes place in Book VII.

Throughout Book VI Thucydides describes Syracuse in terms which make it clear that it was already a potential Athens. Just as he describes Athens in the archaeology as a city so teeming with population that it sent out colonies to Ionia (1.2.5-6), so he portrays Syracuse in the Sicilian archaeology: it is *polyanthropos* (6.3.2) and therefore a major colonizer in Sicily (6.5.2-3). One of the reasons for Syracuse's growth is its security: like Athens, it has walled in outlying territory (6.3.2). As Thucydides makes clear in the first archaeology, large and settled population and walls are two crucial elements in creating *dynamis*.[51] The Egestaean ambassadors warn the Athenians that Syracuse might succeed in "getting hold of all the *dynamis* of Sicily" (6.6.2) and thus join their Dorian kinsmen in the Peloponnese against Athens. Nicias allows that the Syracusans could indeed establish an *arche* in Sicily, but doubts that they would join Sparta in a war against Athens, "*arche* against *arche*" (6.11.2-3). Thus Syracuse has the potential to assimilate *dynamis* and create an *arche* in Sicily like the Athenian one in the Aegean.

Alcibiades and Nicias disagree on the potential strength of the Sicilian cities. The former argues that they are composed of a motley rabble ripe for revolution and unable to function with any efficiency politically or militarily (6.17.2). Nicias, on the other hand, warns that the seven Sicilian cities likely to oppose Athens are "equipped in all respects precisely like our

[51] Compare 1.2.6 and 8.3 and J. de Romilly, *Histoire et raison chez Thucydide* (Paris 1956) 261-262.

own power . . . [παρεσκευασμέναι τοῖς πᾶσιν ὁμοιοτρόπως μάλιστα τῇ ἡμετέρᾳ δυνάμει], especially those against which we sail, Selinus and Syracuse: for they have many hoplites and archers and javelin throwers, and many triremes and a large mob to fill them. And they have a great deal of money, some private, some in the temples at Selinus, and the Syracusans bring in an *aparche* from some of the barbarians" (20.3-4). Curiously, both Nicias and Alcibiades are right. Syracuse in particular, and the Sicilian cities in general, have the raw material to match that of Athens: large populations, armies and fleets, and a great deal of money. But Alcibiades' assessment is also correct: the Sicilian cities are rent by internal division and lack the political and military stability and control necessary for effective action: "It is not likely that such a mob will listen to λόγου μιᾷ γνώμῃ or take action κοινῶς" (17.4).[52] They have only potential power; they cannot match Athens' single-minded *gnome*.[53]

As if to illustrate this very split between the Syracusans' abundant raw materials and deficient leadership Thucydides provides us with the debate between Hermocrates and Athenagoras at Syracuse. The former speaks of the potential Syracuse has to become another Athens (33.6). But he advises the Syracusans to sail to Italy and oppose the Athenians at sea off Tarentum (34.4). As Dover says, "if Hermokrates' proposal had been adopted, and if there had been time (as there was not) to put it into effect, the probable outcome was the annihilation of the Sikeliot fleets and the rapid imposition of Athenian rule on Sicily and South Italy."[54] Hermocrates' ad-

[52] Compare what Pericles says of the Peloponnesians in 1.141.6 (μήτε βουλευτηρίῳ ἑνὶ χρώμενοι) and 7 (ἐν βραχεῖ . . . μορίῳ σκοποῦσί τι τῶν κοινῶν, . . . λανθάνειν τὸ κοινὸν ἀθρόον φθειρόμενον).

[53] Ironically, as we shall soon see, Alcibiades will himself supply them with precisely what they need to make up this deficit!

[54] Dover, *Comm.* on 6.34.4. Westlake (*Essays on the Greek Historians and Greek History* [New York 1969] 182-183) suggests that Hermocrates proposed an impossibly daring plan in order to jolt his audience into an awareness of the issue. There is no need to explain his bad planning in this way. It is quite consistent, as we shall see, with Syracusan and especially Hermocratean deficiency in *gnome* in Book VI.

vice is premature: Syracusan *gnome* is weak, especially in naval *techne*. Athenagoras, on the other hand, proclaims that Syracuse is superior to an army even twice the strength of the reported Athenian force, in cavalry, hoplites and other *para-skeue* (37). His assessment is probably correct, but the debate has revealed the deep rift in the city's political leadership (as Athenagoras acknowledges in 38.3 and 'one of the generals' fears in 41.2). The question is thus raised, whether the city can organize and mobilize its resources (*dynamis*) sufficiently to defend itself against the *dynamis* and *gnome* of Athens.

The first encounter suggests that the answer is no. The head-strong mob of Syracusans allows itself to be tricked into giving the Athenians a foothold on their territory (see especially οἷον δὴ ὄχλος φιλεῖ θαρσήσας ποιεῖν ["as the mob, when it is encouraged, is wont to do"]; 63.2). When battle is joined, a thunderstorm strikes. The inexperienced Syracusans are overcome by fear, the experienced Athenians treat it as a purely natural phenomenon (70.1). The latter are victorious. But the Athenians cannot exploit their advantage won by *episteme* because of the enemy's superior *dynamis*: the Syracusan cavalry prevents the defeat from turning into a rout (70.3).

Following the engagement the Syracusans hold an assembly. Hermocrates, a man known for his superior *synesis*, experience in war and courage (72.2), draws the following conclusions:

> Our *gnome* was not inferior, it was our *ataxia* which did the harm. But even so we were not so deficient as might have been expected, given that we were like amateurs fighting with the most experienced soldiers in Greece. What did the most harm was the large number of our generals and the division of command and the undisciplined anarchy of our soldiers. If we have a few experienced generals and train our soldiers, we can defeat the enemy with our old courage and our new discipline (*eutaxia*). For both will improve, our discipline with the practice that danger affords, and our courage with the confidence of *episteme*. We need to elect a few generals who can command independently: in this way we can act with secrecy, order and zeal. (72.3-5)

The Syracusans elect Hermocrates general, with two others, and vote for everything he requests. Is Hermocrates' assessment correct? Are the Syracusans in fact so nearly the Athenians' equals in *gnome* that better discipline will make them superior to their adversary?

The first answer comes from Alcibiades. In addition to their other decisions, the Syracusans had voted to send ambassadors to Corinth and Sparta to ask for aid against Athens. The ephors were willing to send ambassadors to the Syracusans to ask them not to surrender, but they were not eager to help. At this point, as we have seen, Alcibiades gave his speech "inflaming and stirring the Lacedaemonians" (6.88.10). His advice on the proper Spartan response in Sicily is as follows: send an army as soon as possible and, "what I believe to be even more useful than an army, a Spartan as commander, in order to organize (*syntaxe*) the soldiers already there and to compel the laggards to fight" (6.91.4). Alcibiades holds to his former judgment of the Sicilians: their major deficiency is not in *dynamis*, but in order and generalship; what they most require is a competent commander: "For the Siciliots are rather inexperienced, but nevertheless, if they are unified and organized, they still even now might succeed" (91.2). Mostly convinced by Alcibiades, the Spartans decide to send Gylippus as commander to the Syracusans. It is the most important decision of the war.

The campaign at Syracuse in the following spring, conducted before Gylippus' arrival, vividly reveals the reason why. The new Syracusan generals, including Hermocrates himself, hold a review of the army on the meadow next to the Anapus, where they select a picked group of men to guard the critical approach to Epipolae. While the Syracusans are thus engaged, the Athenians secretly disembark their army nearby at Leon, only six or seven stades away. From there the soldiers rush to seize Epipolae before the Syracusans notice. They succeed first in gaining the high position and then in defeating the late-arriving enemy, which must cover "no fewer than twenty-five stades" on the run and thus arrives "ἀτακτότερον." Superior military strategy (*gnome*) has caused discipline to break down. The Syracusans retire to their city. Hermocrates' first test is a failure.

The Athenians then begin an encircling wall erected with such speed that the Syracusans are astounded (98.2). When the generals lead out the army to try to stop it, they are forced by their troops' complete lack of discipline[55] to decline battle and retire to the city once more (98.3). Additions to the Athenian cavalry make it superior to the Syracusan, which is routed in a battle (98.4). The Syracusans, on the advice of Hermocrates in particular, "no longer wanted to take the risk of opposing the Athenians in pitched battles" (99.2), but preferred now to turn their efforts to building a counterwall against the Athenian wall. Hermocrates admits the inadequacy of his initial assessment and advice. Athenian *gnome* has easily and convincingly won the first two confrontations against Syracusan *dynamis*, courage, and *ataxia*. It will soon win the third.

Again by superior planning and strategy the Athenians demolish the first Syracusan counterwall (6.100, especially section 1), then a second (101.3). Before long the Syracusan army, venturing out of the city, is again defeated and forced back inside. The Athenians, now in complete command of the territory outside the city's walls, press their advantage by building the circumvallation walls without interruption and "everything else progressed favorably for their hopes" (6.103.2; Crawley translation). The Syracusans, believing they can no longer win the war, fall into despondency and begin to treat with Nicias concerning surrender (6.103.2-3). There are rumors about the ill-fortune or treachery of the generals, who are consequently replaced (103.4). Hermocrates is out, a victim of Athenian *gnome* and Syracusan division and suspicion. Thucydides has made his point absolutely clear: in all their engagements, the Athenians are vastly superior to the Syracusans in military know-how. *Dynamis* without *gnome* is impotent. Syracuse, the potential Athens, appears doomed to fall to the real Athens.

This is the situation at the beginning of the second war

[55] Note 6.98.3: τὸ στράτευμα διεσπασμένον τε καὶ οὐ ῥᾳδίως ξυντασσόμενον ("the army scattered and not easily brought into order").

when the Spartans' decisions, based on Alcibiades' advice, begin to take effect, first in Sicily, then in Attica. In both these theaters of the second war, Alcibiades' strategy will be decisive in reversing the positions of Athens and her opponents in the first war. Thus his speech at Sparta is critical in two ways: it causes the Spartans to start the second war and it gives to them and to the Syracusans the *gnome* that had before been Athens' alone. Alcibiades will himself make the difference in Greece, while Gylippus will turn the tide in Sicily. Not only is Athens deprived of her best military leader and strategist (6.15.4), but her enemies have him bestowed upon them. Athens' remaining general in Sicily, conservative and increasingly dependent upon *tyche*, is no match for his new opponent.

The reversal begins immediately and dramatically. In 6.103 the Syracusans are said to be despondent and on the point of making terms with Nicias. Rumors reach Gylippus, who is preparing his crossing at Leucas, that the city is already enclosed by the Athenian blockade (104). He gives up all hope of saving Syracuse but sails nonetheless in order to try to save Italy. Once there, he and his small fleet are scattered by storm and only barely succeed in putting in at Tarentum. Thucydides makes a special point of mentioning here that Nicias missed this golden opportunity to stop Gylippus from reaching Sicily: "Nicias, when he learned that he was coming despised the small number of his ships . . . and took no precautions at all [πω]" (6.104.3). The first Athenian failure of judgment (*gnome*) proves to be costly. Gylippus sails from Tarentum to Epizephurian Locroi, where he learns "more clearly" that Syracuse was not yet completely encircled, but that it was still possible for a relieving army to get into the city through Epipolae. Confronted with the choice of sailing directly to Syracuse or westwards, along the northern coast of Sicily, from where he could march in by land, Gylippus chose the latter. Thucydides makes it clear that it was a wise decision: Gylippus thus avoided the four ships that Nicias sent to stop him after he heard that he had reached Locroi (7.1.2). Gylippus, one step ahead, sails through the straits between Rhegium and Messena and reaches Himera. There he persuades several cities, formerly reluctant to join the Syracusans, to send contingents to meet him. In the meantime, a single Corinthian ship sails into Syracuse "a little before Gylippus," and prevents the Syracusans from surrendering, which they were on the point of voting upon in an assembly (7.2.1). The Syracusans take heart when they hear that Gylippus is in Sicily. He soon arrives at Syracuse, just before the Athenians have completed their encircling wall: παρὰ τοσοῦτον μὲν αἱ Συράκουσαι ἦλθον κινδύνου ("so close did Syracuse come to disaster"; 7.2.4). Gylippus (and indirectly Alcibiades) has saved Syracuse.

The situation is suddenly changed. The Athenians are now confused (3.1) and on the defensive. Nicias declines the battle that Gylippus offers, "and remains quiet [ἡσύχαζε] beside the Athenian wall" (3.3). The Syracusans, now in command of the field, begin a counterwall up Epipolae and nearly take a weak part of the Athenians' wall (4.1-3). Nicias, now finding engagements on land "less hopeful," begins to pay more attention to the war at sea (4.4). He builds three forts at Plemmyrium in order to bring in supplies more easily. It is a costly decision: "This was the first and chief reason for the losses which the crews suffered" (4.6). Forced to go far afield for water and firewood, the sailors were cut down by the Syracusan cavalry.

Gylippus again offers battle, which the Athenians, now losing the war of wall building, are forced to accept. Fighting between the walls "where the Syracusan cavalry is of no use," the Athenians at first win a victory. Gylippus calls together his army and tells them that the mistake (ἁμάρτημα) was not theirs, but his. Now he will correct it. "And he urged them to keep in mind that they would be equal in paraskeue; in gnome it would be intolerable if they, Peloponnesians and Dorians, were not completely confident of defeating Ionians, islanders and a motley rabble of soldiers, and of driving them out of their land" (5.4). Nicias and the Athenians are forced to fight another battle (6.1), though Thucydides gives us the distinct impression that they did not want it. Gylippus leads his army into more open ground, where his cavalry can be used with greater effectiveness, and there routs the Athenians. That night the Syracusans pass the Athenians' wall with their own counter-wall, and thus deprive them of any possibility (παντάπασιν) of investing the city in the future, even if they should be victorious in the field (6.4). Syracuse is now safe from blockade by land, and Thucydides has made it clear why: Gylippus' *gnome* has completely reversed the military situation on land. The Syracusans, previously so inferior in *gnome* to the Athenians that after several defeats they no longer ventured from behind their walls, are now in command of the field. Their *paraskeue*, as before, is a match for that of the Athenians, their *gnome* is now superior. They will not lose to the Athenians in a hoplite battle again. By land, the issue is decided: as Nicias says in his letter to the Athenians, "it has turned out that we, who appear to be besieging others, now suffer this ourselves, at least on land" (11.4). As we showed earlier, Nicias' letter reveals how the Athenians now begin to suffer from precisely those defects and problems that Pericles had predicted would beset their adversaries. Syracuse has, at least in one regard, fulfilled her potential to become the new Athens.

It is, of course, not surprising that Dorians should be superior to Athenians and Ionians in *gnome* on land. But Nicias' letter suggests that the Athenians have now lost their superiority at sea as well: the Syracusans can practice while the Athenians cannot; their ships can be dried out while the Athenians' cannot; the Athenian crews are deteriorating from losses and inaction. It is not long before Gylippus urges the Syracusans to exploit this situation and to test the Athenians at sea: "for he expected that they would accomplish something worth the risk" (21.2). Hermocrates, undaunted by his earlier failures, adds encouragement,

saying that they [the Athenians] did not have an hereditary experience of the sea, nor an everlasting one, but that they were continentals even more than the Syracusans were and had been forced to become a naval people by the Medes. . . . And he said that he knew well that the Syracusans, if they opposed the Athenians' fleet with unexpected daring, would

169

succeed more by such a method against their opponents' dismay than the Athenians would harm by experience the Syracusans' inexperience. He bade them accordingly make a trial of the sea and not hesitate." (21.3-4)

Hermocrates' advice here on the naval war is almost identical to his assessment of the land war in 6.72: the Syracusans' bravery and daring will overcome their inexperience and defeat the Athenians' greater experience (*empeiria*) and knowledge (*episteme*).

As before, Hermocrates' prediction is overly sanguine and premature. In the first engagement the Syracusans, after initially driving back the Athenian fleet, "sailed into [the harbor] in no order [οὐδενὶ κόσμῳ] and, falling into confusion, gave the victory to the Athenians" (23.3). The Athenians sank eleven ships, killed many of the men, and captured the crews of three vessels with the loss of only three of their own ships. Just as had first occurred in the land war, Syracusan bravado and inexperience result in confusion and ἀταξία, which give the victory to the more experienced and better trained Athenians. *Gnome* is all on the Athenian side. Nonetheless, Gylippus takes the three Athenian forts at Plemmyrium by land during the battle, a loss which "first and foremost caused the ruin of the Athenian army" (24.3). The Syracusans confirm their superiority on land.

At this point Thucydides turns his attention to the other theater of the second war. In a long paragraph he describes the impact of the occupation of Decelea upon Attica. This entire paragraph looks back to the first war, with which it contrasts the current situation in the second. The Athenians now suffer from loss of money and of men (27.3), the very resources with which Pericles encouraged them in Book II (13.3-9). Before, the *esbolai* were brief; now the land is occupied continuously. The Lacedaemonian King Agis is always there: "he does not make war ἐκ παρέργου" (7.27.4), as Pericles said the Spartans would before the first war (1.141, 142.9). The result was that "instead of a city, Athens became a garrison" (28.1); we might add, "just as in Sicily," where the Athenians, "seeming to besiege others, were besieged themselves." Thucydides makes this last point himself: "What especially harmed them was the fact that they had two wars simultaneously" (28.3). The other was against Syracuse: πόλιν οὐδὲν ἐλάσσω αὐτήν γε καθ' αὐτὴν τῆς τῶν Ἀθηναίων. Here Thucydides expresses explicitly the comparison that he has for so long been making implicitly: Syracuse is "a city which, taken as a city, is in no way inferior to Athens," and the real Athens has become a garrison instead of a city. The reversal is now almost complete. Athens' enemies in the second war lack only one of Athens' advantages in the first: naval *techne*. It is supplied soon from another theater of the war.

The twenty-five Corinthian vessels anchored at Erineum opposite the thirty-three Athenian ships at Naupactus prepared for a naval battle. They first stationed soldiers along the crescent-shaped shore of the bay in which they were anchored. In the ensuing engagement, the Corinthians disabled seven Athenian ships through the use of specially strengthened prows, which stove in the opposing ships' prows on impact. While they also lost three ships, the Corinthian ships were easily able to escape further damage and pursuit by simply returning to the shores of the bay, which were filled with their own soldiers. Though the battle was more or less a standoff, the Corinthians considered themselves the victors, and the Athenians the vanquished (34.7), because the issue had not been more one-sided (as it usually was when a relatively equal number of Athenian ships fought with an enemy).

This battle, seemingly so insignificant, was decisive in the naval engagements that followed in Sicily. The Syracusans adopted the changes in ship design and tactics that the Corinthians had used at Erineum. They would charge prow to prow; before, this was considered ἀμαθία in a helmsman (36.5), but in the restricted area of the harbor at Syracuse it would give the Syracusan ships with their prows strengthened a decided advantage. In the confined space the Athenians would be unable to use their favorite tactics of breaking the line or sailing around it, in other words, their *techne* (36.4). The Syracusans could retreat to almost any point in the harbor because their soldiers occupied most of it, while the Athenians would have little room to do so. As Thucydides says, "the Syracusans added these inventions [ἐπινοήσαντες] to their *episteme* and *dynamis*" (37.1). The Corinthians had said to the Spartans in 1.71.3, ἀνάγκη δὲ ὥσπερ τέχνης αἰεὶ τὰ ἐπιγιγνόμενα κρατεῖν ("it is necessary that, just as in the skills, innovations always win out"). Their reference was to the Athenians. Pericles had said in 1.142.9, τὸ δὲ ναυτικὸν τέχνης ἐστίν, ὥσπερ καὶ ἄλλο τι ("sailing, like other things, is a matter of skill"). Thucydides has now made it clear that the inventors in naval *techne* are no longer the Athenians, but their enemies.

The results are predictable. The new Syracusan strategy, which includes the use of spear-throwers on the decks of their ships, results in a Syracusan naval victory (41.1). Even after the arrival of Demosthenes' huge relieving force, the Syracusans maintain their newly-won advantage at sea. They win the next naval engagement (52), killing Eurymedon and destroying the vessels on his wing in the process. After this decisive defeat at sea the Athenians, struck by the unexpected reversal, lose heart (ὁ παράλογος αὐτοῖς μέγας ἦν):

> for, coming up against these cities which were the only ones they had met which had the same tropoi as themselves [ὁμοιοτρόποις], with democracies, like themselves, and with ships and horses and large populations, they were unable either to bring about any division in them by political change, which they had offered, or to defeat them by much greater force [*paraskeue*], but they had failed in most of their attempts, and even before this they were beaten at sea, which they would never have expected, and they were much more astounded. (55.2)

With naval *techne* the final Athenian quality has been added to the Syracusan side. The Syracusans are ὁμοιότροποι to the Athenians. Syracuse has become the new Athens.

The Syracusans immediately recognize their new position. No longer fearing for their own safety, they resolve to take the offensive. Their aim now is to defeat the Athenians on land and on sea and prevent their return: καλὸν σφίσιν ἐς τοὺς

Ἕλληνας τὸ ἀγώνισμα φανεῖσθαι ("for the struggle appeared glorious to them within the Greek world"; 7.56.2). They take upon themselves a new role: they will free some Greeks, release others from fear. They will thus be marvelled at by other men and by later generations. As hegemons with the Corinthians and Lacedaemonians, by having improved their fleet to a great extent and by providing their own city as the major risk-taker, they will take part in a worthy contest, and not simply against the Athenians, but with many allies on both sides (7.56.3). It is clear from Thucydides' words that the Syracusans regard this not only as a passing military contest, but as a contest with Athens for fame and reputation. The verb the Syracusans use to describe their city's position among her allies is προκινδυνεῦσαι. It is used on only one other occasion in Thucydides' history: by the Athenians, who use it in reference to their city's role in the Persian Wars (1.73.4). The Syracusans are proud of having improved their fleet, just as the Athenians had when they were invaded by Xerxes (7.21.3). Above all, the Syracusans look forward to being marvelled at (θαυμασθήσεσθαι) by other men and by later generations. That is almost a quotation from the Funeral Oration, in which Pericles said τοῖς τε νῦν καὶ τοῖς ἔπειτα θαυμασθησόμεθα ("we shall be marvelled at both by the ones now and by those later"; 2.41.4). Compare this to the statement in 2.39.4: καὶ ἔν τε τούτοις τὴν πόλιν ἀξίαν εἶναι θαυμάζεσθαι καὶ ἔτι ἐν ἄλλοις ("both among these and even among others the city is worthy of wonder"). We are reminded of Hermocrates' words in 6.33.4-6: "Which these Athenians themselves did, when the Mede unexpectedly failed, and their reputation was augmented because he came, in name, against them; it is not unhoped that the same thing will happen to us." The opportunity has now come for the Syracusans to win the same glory for their defense of Sicily against the Athenians that the Athenians themselves had won for their defense of Greece against the Persians. Thucydides thus draws the comparison between the two cities still more tightly: the Syracusans are now consciously competing for the Athenians' reputation. To emphasize the magnitude of the contest, he appends a catalogue of races at Syracuse (57-58), "second in number only to the total roster of states on the Athenian and Lacedaemonian sides in this war."

With this as a backdrop to the *agon*, Thucydides gives us as *proagon* the paired exhortations of Nicias on the one side and Gylippus and the Syracusan commanders on the other. Commentators have noted the great similarities between this *antilogia* and that of Phormio and the Spartan commanders in 2.87-92. In fact, as Hunter has shown, "the latter can be considered a kind of paradeigma, a model against which to compare the present logoi." But the roles are reversed: Nicias speaks like the Lacedaemonians in Book II, Gylippus and the Syracusans like Phormio. As Hunter demonstrates, Nicias' speech reveals the same errors of judgment and reliance upon *tyche* as that of the Lacedaemonians in Book II, while the Syracusans and Gylippus display the same foresight and command of *gnome* and *techne* as Phormio.[56] Just as Phormio had foreseen his opponents' strategems and plans, so the Syracusans have obviated those of Nicias.[57] Thucydides has provided the reader with a parallel antilogia in order to show how the roles of Athens and her opponent are now completely the antitheses of what they were in the first war—identical form, antithetical content.

As de Romilly has pointed out:

> la bataille de Syracuse devient comme une espèce de contre-épreuve de la bataille de Naupacte. Après de longs tâtonne-ments, les Syracusains ont réussi ce que tentaient vainement les Péloponnésiens à Naupacte: ils ont interdit à Athènes l'εὐρυχωρία, en limitant son champ, sur mer et sur terre; et ils l'ont par là amenée à modifier, progressivement, son armement, son dispositif guerrier, et le principe même de sa tactique; ainsi, dans le combat naval qui s'ouvre, Athènes n'a plus le bénéfice de son expérience.[58]

[56] J. de Romilly, *Histoire et raison chez Thucydide*, 156-157; V. Hunter, *Thucydides: The Artful Reporter* (Toronto 1973) 109-113; Edmunds, *Chance and Intelligence*, 135.

[57] J. de Romilly, *Histoire et raison chez Thucydide*, 158.

[58] Ibid., 159.

The Syracusans are now superior to the Athenians in naval warfare ἐν στενοχωρίᾳ, just as before the Athenians were superior to the Peloponnesians ἐν εὐρυχωρίᾳ. An overwhelming victory follows. Afterwards, the reversals continue, and, in fact, intensify. Hermocrates deceives Nicias into waiting a night before retreating, so the drunken victors will have time after their revels to block the roads out of Syracuse (73). Such deceptions the Athenians used to employ against their enemies. On the retreat thunder and rain terrify the Athenians, "who thought all these things were happening for their own destruction" (7.79.3). We have now come full circle. The experienced Athenians resemble the inexperienced Syracusans of 6.70.1, frightened by a rainstorm. Their *tropoi* now belong to the enemy: *gnome, empeiria, episteme, techne*. Syracuse is the new Athens. The Athenians, on the other hand, have been stripped of their abilities and their resolve. These men, whom Pericles had called the most capable of all men everywhere in dealing with all aspects of life, have become frightened animals.

CHAPTER IV

Books III and VIII: Revolt and Revolution

BOOKS III AND VIII

Almost all the scholars who have approached Book VIII of Thucydides have agreed that it is unfinished.[1] While there is much room for argument about the degree and type of incompleteness, there seems little doubt about the fact itself. The most telling evidence is the total lack of direct speeches in Book VIII, a book which contains Thucydides' account of two of the most important events in the entire Peloponnesian War, the revolts of Athenian subjects in the Aegean, especially Chios and Euboea, and the revolution of the 400 at Athens. That Thucydides would, if he had been given the time and opportunity, have included several full and direct *logoi* in his account of these *erga* seems quite likely.[2] Book VIII is radically

---

[1] See especially the remarks in J. Classen, *Thukydides*, revised by J. Steup (Berlin 1892-1922) Book VIII, "Vorwort zur dritten Auflage" and the bibliography cited there.

[2] See Dionysius of Halicarnassus, *On Thucydides*, 16, where the well-known remark of Cratippus regarding the absence of speeches in Book VIII appears. Bibliography on this question may be found in W. Kendrick Pritchett's translation and annotation of Dionysius' work (Berkeley, Los Angeles, London 1975) 67, n. 7. Some modern scholars support Cratippus' contention that Thucydides decided to abandon the use of speeches in Book VIII because they were "an impediment to the narrative" and "annoying to the hearers" (Pritchett's translation, p. 11). This suggestion remains a possible, but in my view, highly unlikely alternative to the view arguing incompleteness.

different from Book V where, I have argued, the lack of speeches was no sign of incompleteness. In Book V Thucydides dealt with the *erga* that occurred during the years of nominal peace when there was only sporadic fighting. But Book VIII covers nearly two years of crucial events during the second ten-year war. In addition, the narrative itself is loosely strung together and in some places even confused and unclear. It is difficult to follow the movements of fleets and armies, to understand the roles of generals, to appreciate the motivations of decisions.[3] Finally, the book ends *in medias res*: "And coming first to Ephesus (Tissaphernes) sacrificed to Artemis." It seems highly improbable that Thucydides intended this to be the final sentence of his work. His remark in 5.26.1 about finishing his account of the war corroborates this view. On the other hand, we can be virtually certain that 8.109 was the final sentence that Thucydides wrote: at least three other historians, Cratippus, apparently a contemporary of Thucydides, and Xenophon and Theopompus in the next century, began their accounts almost precisely where Thucydides' work breaks off.[4]

Thus Book VIII seems both incomplete and unpolished, a

[3] See especially 8.30.1-2 and 8.64.1-2. For a summary of these difficulties see E. Schwartz, *Das Geschichtswerk des Thukydides* (Bonn 1919) 75: "If one extends the inquiry to the whole eighth book, it becomes apparent, as one might have expected, that even in other passages the relationships are fragile and the narrative falls apart into individual pieces, whose undeniably masterful execution should not conceal the fact that the whole has remained a torso and can only be treated as such."

[4] There is no need to go into the vexed problems associated with the "continuations" of Thucydides' *History*. Ancient evidence may be found in Dionysius of Halicarnassus, *Ad Pompeium Geminum, Opuscula*, ed. Usener-Radermacher (Leipzig 1904) 2:235-236, Diodorus Siculus 13.42.5, Diogenes Laertius, *Life of Xenophon* 2.57, Marcellinus' *Life of Thucydides* 43, 45, as well as in the texts of Xenophon, Theopompus, Cratippus and possibly the Oxyrynchus historian. The most recent and radical approach to the question is that of L. Canfora (*Tucidide Continuato* [Padova 1970]), whose arguments are ingenious but generally unpersuasive. The same might be said about the attempts of most other scholars to solve this difficult problem. There is simply too little evidence to allow for more than almost pure speculation.

truncated first draft. Some historians completed it in antiquity. In modern times, scholars have attempted to polish it, or at least to conjecture about how Thucydides would have polished it. It is unprofitable to conduct such an inquiry along narrow lines, since we can never attain certainty, or even probability, about how Thucydides would have treated details. But it may well prove useful to ask about Thucydides' general approach to the years 412 and 411: what were the major historical events of those years; how might Thucydides have treated those events historiographically.[5] Even in Book VIII, in other words, we can analyze, if only from a broad perspective, Thucydides' principles of selection, emphasis, and juxtaposition. Before, it was only the material in Book VIII itself that could be used as a source for such a study. But if the case made so far in this book is sound, we can add to this evidence that gained from earlier sections of Thucydides' *History*. If Thucydides drew parallels between the opening years of the two ten-year wars, is there not a strong probability that he continued to use this method in his composition of the later years of these wars? In our terms, if Books VI and VII are related to Books I and II respectively, then is not Book VIII connected with III? A comparison of these two books might help us to understand what Thucydides had begun to do in Book VIII. In making these comparisons, we should also be alert to what VIII might tell us about III. For, as we found in previous chapters, segments from the second war often give us valuable insights into how Thucydides shaped episodes in the first.

There are in Book III (which covers the fourth, fifth, and sixth years of the first war) four major foci of Thucydides' attention: the revolt of Mytilene (chapters 2-50); the fate of Plataea (52-68); the stasis at Corcyra (70-85); and the fighting in northwestern Greece (94-114). Though there are brief interruptions in two of the sections, the narrative is quite clearly and neatly divided into these four episodes.[6] That these events

---

[5] For example, would he have found a particular episode worthy of a speech or debate?

[6] Chapter 7 briefly describes the actions of an Athenian fleet in Laconia and western Greece, while 20-24 recount the breakout of half of

were chosen by Thucydides for special emphasis is also proven by his use of highly dramatic techniques in composing them: the speech of the Mytilenaeans (9-14) and the Cleon-Diodotus debate (37-48) in the first; the Plataean-Theban debate (53-67) in the second; the emotion-charged analysis of revolution (82-84)[7] in the third; the pathetic, anecdotal dialogue (113), unparalleled in Thucydides' work, in the fourth. Thucydides has made it clear historiographically that he considers these to be the four most important issues in this part of the first war.

Book VIII lacks this kind of structural clarity. It is composed instead of many small episodes, poorly connected or even completely unconnected with one another. The overall impression is not unlike that gained from the Pentacontaetia, Thucydides' sketchy and rapid-paced account of the years 479-431. But it is still possible to discern the major historiographical components of Book VIII within the disconnected narrative of the first draft. The first such issue is that of the revolt of Athens' subjects. The matter is mentioned initially in 8.2.2 in general terms, and the specific account of the planning of the revolts begins in 8.5 ("first the Euboeans sent an embassy in this winter to Agis concerning revolt from the Athenians"). Other states follow suit (Lesbos in 5.2, Chios and Erythraea in 5.4, the Hellespont in 6.1). A debate ensues at Lacedaemon (6.2-3), where the Spartans decide to give their support first to Chios, and later a conference of the allies is held at Corinth (8.2-4), where a full schedule of revolts is planned. Thucydides then describes the revolt of Chios primarily, and secondarily those of other states as well, in chapters 9-28, which carry the narrative through the end of summer, 412. Chapters 29-60, which cover the multiple events of the following winter, are so varied

---

the besieged from Plataea. These are the only digressions in Thucydides' long account of the revolt of Mytilene. Chapter 104, Thucydides' description of the purification of Delos, is the only interruption in his narrative of the war in western Greece.

[7] Whether chapter 84 of Book III is genuine or not remains, so far as I am concerned, an open question. Scholars have for too long now uncritically treated 84 as spurious. For a good case against this attitude, see E. Wenzel, "Zur Echtheitsfrage von Thukydides, 3,84," *WS* N.F. 11 (1968) 18-27.

and disjointed that it is impossible to characterize their sub-ject simply, but, as we shall see, their major theme is the de-velopment of relationships among Tissaphernes, the Lacedae-monians, and the Ionian Greeks. Chapters 63-98 recount the revolution of the 400 at Athens in the summer of 411, begin-ning with "At this time and even before the democracy at Athens was abolished" (63.3), and ending with the words "and the oligarchy and stasis at Athens ceased" (98.4).[8] The final section, begun at 99 and left unfinished at 109, describes the fighting in the Hellespont.

If we compare Books III and VIII diagrammatically we have the following:

2- 50	Revolt of Mytilene	A	Revolts of Chios, others	5- 28
52- 68	End of Plataea	B	Tissaphernes, Spartans, Ionians	29- 60
70- 85	Stasis at Corcyra	C	Stasis at Athens	63- 98
94-114	Fighting in NW Greece	D	Fighting in Hellespont	99-109.

Even on first sight, these sections of narrative appear similar to one another. In particular, the revolts of part A and the staseis of part C are noteworthy because they are the only such revolts and revolutions in the Peloponnesian War Thucydides has chosen to describe in full historiographical detail. It is worthwhile to see whether or not Thucydides made compari-sons and contrasts between them.

---

[8] This is not to say that Thucydides does not treat the antecedents of the Athenian stasis before chapter 63. In 47-54 he describes the origin of the oligarchical conspiracy on Samos and Peisander's manipulation of the assembly at Athens, which first broached the subject of a change of government. These chapters, which Thucydides might have moved, in his final draft, to join with the major section on the stasis (as he did in the case of the Corcyraean stasis in Book III: see 3.70 and *Comm.*) de-scribe the preliminary actions of the conspirators only, not the real be-ginning of the revolution. Even in his first draft Thucydides made an effort to keep the major part of his narrative of the Athenian stasis to-gether: see especially 8.63.3: ὑπὸ γὰρ τοῦτον τὸν χρόνον καὶ ἔτι πρότερον ἡ ἐν. The words I have underscored reveal his method of pulling to-gether chronologically separated events in order to create narrative unity.

THE REVOLTS: MYTILENE AND CHIOS

The contentions of this section are: that Thucydides carefully measured the revolts of Lesbos in 427 and of Chios in 412[9] against one another, that he contrasted the Athenians' ability to deal with the first revolt with their inability to handle the second, and that he wanted in particular to emphasize the improved effectiveness of the Lacedaemonian response to the second revolt caused by the leadership of Alcibiades. As I compare the two accounts, I shall also point out those places in Book VIII where Thucydides might, in my view, have made changes in later drafts, especially by adding direct speeches to the narrative. We should keep in mind that even the narrative of Book VIII is unpolished and not always carefully structured and ordered, while that of III is a finished product. This makes comparisons more difficult and less secure than those we have made before in Chapters II and III.

Both revolts come after major Athenian losses, the plague and "peak of war" in 430/429, the Sicilian disaster in 415-413.[10] But while the Chians use the consequent Athenian weakness to their advantage, the Lesbians are not so farsighted. Indeed, the primary contrast in Thucydides' accounts is between the Lesbians' haste and lack of preparation on the one hand, and the Chians' prudence and careful planning on the other. In brief, the Lesbians suffer from dissension in Mytilene, in Lesbos, and outside; consequent lack of secrecy, unpreparedness, hesitation, and ἡσυχία; and finally a disastrous split between rich and poor. The Chians benefit from carefully controlled political bonds both inside and outside the island, consequent secrecy, more than adequate preparations, self-confidence, and dominance by the oligarchs of the democratic opposition.

Let us take these contrasts one by one. Before they have had time to complete their preparations for revolt the Lesbian oli-

---

[9] We shall focus most of our attention upon the Chian revolt because that is what Thucydides does. The other revolts are clearly subordinated to that of Chios in his account.

[10] See especially 3.3.1, and Gomme, *Comm. ad loc.* for the phrase τοῦ πολέμου ἄρτι καθισταμένου καὶ ἀκμάζοντος.

garchs' plans are learned (3.2.3) by three hostile (διάφοροι) groups, the Tenedians (outside of Lesbos), the Methymnians (in Lesbos), a faction of Mytileneans (inside Mytilene). Envoys from these groups notify the Athenians of the Mytileneans' forced synoecism of Lesbos and of "all their preparations" for revolt. Their plans exposed, the Lesbians are confronted by the Athenians with the facts. When the Athenians "did not persuade the Mytileneans to cease the synoecism and preparations, in fear they wished to seize them beforehand" (3.3.1). The Athenians sent forty ships to Lesbos, where they demanded that the Mytileneans tear down their walls and give up their ships or face war. The Mytileneans did not obey the command and were thus "forced to fight, unprepared and on the spot" (4.2). Thucydides emphasizes the Mytileneans' unpreparedness by noting it on two other occasions as well, 3.2.1 and 13.2. After a rout in the harbor, they make a vain attempt to convince the Athenians that they plan no revolt! Thucydides says, rather pointedly, that even the Mytileneans themselves had no expectations that this claim would convince the Athenians (3.4.5).

The Chian oligarchical leaders, by contrast, are careful to collect allies and to alienate no one before they are ready to revolt from Athens. They obtain the assistance of the Erythraeans, Tissaphernes, and Alcibiades before sending to Sparta for an alliance (8.5.4-6.3). As a result, their appeal for aid is accepted by the Spartans over that of the Hellespontines and Pharnabazus. They keep all embassies secret from the Athenians (8.7.1), and later, when the Athenians do become suspicious because of the long Peloponnesian delay (8.9.2) in sending ships to Chios, they succeed in temporarily allaying Athenian fears by denying Athenian accusations and sending promptly the seven ships the Athenians demand as a guarantee of their loyalty (8.9.1). In addition, the Chian oligarchs take pains to prevent their own demos from hearing of their plans; "they did not want to have the *plethos* hostile to them before they had some strong base of power, and they no longer expected the Peloponnesians to come, since they were wasting time" (8.9.3). Thus the Chian oligarchs prepared for any eventuality and were able to survive even the usual Peloponnesian delay, which had cost so many other Greeks, particularly the Lesbians, their chances of successful revolt against Athens.

When the fighting against Athens begins in earnest, the differences between the two states become sharper and more critical. Thucydides says that the Mytileneans, even after they won a land battle against the Athenians, "neither made camp nor had confidence in themselves, but retired" (3.5.2). This lack of activity (ἡσύχαζον in 5.2, ἡσυχίαν in 6.1) greatly encouraged the Athenians who called upon the allies to join them. The allies in turn "came more readily when they saw so little vigor shown by the Lesbians" (6.1), and soon the Mytileneans were nearly hemmed in by the besieging armies and fleets. Thucydides emphasizes that the Chians, on the other hand, put forth exceptional effort, not only in the cause of their own revolt, but on behalf of others as well: "After this, during the same summer, the Chians, whose zeal continued as active as at the beginning, and who even without the Peloponnesians had sufficient forces to cause the revolt of the cities, and who wished at the same time to have as many companions as possible to share in the risk, made an expedition with thirteen ships of their own to Lesbos" (8.22.1). There they effected the revolts of Methymna and Mytilene. Though these cities were soon recaptured by the Athenians (23.2-4), Thucydides clearly found it significant that the Chians had been so vigorous in their efforts. They also caused the revolts of Lebedus and Haerae (19.4). Thus, while the Mytileneans' inactivity had made the Athenians' allies more willing to assist Athens in putting down the revolt, the Chians' vigor made the allies eager to join in their revolt.

Finally, and perhaps most significantly, the Mytilenean ὀλίγοι lost control of the demos, while the Chian leaders prevented a fatal split between rival factions by moderate but firm action. Even this contrast was caused, at least in part, by the difference in planning. The Mytileneans had been forced to fight before they could bring in all their provisions, including grain from the Pontus (3.2.2). The result was that when they were besieged, they eventually began to run short of food. The Lacedaemonian commander in the city, Salaethos, was forced to give the demos hoplite equipment for a desperate sally against the Athenians. As soon as they acquired heavy armor the demos "no longer obeyed the *archontes*, but formed into groups and demanded that the *dynatoi* bring the grain out into public and distribute it to everyone, or they would themselves make terms with the Athenians and betray the city to them" (3.27.3). The *dynatoi*, realizing that they could not stop the demos from carrying out its threat, surrendered to the Athenians.

After the Chians sustained several serious defeats by land (8.24.3), they no longer went out to face the Athenians but retired behind their walls. There, they were so well provided that Thucydides is led to write his well-known disquisition on the Chians' *eudaemonia* and *sophrosyne*:

> For the Chians, after the Lacedaemonians, alone among those of whom I know, had good fortune and good sense at the same time; the more their city prospered, the better they ordered it. And even this revolt, if they seemed to have committed it somewhat unsafely, they dared to make only after sharing the risk with many and good allies and after they saw the Athenians themselves no longer denying that their position was extremely weak after the disaster in Sicily. And if, in the course of human uncertainties they failed, they shared their error with many to whom it seemed that the Athenians would soon be completely defeated. (24.4-5)

But even with these advantages the Chians were so hard pressed by land and sea that a faction arose and attempted to give the city over to the Athenians. The leaders' response is a perfect illustration of Chian *sophrosyne*: "When the *archontes* discovered the conspiracy they took no action themselves [ἡσύχασαν], but bringing Astyochus the [Lacedaemonian] admiral out of Erythrae with four ships which he had, they carefully considered how they could most moderately [μετρι-ώτατα] put an end to the plot, either by taking hostages or by some other means" (24.6). This sentence, and the entire preceding paragraph, are unique in Thucydides' entire work for their exceptionally high praise of a city and its government.[11] Thucydides has gone out of his way to stress the Chians' virtues in his account of their revolt: prudence, foresight, resolution, magnanimity, moderation. They avoided every pitfall into which the Mytileneans had fallen fifteen years before. The contrast is designed not so much to denigrate the Lesbians as to emphasize the Chians' extraordinary virtue.

While there are thus major differences between the perpetrators of the two revolts, the most significant contrast is the one that Thucydides draws between the Sparta of the first revolt and the Sparta of the second. In short, this contrast is between Sparta without Alcibiades and Sparta with Alcibiades. Thucydides' judgment on this point is so strong that it influences his historiographical decisions in composing narratives and speeches in the two episodes. A comparative study of the Spartan responses to the two revolts reveals clearly Thucydides' view of the significance of Alcibiades to Sparta.

The Mytileneans had sent two embassies to Lacedaemon (3.4.5 and 5.2). The first achieved virtually nothing, only the dispatch of two officials who asked the Mytileneans to send a second legation. Valuable time was lost in this process (see 3.5.2-6.1). The second, which met with the Peloponnesians at Olympia, gained its object, an alliance and a promise of assistance for the revolt (15.1). Thucydides gives us the speech of the Mytilenean ambassadors to the Spartans and their allies. The bulk of it (9-13.1) consists of the Mytileneans' presentation of their reasons for revolt, a presentation that takes the form of an ally's view of the history of the Athenian empire from 479 to 428. In this discussion of their *prophaseis* and *aitias* (13.1) the Mytileneans try to persuade the Peloponne-

---

[11] Thucydides' remarks (8.97.2) about the government of the 5000 at Athens are similar (see especially εὖ πολιτεύσαντες and μετρία), but the introductory words τὸν πρῶτον χρόνον certainly undercut the force of the judgment and, if anything, emphasize the contrast between Athens and Chios rather than the comparison. One should also note that, considered in this context, the words μετὰ Λακεδαιμονίους in 8.24.4 serve to make the contrast between Sparta and Athens even greater than that between Chios and Athens.

sians that they have the right to revolt from Athens: they are concerned primarily with the morality of their action (see τοῦ δικαίου καὶ ἀρετῆς in 10.1). Only a short section of the speech(13.2-7) assesses the possibilities of success for the revolt. The Mytileneans argue that the moment for action has now arrived (13.3). The Athenians are worn out by plague and economic difficulties, their ships are away, some in Peloponnese, some in Lesbos: "So that it is not likely that they have a surplus of ships, if you attack them a second time this summer by sea and by land simultaneously, but they will either not defend against your attack by sea or they will withdraw from both places" (13.4).

The Peloponnesians accordingly plan a double invasion of Attica. They summon an army to the isthmus and begin to assemble a fleet that they will transport across the isthmus for the attack upon Attica by sea. But at this point the Athenians make a great demonstration of their power to prove a point (16.1). The Lacedaemonians are awed by this display and "considered the things said by the Lesbians to be untrue" (3.16.2). This *paralogos*, plus the delay and lack of enthusiasm of their allies in mustering, induced the Lacedaemonians to return home. The double invasion of Attica, suggested by the Lesbians and promised by the Peloponnesians, was aborted. In order to lend some assistance the Lacedaemonians then prepared to send a fleet of forty ships to Lesbos under the command of Alcidas. These preparations took some time: the fleet was not ready to sail until the following spring (3.26.1). In the meantime, the Peloponnesians succeeded in getting one trireme to Lesbos carrying the Lacedaemonian Salaethos, who managed to slip past the Athenian lines into Mytilene. There he told the leaders that an invasion of Attica was planned along with the dispatch of forty ships to Lesbos in the following spring. The Mytileneans took heart at this news, which strengthened their resolve not to give in to the Athenians (25.2).

But, as on so many previous occasions (see 3.13.7) the Lacedaemonians failed to support sufficiently a city in revolt from Athens. Though their invasion of Attica in spring, 427 was one of the most severe that they carried out in the war, the fleet accomplished nothing. Under the incompetent command of Alcidas the forty ships that were supposed to sail quickly to Lesbos (29.1) wasted precious time on the voyage (27.1). Thucydides emphasizes their delay by stating it three times: ἐνεχρόνιζον in 27.1, ἐνδιέτριψαν and σχολαῖοι κομισθέντες in 29.1. Finally, even Salaethos gave up hope of their arrival (27.2) and armed the demos for a sally. As we have already seen, the revolt quickly fell apart, the victim of stasis in Mytilene. Thucydides makes it clear that one of the two major reasons for Salaethos' decision was his loss of faith in the forty Peloponnesian ships.[12] Salaethos had good reason for this lack of confidence. When Alcidas reached Icarus and Myconus, he heard rumors that Mytilene was taken. Wishing to check these reports, he sailed to Ionia. By the time he put in at Embaton on the coast and heard the full story, Mytilene had been in Athenian hands, Thucydides says, for seven days (29.2). Alcidas was in large part responsible for the surrender of Mytilene and the failure of the Lesbian revolt. As we shall see, he would soon cost Sparta far more dearly in the Aegean and in Ionia generally.

Before following Alcidas' voyage to its miserable conclusion let us look, for comparative purposes, at the initial Spartan responses to the proposals of Chios and the other states that wanted to revolt from Athens in 412. Two sets of envoys came to Lacedaemon in that year, one from the Chians, Erythraeans, and Tissaphernes, the other from Pharnabazus and the Hellespont.[13] Both groups asked for Peloponnesian assistance with revolts. Thucydides tells us that a "great dispute" (πολλὴ ἅμιλλα) arose at Sparta over whether to send ships and an army first to Ionia and Chios or to the Hellespont.[14] The Spartans decided in favor of Chios and Tissaphernes "by a

[12] The other, previously mentioned, was the dwindling food supply (3.27.1).

[13] The Euboeans and Lesbians appealed to Agis at Decelea at about the same time.

[14] Ἅμιλλα occurs only here in the text of Thucydides with the meaning of debate, dispute; elsewhere in Thucydides it denotes a military confrontation.

great margin." Thucydides gives us one of their reasons: "For Alcibiades joined in arguing on their behalf" (6.3). Did Thucydides plan in his final draft to compose a speech at this point in his narrative of the Chian revolt? We cannot know with any certainty, but a speech by the Chian envoys or by Alcibiades here would have made a nice counterpoint to the Mytilenean speech at Olympia.

In any event, the Spartans soon disappointed the Chians' hopes, much as they had the Mytileneans' in 428/427. Just as in 428, they voted to send forty ships to assist in the revolt. First they decided to send out ten of their own ships with Melanchridas as nauarch. But when an earthquake occurred, they decided to send Chalcideus in place of Melanchridas and they prepared five ships instead of ten in Laconia (6.5). In the following spring when the Chians urged them to send the ships before the Athenians got wind of their revolt, the Lacedaemonians sent three men to Corinth to move the ships in preparation there across the isthmus "as soon as possible" for the voyage to Chios. There were altogether, including the ships which Agis was preparing for Lesbos, thirty-nine ships at Corinth. There the allies held a council in which it was decided to sail first to Chios with Chalcideus as commander, then to Lesbos with Alcamenes as commander, and last to the Hellespont with Clearchus as commander. The fleet was to be divided into two parts, the first to sail "immediately," the second to wait and distract the Athenians' attention. When they were ready, they accordingly moved twenty-one ships across the isthmus. But at this point the Corinthians objected to sailing before the Isthmian Games had been celebrated. In spite of Agis' offer to sail alone immediately and privately, a delay occurred in which the Athenians discovered the Chians' plans. It was then that they demanded that the Chians give them ships as a pledge of their loyalty. The Chian leaders, in order to keep the demos, still unaware of the planned revolt, in the dark, sent seven ships: "They did not want to have the *plethos* hostile to them until they had some firm basis for revolt, and they no longer expected the Peloponnesians to come since they were wasting time" (8.9.3).

We are now at precisely the point when Salaethos was driven to arm the demos at Mytilene because of shortage of food and desperation at the delay of the forty Peloponnesian ships under Alcidas. Note how Thucydides echoes even the language of 3.27.1-2. Compare ἐνεχρόνιζον in 3.27.1 and ἐνδιέτριψαν in 3.29.1 with διέτριβον in 8.9.3, and ὁ Σάλαιθος καὶ αὐτὸς οὐ προσδεχόμενος ἔτι in 3.27.2 with καὶ τοὺς Πελοποννησίους οὐκέτι προσδεχόμενοι ἥξειν in 8.9.3. But note also the difference in the Chian situation. The Chian leaders, who have not yet played their hand, are able to forestall Athenian suspicion and are careful to avoid antagonizing their own demos before they have a firm basis for action. With these words Thucydides seems to be contrasting the Chian oligarchs' successful control of their demos with the Lesbian oligarchs' disastrous split with theirs. In short, Thucydides tells us, the Chians are able, at least temporarily, to survive the Peloponnesian delay that had wrecked the Lesbians' chances of successful revolt. Section 8.9.3 looks back to 3.27.

At this time the Isthmia took place. During the games the Athenian *theoroi* became more fully aware of Chian intentions. When they returned home, they informed the Athenians who took "immediate" steps to prevent the twenty-one Peloponnesian ships from leaving Cenchreae (8.10.1). When the latter did set off after the Isthmia ended, the Athenians sailed against them, first with an equal number of ships, then later with thirty-seven. The Peloponnesians were eventually forced to make a landing at Speiraeos, a deserted beach at the edge of Epidaurian territory. There the Athenians attacked the Peloponnesian vessels, disabling most, made a landing, and killed the Lacedaemonian commander Alcamenes in a confused and violent struggle. They then proceeded to blockade the enemy force, which was soon joined by the Corinthians and other inhabitants in the vicinity. The Peloponnesian position was extremely difficult since it appeared almost impossible to maintain guard over the ships in such a deserted place. In this *aporia* they considered burning them, but then decided to haul them up on shore, guard them with their land forces, and wait for an opportunity to escape (8.11.2). They

189

were as useless to Chios as Alcidas' fleet had been to Mytilene. Once again, Peloponnesian delay and hesitation had given the Athenians the upper hand and forced a city in revolt into a desperate position. The two situations are quite similar: a promised fleet of forty Peloponnesian ships fails, because of gross incompetence and delay, to reach a city in revolt from Athens. It is only at this point that the two cases diverge from one another. Let us follow first Alcidas' actions in Book III and then Alcibiades' in Book VIII.

When Alcidas reached Embaton, where he learned that Mytilene had been taken seven days before, he held a council to decide what to do under the circumstances. Thucydides reports first the speech of one Teutiaplus, an Elean. It is the strangest speech in all of Thucydides:

> Alcidas and other Peloponnesian leaders, it seems best to me to sail straight to Mytilene, just as we are, before we are heard of. For it is likely that men who have recently taken a city will be caught totally unawares, especially by sea, from which they expect no enemy whatsoever, and where our strength happens to lie. It is probable that their soldiers are carelessly, in the manner of victors, dispersed and scattered among the houses. If we fall upon them suddenly and at night I expect that, together with those inside the town, *if there is anyone still left who is sympathetic to us*, we will gain command of the situation. Let us not shrink from the danger, but recognize that delay in war is nothing other than this: what a general avoids in himself and, when he sees it in an enemy, attacks; that is best. (my italics; 3.30)

It is no wonder that this speech has puzzled readers of Thucydides. Why did he include it? After all, Alcidas did not accept his advice ("And he, saying such things, did not persuade Alcidas" [3.31.1]). From whom did he hear of it? What purpose does it serve? It has recently been defended on the grounds that it contains good advice on the efficacy of surprise in war, a matter which Thucydides often stressed, sometimes if only to emphasize the failure to use it.[15] But this does

[15] See D. Lateiner, "The Speech of Teutiaplus (Thuc. 3.30)," *GRBS* 16 (1975) 175-184. H.-P. Stahl (*Thukydides Die Stellung des Menschen*

not explain why Thucydides composed this short speech here, in his account of Alcidas' voyage through Ionia. There were many other occasions on which such a speech would have been far more apposite. The same might be said of the following indirect speech of "some exiles from Ionia and the Lesbians who accompanied Alcidas on his voyage." These men recommended to Alcidas that, "since he was afraid of this risk [the suggestion of Teutiaplus], he should take one of the cities in Ionia or Aeolic Cyme, so that, using the city as a base he could bring about the revolt of Ionia [and there was some hope of this, for he had not come against anyone's wishes] and take away this, the greatest Athenian source of revenue; at the same time, if the Athenians should blockade them, that would become expensive for them. And they thought that they could persuade Pissouthnes to join them in the war" (3.31.1). Thucydides says that they did not persuade Alcidas either, for he clung to his own opinion, that, since they were too late for Mytilene, they should return to Peloponnese as soon as possible (31.2).

Alcidas then proceeded along the coast south from Embaton and put in at Myonnesus, where he put to death the many captives whom he had taken on the voyage. When he arrived at Ephesus, some ambassadors came to him from the Samians at Anaeae who gave him yet a third piece of advice: "they said that he was not freeing Greece well if he killed men who neither raised a hand against him nor were his enemies, but were allies of the Athenians by compulsion. And if he did not stop, he would turn few enemies into friends, and would turn many friends into enemies" (3.22.2). Thucydides says that this time Alcidas was persuaded and released whatever Chians he still had and some of the others. He then explains why Alcidas had so many prisoners: "For men, seeing the ships, did not flee, but rather came up to them as if they were Attic vessels,

---

im geschichtlichen Prozess [Munich 1966] 106-109) presents a far better analysis of the purpose of Teutiaplus' speech: it serves to emphasize the fact that Alcidas' mission ended with precisely opposite results from its intentions. Rather than saving the Mytileneans, Alcidas nearly caused their massacre! (see 3.36.2.) This is correct and valuable, but, as we shall show, only part of the story.

and they had not the least expectation that, as long as the Athenians controlled the seas, Peloponnesian ships would ever come to Ionia" (32.3). Alcidas then, when he was seen by some Attic ships, set sail "quickly" (at last!) and took flight: "Fearing pursuit he sailed across the open sea like a man who would not willingly land at any place other than the Peloponnese" (33.1). So ends Thucydides' description of Alcidas' useless and inglorious voyage.

The narrative of 3.29-31.1 is exceptional in Thucydides' history for its bitterly ironic tone and its almost personal attack upon a commander's incompetence, cowardice, and cruelty. The only passages remotely like it involve Cleon, probably a personal enemy of the historian.[16] Thucydides has done his utmost to reveal Alcidas' stupidity and sloth, to emphasize by direct and indirect speeches his sins of omission and of commission. Thucydides' irony builds in intensity until it reaches its climax with the words οὐ καλῶς τὴν Ἑλλάδα ἐλευθεροῦν αὐτόν ("he was not freeing Greece well"), and his personal attack upon Alcidas' character does not end until the final words of the episode, ὡς γῇ ἑκούσιος οὐ σχήσων ἄλλῃ ἢ Πελοποννήσῳ ("like a man who would not willingly land at any place other than the Peloponnese"). Why has Thucydides made such a point of exposing Alcidas' mistakes and, in particular, his missed opportunities?

The answer, I suggest, can be found by comparing Alcidas' inaction in 428-427 with the actions of Alcibiades in 412 at a similar stage in the revolt of Chios. We left the twenty-one Peloponnesian ships which were supposed to sail to Chios on the beach of Speiraeos besieged by an Athenian fleet of thirty-seven triremes. The Chian oligarchs were in serious danger: their intention to revolt was now clearly revealed to the Athenians, and the help promised by the Lacedaemonians, long delayed by Peloponnesian inefficiency and bickering, was now cut off from any opportunity of crossing the Aegean, at least for the foreseeable future. When the news of the disaster at Speiraeos was brought to Sparta, the Lacedaemonians fell into despondency: "They lost heart since they had failed in this,

---

[16] See especially the acerbic irony of 4.27.3-28.5.

their first effort of the Ionian war, and they no longer intended to send the ships from Laconia, but even wanted to recall some which had already set off" (8.11.3).[17] At this point it appeared that Chios would suffer the fate of Lesbos. Just as Alcidas had lost heart for his mission when he heard of the surrender of Mytilene and had determined to return as quickly as possible to Peloponnese, forsaking his allies, so the Lacedaemonians reacted in 412 when they heard the bad news from Speiraeos. All thoughts of Chios were forgotten in the general despondency. The revolt seemed doomed.

Enter Alcibiades, with advice resembling that of Teutiaplus in Book III. In a short indirect speech which Thucydides might have rewritten as a direct speech in a later draft, he urged Endius and the other ephors "not to shrink from [ἀπο-κνῆσαι] the voyage, saying that they could sail in first before the Chians heard of the misfortune of the ships, and when he reached Ionia, he would easily persuade the cities to revolt by citing the weakness of the Athenians and the zeal [!] of the Lacedaemonians. For he would appear more credible than others" (8.12.1). Note especially the similarity of πρὶν τὴν τῶν νεῶν ξυμφορὰν Χίους αἰσθέσθαι to πρὶν ἐκπύστους γενέσθαι in 3.30.1, and of μὴ ἀποκνῆσαι τὸν πλοῦν to μὴ ἀποκνήσωμεν τὸν κίνδυνον in 3.30.4. One might even compare the irony of τὴν τῶν Λακεδαιμονίων προθυμίαν (see ἀθυμήσαντες in 8.11.3) with that of εἴ τις ἄρα ἡμῖν ἐστιν ὑπόλοιπος εὔνους in Teutiaplus' speech (3.30.3). In any event, Alcibiades' advice to the ephors is certainly close to that of Teutiaplus to Alcidas: ignore the recent setback, seize the moment, and take swift and effective action. The only real difference is in the outcome: Alcibiades persuaded the ephors to accept his advice (12.3). We are not told why, at least explicitly, but Thucydides does suggest the reason. Alcibiades added personal incentive to his appeal: "He said to Endius privately that it would be a good thing for him to get the credit for causing the revolt of Ionia and for making the king an ally of the Lacedaemonians, and not to allow this to become Agis' contest [for he, Alcibiades, was a personal enemy of Agis"; 8.12.2]. By a clever

[17] For a possible identification of these ships, see Classen-Steup *Thukydides*, on 8.11.3.

193

stroke Alcibiades fulfilled three parties' aims: the Spartans' desire to help Chios, Endius' wish to get credit for this exploit, and his own plan to prevent Agis from acquiring more prestige. There is little doubt that Endius passed this argument on to the other ephors and that it had a significant impact upon their decision. Thucydides had indicated a few chapters before that Agis was already using his independent and semipermanent position as commander at Decelea to built up considerable personal power and influence (8.5.3). Note in particular the last sentence of that section: "The allies, so to speak, obeyed him [Agis] at this time much more than they did the Lacedaemonians in the city; for having power he was immediately accessible" (8.5.3). No doubt the ephors at Sparta were becoming increasingly jealous of Agis' prestige and concerned with his frequent interventions into policymaking.[18] Alcibiades played upon these concerns with Endius, who used them to persuade the other ephors to send help immediately to Chios. Thus while Teutiaplus had used general arguments of strategy and tactics to try to persuade Alcidas to take action, Alcibiades concentrated on personal matters, his own superior credibility in Ionia and the necessity of preventing Agis from gaining credit the ephors deserved themselves. His success proves the correctness of his approach.

[18] The last couple of instances must have been particularly galling to the ephors. Agis had acquiesced in the Lacedaemonians' desire to send the fleet to Chios before Lesbos, his own preference (8.8.2). But then, when the Corinthians had argued for delay, Agis' offer to take the expedition under his own "private" (ἴδιον in 8.9.1) leadership must have seemed too aggressive to the government at Sparta. That had been avoided because of Corinthian objections, but later, when the expedition did set off, another incident occurred that must have stimulated the ephors' jealousy. They had given orders to Alcamenes, the admiral of the fleet, to notify them when he set off from the isthmus (11.3). When the horseman arrived in Lacedaemon bearing this news, there was great enthusiasm among the ephors (ὡρμημένων αὐτῶν in 11.3), and they prepared to send the five ships from Lacedaemon with Alcibiades and Chalcideus "immediately." But when the news then arrived of the fleet's disastrous encounter with the Athenians, they lost heart. They must also then have heard that Agis had sent an agent named Thermon to Speiraeos to inquire into the situation there. That would have seemed to be an embarrassing interference to the ephors.

Chalcideus and Alcibiades sailed with only five ships from Laconia toward Chios. On their way across the Aegean they too, like Alcidas before them in Ionia, picked up all with whom they met. But Thucydides makes a special point of telling us that they did so for a purpose, "to prevent news of their coming" (14.1), and that they let them go once they had reached the continent. These two pieces of information, as insignificant as they might appear in their context, provide the reader with another point of comparison between the two episodes and accentuate the useless cruelty of Alcidas' capture and murder of men whom he chanced upon on his voyage through Ionia.

Once in Ionia Chalcideus and Alcibiades set about their work with vigor and speed. They met with Chian collaborators who told them to sail unannounced to Chios, which they did, so suddenly in fact that the demos was astounded and panicked at their arrival. The oligarchs were prepared, however: they had arranged for the council to be in session when the ships arrived. When Chalcideus and Alcibiades told the boule that "many other ships were on the way" (8.14.2) and suppressed the news of the defeat at Speiraeos, the Chians and Erythraeans revolted from the Athenians. It is clear that success resulted from the kind of actions recommended by Teutiaplus and spurned by Alcidas: "If we fall upon them suddenly and at night, I expect that, together with those inside the town, if there is anyone still left who is sympathetic to us, we will gain command of the situation" (3.30.3). Alcibiades and Chalcideus have done precisely that. Their sudden arrival startled the potential opposition and renewed the confidence of the oligarchs, who had almost lost hope in the Lacedaemonians and their promises. The revolt swiftly ensued.

Success followed success. Crossing in only three ships to Clazomenae, Alcibiades and Chalcideus brought about a third revolt. Soon the Clazomeneans were busy constructing a fort on the mainland and making preparations for war against Athens (14.3). Such haste was necessary. It was not long before the Athenians heard of the revolt of Chios and took immediate action to deal with this "great and manifest danger"

(15.1). First eight, then twelve ships were sent across the Aegean from their position near Speiraeos, and another thirty were hastily made ready at Peiraeus. But for the time being the Lacedaemonians and Chians controlled the seas in Ionia. Alcibiades made the most of the opportunity. He decided not to wait for additional ships from Peloponnese, but with only the Chians and Chalcideus he determined to cause the revolt of as many cities as possible and thus "to gain credit for the Chians and himself and Chalcideus and, as he had promised, for Endius, who had sent him out" (17.2). With some twenty-five ships he sailed to Miletus, where he had close friends among the political leaders. Barely escaping from the Athenian fleet, which now numbered twenty, he arrived at Miletus just in time to effect its revolt. The Athenians arrived shortly thereafter on the same day, only to be confronted with a fait accompli. When the Milesians did not receive them into the city, they blockaded the city from Lade.

Alcibiades had thus accomplished what "some of the exiles from Ionia and the Lesbians" had urged Alcidas to do in 427, namely, "to take one of the cities in Ionia or Aeolic Cyme so that, using this city as a base, he might cause the revolt of Ionia [and there was reasonable hope of this—for he had come against no one's wishes] and take away this, the greatest source of revenue, from the Athenians, and in addition, cost the Athenians some money if they blockaded them" (3.31.1). One might almost think that Thucydides included these indirect remarks, which Alcidas failed to accept, for the sole purpose of emphasizing that Alcidas here missed an opportunity of which Alcibiades was later to take full advantage. Possibility becomes probability when we read the next sentence in 3.31: "And they thought that they could persuade Pissouthnes [satrap of Lydia] to join the war." Note what Thucydides says in 8.17.4: "And immediately after Miletus revolted the first alliance between the King and the Lacedaemonians was concluded through Tissaphernes [satrap of Lydia] and Chalcideus." Even the consequence of seizing a base in Ionia has been correctly predicted in Book III! The revolt of Miletus leads directly to an alliance with the King, through his Lydian satrap.

It is, I think, readily apparent that Thucydides has written his account in Book III with the events of Book VIII in mind. He has done his utmost to reveal the opportunities missed by Alcidas because they were taken fifteen years later, at a similar point in the second war, by Alcibiades. He has gone out of his way to emphasize Alcidas' incompetence, sloth, and cowardice because those features make such a telling contrast with the efficiency, vigor, and bravery displayed by Alcibiades in a similar mission. He has stressed Alcidas' cruelty by the ironic words he put into the mouths of the Samian ambassadors: "he was not freeing Greece well if he killed men who neither raised a hand against him nor were his enemies. . . . And if he did not stop, he would turn few enemies into friends, and would turn many friends into enemies" (32.2). Alcibiades, on the other hand, proved to be, as he had promised, "πιστότερος than others" in causing the Ionians to accept Sparta's offers to revolt from Athens (8.12.1). We might now make a guess as to who those "others" were: it seems probable that Thucydides had Alcidas principally in mind, though the words refer, on the surface, to other Lacedaemonians in 412.

For these reasons Thucydides took the unusual step of composing in 3.30-31 one direct and one indirect speech that offered advice not taken and wrote a second indirect speech in 3.32 to point out Alcidas' useless, in fact, counterproductive, cruelty. Thucydides wrote these three chapters from the perspective of Alcibiades' exploits in the year 412. They are designed in part to accentuate the shortcomings of Alcidas, an all-too-typical Spartan commander. But their major purpose, I think, is to stress the crucial importance of Alcibiades to Sparta in the second war. Without him, there would have been no Chian revolt, no Erythraean revolt, no Clazomenian revolt, no Teian revolt, no Milesian revolt, and no alliance with Persia. To Thucydides, the matter is as simple as that. After the disaster at Speiraeos the Spartans were despondent. Half of the fleet was grounded on a deserted beach in the Peloponnese and morale was so low that there was talk of burning the ships. Chios and the Aegean were forgotten in the general mood of dismay and apathy. The Spartans were on the point of giving up the war in Ionia. A few days later several major cities in

Ionia were in revolt, Sparta controlled the eastern Aegean, and a vital alliance had been concluded with the King of Persia because one man had sailed with five ships to Ionia—not with forty ships, which Alcidas had commanded, but five. In a matter of days he had turned the war around with those five ships. That, in Thucydides' judgment at least, was the importance of Alcibiades to Sparta.[19] Given this view, it is not hard to understand his extraordinarily high opinion of Alcibiades' military value to Athens (6.15.4).

THE SPARTANS AND THE "FREEDOM OF THE GREEKS"

In chapters 29-60 of Book VIII Thucydides narrates the events of the winter, 412/411. These events are many and varied, and Thucydides' account is correspondingly complex and disjointed. In spite of this disunity, however, we can discern in this narrative one subject or theme of overriding significance: that of the Lacedaemonians' attitude toward the Greeks of the Aegean and of Ionia. This issue dominated the almost constant diplomatic negotiations between the Spartans and Tissaphernes in that winter, as well as the Spartans' own internal disputes and decisions. We can see Thucydides' emphasis upon it in his very structuring of the winter's events. The section ends at chapter 58 with the text of the third and last treaty drawn up between Persia and Sparta, the product of the numerous conferences held in the winter to discuss the rights and duties of the two sides in the Aegean and in Asia. It had begun at chapter 29 with a dispute about how much Tissaphernes was to pay the Peloponnesian fleet and with the text of the second treaty between Persia and Sparta (37). About half of the chapters in this section deal with Spartan-Persian or Spartan-Spartan discussions and debates about the correct treatment of the Ionians. The primary result of the winter's activities was the development of separate Spartan policies toward the Greeks of the Aegean and the Greeks of Asia.

[19] Note R. Meiggs' remark (*The Athenian Empire* [Oxford 1972] 314): "Had Alcidas shown energy and determination Chios, which had the largest fleet after Athens in the Aegean, might have anticipated the course she was to follow in 412."

There is a second, minor theme in chapters 29-60, the origin and early development of Athenian stasis, which Thucydides treats in 47-56. We shall discuss these chapters separately, after first examining the major subject of this section.

The evolution of a Spartan policy toward the eastern Greeks was a slow and painful process. It was closely tied to the issue of Spartan relations with Persia. The Spartans needed Persian money and naval support for their war against Athens. The Persians needed, and demanded in return, Spartan military assistance in regaining the rich cities of Asia and the Aegean from the Athenians, who had gradually taken these cities and their tribute away from the Persian empire in the course of the fifth century. Sparta was thus caught in an extremely difficult and delicate position: in order to obtain the help she needed, she was forced to cede to Persia the very cities that she claimed she had come to the Aegean to liberate from Athens. Furthermore, she needed to maintain her credibility with those same cities, for she encouraged and supported their revolts from Athens, indeed, required their revolts in order to keep Athens' fleet strung out and constantly occupied. But the real problem was caused by the fact that the Persians' demands for territory and the Ionians' claims to liberty conflicted with one another.

This was very nearly the dilemma faced by the Spartans in Boeotia in the summer of 427. After besieging Plataea for over two years, the Spartans and Thebans had forced the starving inhabitants to surrender on the condition that they would have their fate determined by Lacedaemonian judges. Five *dicastai* accordingly came to Plataea to decide how to deal with the two hundred Plataeans and twenty-five Athenians left in the town. Their solution was simplicity itself: ask them individually whether they had done any service for the Lacedaemonians and their allies in the war; if they said no, they would immediately be put to death. When the Plataeans asked to speak more at length in their own defense, the Spartans agreed. A debate between the Plataeans and the Thebans follows, in which the issues at stake are examined and dramatized.

The Plataeans' defense depends upon the distinction that they draw for the Spartans between immediate expediency and long-term (both past and future) justice (3.56.3-7). Immediate expediency means granting a favor to the Plataeans' bitter enemies, the Thebans, because they happen now to be useful allies for the Spartans. But to do this (i.e., to put the Plataeans to death) is to "show yourselves to be not good judges of what is right, but rather men who care for what is expedient. And if they [the Thebans] appear to you to be useful now, how much more were we and the other Greeks then, when you were in greater peril?" (56.3-4). The Plataeans go on to describe their own *arete* in the Persian wars, when they were praised for preferring to "dare the best course with its dangers rather than to do what was expedient and safe" (56.5). And now the Spartans should decide the same kind of case in the same way and "realize that expediency is nothing else but lasting gratitude for good allies combined with some attention to your own immediate interest" (56.7). So much for the contrast between current expediency and historical justice.

In chapter 57 the Plataeans introduce the subject of future justice: "Consider carefully that you are viewed as an exemplum of honor by the Greeks generally. But if you judge us unjustly (for this is not an insignificant case which you are judging, but we are both renowned), take care that men will not think that you, better men though you are, made an unjust decision concerning good men such as us. . . . It will seem terrible if Lacedaemonians sack Plataea." The Plataeans, after recalling their services to Greece in chapter 58, return to the theme of future justice in 59: "It is not for your glory, Lacedaemonians, to offend in this way against the common laws of the Greeks; . . . Fate is unfathomable and may fall upon anyone unjustly." And they conclude: "be our saviors and do not, while freeing the other Greeks, destroy us."

These pleas fell upon deaf ears. After the sophistical and vengeful Theban speech, the five Lacedaemonian judges decided that their earlier decision was the right one. The Plataeans were led out, one by one, asked the single question, and put to death to a man. Thucydides tells us, in no uncertain terms, the basis for this decision: "The Lacedaemonians treated the Plataeans in this way because of the Thebans, whom they considered to be useful for the war currently being waged" (3.68.4). Here Thucydides makes it quite clear that the Spartans preferred immediate expediency to considerations of past or future reputation. The past reputation was that of the Plataeans; the future one was that of the Spartans themselves. By their current action, Thucydides implies, the Spartans heightened the former and diminished the latter. The paradeigma that they established made their claim to be liberators of Greece difficult to maintain, as the Plataeans had warned. Thus were future interests callously, and, we might add, stupidly, sacrificed to immediate expediency. It was not enough to destroy the city of Plataea; the Plataeans themselves must be exterminated to satisfy Theban anger.

It appeared that the Spartans would make the same decision in similar circumstances in the second war. Their first treaty with the King indicates how far they were willing to sacrifice the freedom of Greek cities to the expediency of Persian money and military support. In return for the latter the King acquired the right to "all the territory and cities which he and his ancestors had held" (8.18.1). With one stroke the Spartans had apparently agreed to return to Persian rule the Greek cities of Asia Minor, the Aegean, the Hellespont, Thrace, and Greece north of the Isthmus of Corinth! A high price indeed.

Their actions in the first part of the winter, 412, especially those of the admiral Astyochus, do little to belie this picture of a Sparta ready to sacrifice Greek liberty for Persian support. First, at the instance of Tissaphernes, they attacked Iasus, which housed the satrap's enemy and Athens' friend Amorges. They took it by surprise, pillaged it, thus acquiring considerable booty, and gave it to the Persians to garrison (28). In the following winter Astyochus and Tamus, the hyparch of Ionia, sailed to Clazomenae and ordered the pro-Athenian inhabitants to move to Daphnous and to join the Peloponnesian side. When they refused, the Peloponnesians attacked the city in vain. Delayed by a storm for eight days in the nearby islands, "they plundered and consumed everything which the Clazomenians had stored there" (31.4). Then, when the Chians and their Lacedaemonian commander Pedaritus refused to accept his request to support a second revolt of Lesbos because of the failure of the first, Astyochus "threatened the Chians many times that he would not help them if they needed him."[20] This dissension in the Lacedaemonian command would soon, as we shall see, seriously hurt the Chians' chances of breaking the siege.

In the meantime, while they were enjoying such military and economic success, the Spartans determined to make a more favorable treaty with Tissaphernes because "the first one seemed to be defective and more advantageous to him than to them" (36.2). One thus expects some change in the Lacedaemonian concessions to the King on the question of Greek liberty. Not at all. The King retains his claim to "all the territory and cities that he and his ancestors had held" (37.2), though perhaps not quite so unconditionally as before.[21] The only addition to the treaty of any substance was the clear stipulation (37.4) that the King support the Lacedaemonians financially as long as they were in his land or he had sent for them.[22] Otherwise, the two sides made essentially the same agreement as before. The Greeks of Asia, the Aegean, the Hellespont, Thrace, and the mainland to the Isthmus were still nominally the property of the Persian King.

After the second treaty the dispute between Astyochus and Pedaritus broke out anew. When Astyochus continued to pay no attention to the Chians' requests for help despite their constant defeats at the hands of the Athenians and internal dissension and fears, Pedaritus finally was led to send accusations to Sparta against the Lacedaemonian admiral. The Spartans dispatched in response eleven advisors to Astyochus, of whom one was Lichas, son of Arcesilaus. They were told to act as they

---

[20] See 8.32.3-33.1.

[21] The phrase βασιλέως ἔστω ("let it belong to the King") in the first treaty was changed to "let neither the Lacedaemonians nor their allies go to these cities for war or for any harm, nor let the Lacedaemonians or their allies take tribute from these cities" (37.2).

[22] As Classen-Steup (*Thukydides, ad* 8.37.2) says, "Above all, however, the commitment to the payment of wages . . . was, for the Peloponnesians, a more important addition."

saw fit in the interests of Sparta, not only concerning Astyochus but concerning other matters as well (8.39.2).

These eleven Spartiates, like the five who had been sent as judges to Plataea, were thus put into a position of total authority over a Lacedaemonian affair abroad. The need for better leadership became most apparent while they were en route to Ionia. Astyochus was finally persuaded, against his wishes, by the desperate appeals of the Chians to move his forces from Miletus to Chios. But before he could do so, word reached him of the approach of the eleven Spartan advisors and the fleet of twenty-seven ships from Lacedaemon. Thinking their safety to be his highest priority, he "immediately gave up the voyage to Chios and sailed for Caunus" (8.41.1) to provide a convoy for the approaching fleet. Despite the need for haste, however, Astyochus put in at Cos on the way. The city was unwalled and had just been devastated by an earthquake which was "by far the greatest in living memory" (8.41.2). Astyochus completely sacked the ruined city, whose inhabitants had fled to the mountains, and overran and plundered the countryside, releasing only the free citizens whom he captured.[23] This wanton act reminds us of Thucydides' words in 1.23, where he introduces his subject by saying that this war brought unparalleled suffering to Greece, not only in the destruction of cities but in exiles and murder of men and even in natural disasters, such as earthquakes, which struck more widely and violently than ever before. Thucydides makes it clear that all these afflictions beset Cos in rapid succession, Astyochus adding human violence to the recent natural destruction. These were the men who came to Ionia bringing freedom to the Greeks. The Plataeans had said, "It will seem terrible for the Lacedaemonians to sack Plataea," and "do not, while freeing the other Greeks, destroy us" (3.57.2 and 3.59.4). What was now to become of Ionia? The Spartans seemed intent upon destroying what they did not cede to Persia.

Enter the eleven Spartan commissioners. A conference was

[23] Note the verb ἐκπορθεῖν, used on only one other occasion in Thucydides, the Athenians' savage attack upon Aeginetan Thyrea (3.57.3), one of the most vicious actions of the war.

arranged with Tissaphernes at Cnidus "concerning those things which had already been done, to see if any of them was dissatisfactory, and concerning the war to come, to see in what way it could best and most expediently be waged" (8.43.2). In ξυμφορώτατα we recognize the issue that had concerned the Spartans at Plataea. Would their decision then be repeated now at the expense of the Ionians? The answer would come from the attitude that the commissioners took toward Tissaphernes. How necessary was his assistance?

The Spartan Lichas is singled out among the eleven commissioners with the words μάλιστα δὲ ὁ Λίχας ἐσκόπει τὰ ποιούμενα ("and Lichas especially investigated what had been done") in 43.3. Note that the verb is the same one used by Thucydides to refer to the discussions held by the Athenian oligarchical conspirators concerning Alcibiades' "offer" to bring Persia over to the Athenian side (8.48.3). In both cases Thucydides uses this verb to refer to detailed scrutiny of a particular issue. Did he intend to dramatize these issues in a later draft by means of formal speeches? There follows in indirect discourse a speech of striking force and content: "he said that neither treaty, that of Chalcideus or that of Therimenes, was well constituted; it was terrible if the King should now lay claim to hold sway over the territory which he and his ancestors had ruled. For it would thus be in his power to enslave all the islands again and Thessaly and Locroi and all the land down to Boeotia, and the Lacedaemonians would thus be bestowing upon the Greeks Persian rule instead of freedom. He therefore asked Tissaphernes to make another treaty, or they would certainly not use these former ones, nor did they want any financial support on these conditions" (8.43.3). Here was a vigorous attack upon Spartan policy in the East, delivered by a man who clearly interested Thucydides, as we can see elsewhere in his narrative.[24] There is some reason to suppose that the historian planned to give Lichas a formal speech on this occasion. He tells us that his words greatly angered Tissaphernes who went off "in a rage without having accomplished anything" (43.4). It was no wonder; Lichas had

[24] See especially 8.52, 84.5.

just exposed his treaties for what they were, shabby deals in which both sides bargained with the future of the Greek cities of Ionia and the mainland. In the process, he had enunciated a new principle for Spartan policy, one which the Plataeans had described this way: "realize that expediency is nothing else but lasting gratitude for good allies combined with some attention to your own immediate interest" (3.56.7). Note also the ironic reference of Lichas' words: καὶ τὰ μέχρι Βοιωτῶν, καὶ ἀντ᾿ ἐλευθερίας ἂν Μηδικὴν ἀρχὴν τοῖς Ἕλλησι τοὺς Λακεδαιμονίους περιθεῖναι (8.43.3). The mention of "Boeotians" might remind the reader of the debate at Plataea between Thebans and Plataeans, the words ἀντ᾿ ἐλευθερίας . . . Μηδικὴν ἀρχήν of the Plataeans' appeal on that occasion to their defense of Greek liberty against Persian aggression (see especially 3.54.3 and 58.5). Finally a Spartan had come forward to argue this proposition, to put, that is, the interests of the Greeks on the same level as the interests of the Spartan and Persian states. That Lichas was effective, and indeed, that he convinced his fellow councillors, can be seen in the next sentence: "The Lacedaemonians intended now to sail to Rhodes, whither they had been invited by the leading citizens, hoping to gain a powerful island to their side with many sailors and soldiers; they also thought that with this alliance they would be able to pay for their crews without asking Tissaphernes for money" (44.1). Here was the first instance of Lichas' new policy, a conscious attempt to win back the support of the Ionians lost through Astyochus' cruelty and hostility.[25] It also marked, we might add, a radical change in perspective from that taken by the five Spartan judges at Plataea.

It is possible that Thucydides intended to include here an opposing speech delivered by one of the other councillors or by Tissaphernes himself. The latter is perhaps the more likely candidate, especially in view of Thucydides' introductory words: καὶ πρὸς τὸν Τισσαφέρνην . . . λόγους ἐποιοῦντο οἱ ἕνδεκα ἄνδρες τῶν Λακεδαιμονίων ("the eleven Lacedaemonians held a conversation with Tissaphernes"; 8.43.2). His

[25] Astyochus was later to hire himself out as an informer in the service of Tissaphernes and Alcibiades (50.3).

205

speech on this occasion would have made an effective parallel to that of the Thebans in Book III, and the outcome of the debate would have furnished Thucydides with an opportunity to draw a striking contrast with the result of the debate at Plataea. There, he says, the five Spartan judges had made their decision principally because "they considered the Thebans to be useful for the war currently being waged" (3.68.4). In 412, Lichas and his fellow commissioners, faced with the same kind of choice between short-term expediency and future reputation, had sent Tissaphernes packing: ἀγανακτῶν δὲ ὁ μὲν Τισ-σαφέρνης ἀπεχώρησεν ἀπ᾿ αὐτῶν δι᾿ ὀργῆς καὶ ἄπρακτος ("Tissaphernes, vexed, angry and having accomplished nothing, left them"; 8.43.4).

Lichas' speech was of great significance for two reasons. First, as Thucydides makes clear in 8.52, it "verified" (ἐπηλή-θευσεν) Alcibiades' interpretation of Sparta's intentions in Ionia and thus strengthened his argument that Tissaphernes should, in the long run, favor the Athenians rather than the Peloponnesians. Alcibiades had told Tissaphernes (8.46.3) that the Athenians were "more convenient" partners in empire for the Persians than the Spartans. For the former would be content to enslave the Greeks in the Aegean and leave the Asiatic Greeks to the King, while the Spartans were not likely to free the Greeks from the Athenians only to have them subjugated by the Persians. Tissaphernes should thus try first to wear out both sides, then, if necessary, use the Athenians as allies in order to defeat the dangerous Spartans. Lichas' vehement attack upon Tissaphernes confirmed Alcibiades' prediction and convinced the satrap to initiate a new policy of "hostile neglect" toward the Lacedaemonians, one which Thucydides says was soon to reduce the effectiveness of the Peloponnesian fleet (46.5).[26] Thus one result of Lichas' speech was the alienation

---

[26] The other half of this prediction, that the Athenians were willing to share in the enslavement of the eastern Greeks, was soon borne out by the Athenian oligarchical leaders, who showed themselves willing to give the King "all of Ionia and the islands adjacent to it and other things as well" in return for Persian money (56.4).

of Tissaphernes from the Spartans and the consequent weakening of Persian support for their navy.

The second result was that the Spartans began to assume a more active role in conducting the war in Ionia. Their first attempt to put, Lichas' policy into practice was a complete success: not only did the Peloponnesians cause the successful revolt of Rhodes from Athens, but they collected thirty-two talents from the Rhodians after their secession (8.44.4). Tissaphernes, partly through fear that they might begin to plunder the continent in search of booty and money, made a new treaty (8.59) with the Lacedaemonians that went a long way toward meeting Lichas' objections to the old ones, and toward fulfilling his demands for a more equitable agreement. The principal change in the new treaty is the reduction of the Persians' territorial claims from "all the land and cities ruled by the King and his ancestors" to "the land of the King in Asia," (8.18.1 and 8.37.2; 8.58.2). Though the third treaty also contains new sanctions against Lacedaemonian attacks upon the Asiatic mainland, it is clear that Lichas had gained, at least partially, his major object: the enunciation of a new principle of Spartan foreign policy, the protection of the freedom of the Greeks in the Aegean and in Europe. Lichas adhered to this principle until his death, even when it necessitated clear acknowledgment of the Persian right to rule Greek cities on the mainland. That was a price Lichas was willing to pay, at least until the war was won (see 84.5).

THE REVOLUTIONS: CORCYRA AND ATHENS

In chapters 47-56 of Book VIII Thucydides interrupts his account of Persian-Spartan negotiations to report the origin of the oligarchical conspiracy against Athenian democracy. This section begins with a description of Alcibiades' machinations to return to his native city, a move forced upon him by recent Spartan suspicion of him and even an attempt to have him killed (45.1). Alcibiades based his plans upon a change of government at Athens: if he could use his close association with

Tissaphernes to convince aristocratic leaders of his power, then he hoped to return to Athens at the head of an oligarchical faction that would overthrow the democracy which had exiled him. With this scheme in mind he sent word to the most powerful men in the Athenian force at Samos "to remind the aristocrats about himself, that he wished to return under an oligarchy, not the mob rule and democracy which had driven him out, and that he would make Tissaphernes their friend and ally" (47.2). A group of these men were interested enough in Alcibiades' message to cross from Samos and hold discussions with him on the continent. There he assured them that he could make first Tissaphernes and then the King himself their ally if only the democracy were removed and credibility were thus established with the King. The leaders returned to Samos where they established a conspiracy of like-minded aristocrats and even proclaimed openly in camp that if the democracy were removed in the city, the Athenians could count on the King as an ally and paymaster for the war against Sparta. The democrats at Samos, though irked at these proposals, were nonetheless quiet because of their hope of tapping the King's money, now desperately needed for the fleet. The conspirators, having thus broached the subject of a change of government and having found no substantial opposition, then held another meeting among themselves, with the majority of the members present, and "examined carefully ($\dot{\epsilon}\sigma\kappa\acute{o}\pi\sigma\nu\nu$) the proposals of Alcibiades" (48.3).

This private discussion among prominent Athenian oligarchs produced frank and intriguing disagreement. Thucydides tells us that Alcibiades' proposals appeared advantageous and trustworthy to the others, but not to Phrynichus, one of the generals. He then reports (48.4-7), in indirect discourse, Phrynichus' objections, which include not only correct and perceptive remarks about Alcibiades' motives in urging a change in government, but also a penetrating and candid analysis of the attitude of Athens' allies toward Athenian democrats and oligarchs, particularly the latter. This speech, which we shall presently examine in detail, failed to convince the conspirators, who went ahead with their plans. Peisander and others were sent to Athens to introduce the matter of Alcibiades' return and alliance with Tissaphernes to the assembly. There follows (50-51) a dramatic account of Phrynichus' attempts to discredit Alcibiades with the Spartans, Alcibiades' counterattempts to discredit Phrynichus with the Athenians, and Phrynichus' close brush with death. Thucydides reports Peisander's proposals to the Athenian assembly, his successful attack upon Phrynichus, whom he brands a traitor, and his widening of the conspiracy to include the aristocratic clubs in Athens.

An examination of Phrynichus' indirect speech reveals three major attacks upon the arguments presented by the conspirators for accepting Alcibiades' proposals. First, he exposes Alcibiades as a man who cared nothing for oligarchy or democracy, but only for his own interests, in this case his reestablishment, through associates, in his native city. Rather than involving themselves with Alcibiades, a dangerous ally, they should make it their major concern to avoid stasis, which would work only in Alcibiades' favor. Second, Phrynichus casts doubt upon the proposition that the King would transfer allegiance from the powerful Spartans, of whom he had nothing to complain, to the Athenians. This argument countered the assumption that the Athenians could expect Persian money if they changed government. The third and most fully developed line of attack in Phrynichus' speech is worth quoting in full:

He said he knew well that of the allied cities to which they promised oligarchy, since they themselves would not have a democracy, the ones in revolt would not come over more quickly nor would the ones that remained be more secure. For they did not want to be subjects with oligarchy or democracy, but with whichever of these they got to be free. They believed that the so-called aristocrats gave them no less trouble than the demos, since they were the proposers and supporters of evil motions to the demos, from which the aristocrats themselves for the most part benefited. If it were up to them, the allies would perish, without trial and more violently, while the demos was their refuge and the aristocrats' governor. And he knew positively that the cities thought in this way, knowing things as they did from actual experiences. (8.48.5-7)

These remarks remind us of the debate between Cleon and Diodotus on the fate of Mytilene, and particularly of Diodotus' remarks in 3.47. But note how the perspective has changed. While Diodotus was concerned with the question of how the Athenians should regard the *oligoi* and the demos in the allied cities, Phrynicus is interested in how the allied cities view the *oligoi* and the demos of Athens. Just as Diodotus had argued then that the demos in the allied cities was the real friend and supporter of the Athenians, especially when their oligarchs revolted, so now Phrynichus argues that, so far as the allies are concerned, the Athenian demos is their refuge in times of trouble, and their safeguard against the oppressive aristocracy.

That Thucydides agreed with most of Phrynichus' points we can see from the text itself. He expresses his approval of his attack upon Alcibiades with the parenthetical and unusually revealing phrase ὅπερ καὶ ἦν in 48.4: "Alcibiades, Phrynichus thought [and he was certainly correct], cared nothing for oligarchy or democracy." Even more importantly, Thucydides only a few chapters later renders precisely the same verdict on the allies' attitude toward Athenian politics that Phrynichus gave in 48.5. In chapter 64 Thucydides describes the events at Thasos during the following summer. Peisander and his fellow-conspirators, on their way to Athens to overthrow the democracy, stop at Thasos and end democratic government there, hoping thus to win the Thasians' support for their enterprise. But in the second month after their departure the Thasians "fortified the city, since they had no more need of aristocracy with the Athenians, and were expectant, daily, of freedom from the Spartans" (64.3). Affairs then turned out for them exactly as they wished: the city was reformed without danger and the demos which would have opposed this change was abolished. Thucydides comments, "Thus events in Thasos and, it seems to me, in many other subject states as well, occurred contrary to the expectations of the Athenian oligarchs.

For the cities, as soon as they got a moderate government and liberty of action, went on to absolute freedom rather than preferring halfway reform from the Athenians" (8.64.5). Not only did events completely corroborate Phrynichus' analysis, but Thucydides expressly repeats that analysis himself. Thucydides clearly found Phrynichus' remarks to the conspirators percipient. Did he intend to raise them to the level of a direct speech in a final draft? We cannot be certain, but we can say, based upon Thucydides' description in 8.50-51, that the historian was much interested in and informed about the battle of intrigue waged between Alcibiades and Phrynichus.

Thucydides' account of the stasis at Athens follows this portrayal of the inception of the oligarchical conspiracy. It is clear that he went out of his way to present, as far as he could, the revolution in a single, unified account, just as he had done with the stasis at Corcyra at a similar point in Book III. In both Books III and VIII he delayed the narratives of the staseis: in III he waits until he has completed the account of the end of Plataea before treating events at Corcyra (see Oἱ γὰρ Κερκυραῖοι ἐστασίαζον in 70.1); in VIII he postpones discussion of the early events leading to the fall of democracy at Athens until he can treat the entire subject in a continuous narrative. (See ὑπὸ γὰρ τοῦτον τὸν χρόνον καὶ ἔτι πρότερον ἡ ἐν ταῖς Ἀθήναις δημοκρατία κατελέλυτο ["at this time *and even before* the democracy at Athens was dissolved"] my italics, in 63.3.) Though he cannot completely finish his narrative of the Corcyraean revolution until 4.48, because the last oligarchical opposition was not extinguished for two years, and though he treats the beginnings of the Athenian oligarchical conspiracy a few chapters before the main narrative in 63-98, because the initial developments occurred at Samos in the preceding winter, it is clear that Thucydides did his best to make his accounts of these two revolutions stand out as dramatically unified and independent pieces of narrative. They are the only such descriptions of stasis in his *History* as we have it, though we know from his own words that almost every city in Greece was convulsed by revolution during the course of this war (see 3.82.1-3). Why select these two, only these two, for such special treatment?

One reason is certainly their significance for the war as a whole. Civil strife and disunity were, Thucydides tells us (2.65.12), the principal factors leading to Athens' defeat in the war, while the stasis at Corcyra effectively removed from Athenian power a sizable fleet, one in fact that had been instrumental in convincing the Athenians to embark upon the war (1.44.2). Secondly, both revolutions were extraordinarily intense: the Corcyraean one did not end until, as Thucydides stresses (4.48.5), one side was virtually exterminated; the Athenian one resulted in the city's being split, quite literally, between the democrats at Samos and the oligarchs in control at Athens, an almost fatal division that resulted in the loss of Euboea and near-capitulation to Sparta. Thirdly, it appears that Thucydides took the trouble to describe in detail the developments at Corcyra and to make at this point in his narrative general remarks on the course of stasis in the cities of Greece because Corcyra was the first of the revolutions that occurred during the war (3.82.1). It could thus be used as an exemplum of stasis generally. That this was one of Thucydides' major reasons for emphasizing the stasis at Corcyra is clear from 3.82.3-83, a passage almost unique in the entire work for its paradigmatic quality. These chapters were designed to serve as a description of stasis in the abstract, stasis per se; they serve as an analysis that can safely be applied to the other staseis which occurred during the war as well. Thucydides says as much in 82.2, though he allows for divergences from the norm depending on local circumstances. But even these are differences of degree, not differences in kind.

It is this third function, the paradigmatic, of Thucydides' account of stasis at Corcyra, that stands out for the reader as its most important and remarkable aspect. He tells the reader that in later revolutions factions refined the methods of attack and reprisal, basing their improvements upon what they learned from earlier cases (82.3). Thus not only did he consider Corcyra an exemplum, but so did other Greek cities beset by revolution. The result was that as the war progressed

Greece experienced a whole series of staseis in which factional leaders developed more and more sophisticated methods of revolutionary action. Hellas became a school for revolution.

The culmination of these revolutions was the oligarchic coup at Athens in the summer of 411. Thucydides emphasizes that it was planned and carried out by exceptionally clever and capable men (8.68.1-4). Plans were carefully made, trustworthy associates were chosen, military precautions were taken. But the basis of success was the slow and subtle takeover of the demos and its governmental organs by the conspirators. In this respect, the Athenian oligarchic coup was the exact antithesis of the attempted oligarchic takeover at Corcyra. Both revolutions were instigated by oligarchs returning to their city with plans for an overthrow of the ruling democracy (see 3.70.1). But in Corcyra the aristocratic conspirators, after the failure of their initial plans, burst suddenly into the boule bearing daggers, killed the leader of the demos and the bouleutai, even some private citizens nearby, and then tried to force the assembly to obey their will.[27] The Athenian conspirators, on the other hand, after elaborate preparations and precautions, supplanted the boule so quietly that they did not even need to use the swords they had hidden on their persons or the bodyguard they had assembled in case of violence.[28] Their manipulation of the assembly was even more brilliant: they used perfectly legal and open methods to destroy the constitution and to form a new government.[29] Only after they were in total control of the city did they "kill a few men, whom they thought they should remove, and arrest others, and banish others" (70.2). Every step was taken with a purpose and a consideration of its consequences. With such intelligent leadership, says Thucydides, "it was no wonder that the enterprise, though large, went forward. For it was a difficult thing to bring to an end the freedom of the Athenian demos 100 years after the tyrants were overthrown, a demos which was not only no subject-slave itself, but for over half that period

[27] See 3.70.3-5 and 3.70.6-71.1.

[28] 8.69.1-70.1.

[29] 8.67.

213

had grown accustomed to ruling others" (8.68.4). The conspiracy succeeded completely in attaining its initial objects, the dissolution of Athenian democracy and the establishment of an oligarchical government to take its place. It failed to hold its position primarily because of internal jealousy, "in which," says Thucydides, "oligarchy emerging from democracy is often destroyed" (8.89.3). The Corcyraean oligarchs, on the other hand, overplayed their hand from the first, resorted to senseless violence, and were driven from the city within days and exterminated in two years.

Thus the two accounts of stasis in Thucydides' *History* stand as portraits of the two extremes of civil war, one naive and uncontrolled, the other cunning and carefully contrived. They characterize, in their paradigmatic aspects, a whole process that Thucydides tells us was spawned and nurtured by the war, the progress of revolution from one Greek city to another. Thucydides gives us a case history of the first, accompanied by a systematic diagnosis, and a lengthy and detailed description of one of the last and most complex. That is all we need to fill out the picture. We have the two ends of the process and the mechanism that dictated its growth: "There were revolutions in the cities, and the ones that came later, through their knowledge of the earlier ones, carried substantially forward the novelty of their plans, in both the intricacy of their attacks and the extraordinary nature of their reprisals" (3.82.3).

The last well-defined sections of Books III and VIII deal respectively with the campaigns in northwest Greece and the naval battles in the Hellespont. Thucydides devotes the bulk of his narrative of the sixth year of the war (3.89-116) to Demosthenes' campaigns in Aetolia and Acarnania (94-98, 100-103, 105-114). The major subject of his truncated account of the summer of 411 (8.99-109) is the naval fighting in the Hellespont (99-107), which continued through the remainder of the year (Xenophon, *Hellenica*, 1.1.1-8) and ended with the Athenian victory at Abydus. Both sections describe the first fighting in new theaters of the war, areas where radically different types of warfare from those hitherto practiced were developed: guerilla fighting in Aetolia and Acarnania, combined land and sea fighting in the narrow channel of the Hellespont. In the former, Demosthenes learned through a costly defeat and a stunning victory the value of using light-armed troops against hoplites in difficult terrain, a lesson which he was to put to good use in the following year at Pylos; in the latter Alcibiades learned the necessity of following up a naval victory in the straits with an assault upon the enemy's position on land, a lesson which he applied with brilliant results the next summer at Cyzicus.[30]

[30] Compare 3.98 and 106-114.1 with 4.29-33, especially 30.1, for the lessons that Demosthenes learns, and Xenophon, *Hellenica* 1.1.5-7 with 13-23, especially 14, for Alcibiades' learning through experience.

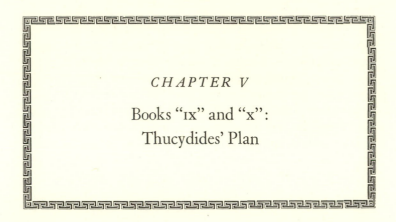

CHAPTER V

Books "ix" and "x":
Thucydides' Plan

If we were on difficult ground in the last chapter in dealing with Book VIII of Thucydides, the terrain becomes far more treacherous in the present chapter which tries to assess the projected shape of the *History*'s conclusion, the account of the last six years of the Peloponnesian War. That Thucydides did intend to complete his *History* of the war is, I think, indisputable: "The same Thucydides the Athenian has composed[1] also these things successively, as each event occurred, by summers and winters, until the Lacedaemonians and their allies ended the empire of the Athenians and tore down the long walls and the Peiraeus. To this point the war, taken as a whole, lasted twenty-seven years" (5.26.1). But Thucydides failed, for whatever reason, to finish his account, and we are left with a truncated work.[2] It is, of course, impossible, and indeed profitless, to attempt to reconstruct the last part of Thucydides' *History*. Such is not the aim of this chapter. It is, however, quite useful, in accordance with the general argument of this book, to see whether or not Thucydides' narrative of the concluding years of the first ten-year war is in any way influenced by the

[1] The perfect tense does not necessarily mean that when Thucydides wrote these words he had already finished his account of the war. Much less do I think that this sentence is an interpolation and that 5.1-83 was put together by Xenophon (see L. Canfora, *Tucidide Continuato* [Padova] 1970).

[2] The so-called "evidence" from antiquity on Thucydides' death is worthless and speculation is futile.

final events of the second ten-year war. To answer this question we have to compare two kinds of evidence, that furnished by other ancient sources on the last years of the Peloponnesian War, and that which we have in Books IV and V of Thucydides. Since our knowledge of the end of the war, gained primarily from Xenophon and Diodorus, is sketchy and in many cases unreliable, this comparison must be made on only the broadest lines. It seems, nonetheless, to be well worth making. For, if we can find evidence that Thucydides shaped Books IV and V to some degree in accord with the events of 410-404, then we shall have strengthened our case that he saw the two ten-year wars as parallel conflicts offering opportunities for meaningful comparison and contrast. In addition, we might thereby be enabled to hazard one or two conjectures about Thucydides' plan for the conclusion of his *History*.

In this study we shall concentrate upon several major episodes of Books IV and V that seem to offer points of comparison with events of the years 410-404: the conflict at Pylos (4.2-41); Brasidas' campaigns in Thrace (4.78-135); and the Melian dialogue (5.84-116).[3] In each of these episodes we have enough material to ascertain Thucydides' point of view, that is, his attitude toward the major figures involved and his intention in portraying the episode in a dramatic manner. We shall examine each of these three sections of narrative from the perspective of the last years of the second ten-year war in order to see what the latter might have to tell us about Thucydides' treatment of events in Books IV and V.

SPARTAN PEACE OFFERS: PYLOS AND CYZICUS

Our comparison of Thucydides' treatments of the two ten-year wars has taken us to the end of Books III and VIII, which deal with, respectively, the last events of 426/425 and of 411/410.[4]

---

[3] The reasons for treating here the Melian dialogue, which does not appear in the first ten-year war, but in the seven years of uneasy peace, are explained on pp. 247-249.

[4] In Book VIII Thucydides did not quite complete his account of the fourth year of the second ten-year war. He would have gone on to

Book IV begins with a lengthy account of the campaign at Pylos, which takes up most of its first 41 chapters. "Book IX," had it been written by Thucydides, would have commenced with a narrative of the first significant encounter of the year 410/409, the Battle of Cyzicus. Like Pylos, Cyzicus was a critical Athenian victory. There are several notable similarities between these two campaigns: both were combined sea and land operations in which the Athenians captured sixty Peloponnesian vessels, virtually the entire navy of their opponents; both defeats shocked the Spartans so gravely that they sent embassies to Athens asking for peace; both offers were turned down by the Athenians, who were persuaded to reject them by the leading demagogues of their day, Cleon in 425 and Cleophon in 410. Occurring, as they did, at similar points in Thucydides' narrative of the two ten-year wars, there is reason to think that the historian might have treated them as parallel events. Let us first examine the extant sources for Cyzicus to ascertain, as precisely as possible, what happened during and after the battle, before reviewing Thucydides' treatment of the campaign at Pylos and its aftermath. Then we shall be in a position to assess what he might have planned to do with the events of 410.

Our main sources for Cyzicus are Xenophon, Plutarch, and Diodorus. In the spring of 410, according to Xenophon's account (*Hellenica* 1.1.11-18), Alcibiades, after escaping from Tissaphernes, joined the Athenian fleet at Cardia, to which it had been forced to retire because of the threat of attack from Mindarus' sixty ships in the Hellespont. The Athenian fleet was numerically inferior because contingents had been sent in the preceding winter throughout the Aegean to collect money; only forty ships had been left in the Hellespont (1.1.8). After he learned at Cardia that Mindarus had moved his fleet from Abydus to Cyzicus, Alcibiades went by land to Sestus and ordered the Athenian fleet to join him there. After it arrived,

---

describe the Battle of Abydus, which occurred in the fall of 411, had he finished that year's narrative (See Xenophon, *Hellenica* 1.1.2-7), as well as the escapades of Alcibiades in the following winter (*Hellenica* 1.1.9-10).

Alcibiades, according to Xenophon (*Hellenica* 1.1.12), was already on the point of leaving to attack Mindarus when Theramenes and Thrasybulus, both of whom had been collecting money, arrived with twenty ships each from Macedonia and Thasos respectively. We may doubt Xenophon's claim that Alcibiades intended with forty-six ships to seek a sea battle against Mindarus' sixty, especially since Diodorus (Ephorus) gives us a seemingly more plausible version.[5] According to his account (13.49), the Athenians at Cardia, in fear of attack from Mindarus, sent word to Thrasybulus, Theramenes, and Alcibiades to join them as soon as possible. Then, when the whole fleet was gathered together at Cardia, the generals became eager for a decisive battle and determined to sail to Cyzicus, which Mindarus was besieging with the help of Pharnabazus and his large army.

Despite the apparently greater probability of Diodorus' version, we cannot summarily reject Xenophon's account. His explicit remark that Alcibiades intended to seek battle with Mindarus before the other forty ships arrived may have been based on solid evidence. Otherwise, why would he make such a statement? Xenophon knew, after all, and reported that Thrasybulus and Theramenes did, in fact, join Alcibiades with their forty ships in time for the battle. He could have omitted the remark altogether. It seems probable that he had the information on good authority and recorded it with confidence in its veracity. I agree, then, with Busolt against Grote, that it was Alcibiades' plan to attack Mindarus' fleet of sixty ships with only forty-six of his own.[6] Why he intended to do so, Xenophon does not tell us, but we may venture a guess. When he joined the Athenian fleet at Cardia, Alcibiades desperately needed to demonstrate to the Athenians his value as a general.

---

[5] There were forty ships at Cardia when Alcibiades arrived with "five triremes and a light vessel." Since the whole fleet, after Thrasybulus and Theramenes added their forty vessels, is said by Xenophon to have numbered eighty-six ships (1.1.13), we must assume that Xenophon counted the "light vessel" in the number of fighting ships.

[6] G. Busolt, *Griechische Geschichte bis zur Schlacht bei Chaeroneia* (Gotha 1893-1904) 3: ii, 1526, n. 3. Hereafter cited as Busolt, *Gr. Ges.* George Grote, *A History of Greece* 12 vols. (London 1869) 7:3.

He had just failed in his (clearly final) attempt to deliver his promised Persian money and support to Athens. It was this hope, indeed expectation, that had induced the Athenians to restore him from exile and to elect him general. When Tissaphernes threw him into prison on his arrival in the preceding winter, Alcibiades knew that that game was up. When he escaped from Tissaphernes, he recognized, and so did the army, that his promises of Persian aid could not be kept. His enemies at Athens, still numerous and influential, would soon begin to make trouble for him. The only means of forestalling political pressure was military success. Alcibiades needed a victory, and quickly, to secure his position with the Athenians.[7]

When the other two generals arrived with their fleets, Alcibiades ordered them to follow him up the Hellespont in battle-readiness. The combined fleet of eighty-six ships, sailing at night to avoid being seen, reached the island of Proconnesus early in the morning. There they learned that Mindarus and Pharnabazus were already in Cyzicus.[8] Alcibiades let his rowers rest for a day while detaining all ships, large and small, which came to the island, and forbidding, on penalty of death, all ships on the island to cross to the mainland. The number of Athenian ships must not be divulged to Mindarus, who, if he was to be lured into engaging at sea, must remain ignorant of Athenian superiority in numbers. The following day Alcibiades held a meeting of his troops in which he told them "that it was necessary to fight on sea, on land, and against fortifications;[9] for, he said, they had no money, while the enemy had

[7] Busolt, *Gr. Ges.* 3: ii, 1526.

[8] The city had evidently been taken without a struggle. It was, as Thucydides (8.107) says, unwalled, and probably put up no resistance to Mindarus' large fleet and Pharnabazus' army. Diodorus' (Ephorus') account of a siege (13.49.4) is exposed by Busolt (*Gr. Ges.* 3: ii, 1527, n. 1) as fabrication.

[9] What Alcibiades can mean by τειχομαχεῖν is not immediately clear, since Cyzicus was, according to Thucydides (8.107.1), unwalled at this time. In all likelihood, the Spartans, together with Pharnabazus, had begun building a bulwark after taking the city shortly before Alcibiades' arrival. Alcibiades thus warned his men that they would be

as much as he wanted from the King" (*Hellenica* 1.1.14). Alcibiades, in other words, sought a decisive victory at all costs, even if it meant landing, fighting on foot against Peloponnesian and Persian soldiers, and attacking fortifications. The Athenians' financial position had now necessitated risk taking. So, we might add, had Alcibiades' precarious political position.

After the assembly the fleet set out for Cyzicus in a heavy rain. A less enterprising commander might have delayed his attack, but Alcibiades used the fortuitous storm for cover: Mindarus would not know of the size or approach of the Athenian fleet until the last possible moment. When the fleet was close to Cyzicus, the storm lifted and Alcibiades saw the enemy's vessels practicing maneuvers so far out from the harbor that they were cut off from retreat by the rapidly advancing Athenian fleet. The surprise was complete. The Peloponnesians did not even try to put up a fight at sea but fled to the nearest unprotected shore, where they anchored their ships next to one another and prepared to oppose the Athenians. Alcibiades landed with twenty ships and defeated the hastily organized enemy. The Lacedaemonian commander was killed and his men were driven into flight. The Athenians captured the entire Peloponnesian fleet, except for the Syracusan contingent that was burned by its own sailors, and took it back to Proconnesus. In a matter of hours the Peloponnesians had lost sixty ships, their high admiral, and control of the Hellespont. Cyzicus was evacuated by Pharnabazus and the remaining Peloponnesians. The famous dispatch sent by Mindarus' secretary to Sparta, but intercepted by the Athenians, sums up the battle with Spartan succinctness: "Ships lost, Mindarus dead, men starving, we know not what to do." The defeat was nearly total (*Hellenica* 1.1.23).

Such is Xenophon's account of the Battle of Cyzicus. His only remarks following the narrative of the battle itself concern the help given by Pharnabazus to the defeated Peloponnesians, whom he fed and clothed for two months while he be-

---

called upon to make an assault upon the fortified Peloponnesian position even after landing and fighting on shore.

gan construction of a new fleet. Xenophon says nothing about the effects of the defeat upon the government at Sparta. Our evidence for the Lacedaemonian offer of peace following the battle and its rejection by the Athenians comes mainly from Diodorus 13.52-53. Though his (Ephorus') testimony is generally not to be preferred to that of Xenophon, there are two reasons why, in this case, we should treat his evidence more confidently.[10] First, Diodorus' report of a Spartan embassy to Athens contradicts nothing in Xenophon. The fact that the embassy's request was refused may have led Xenophon to omit the incident altogether. His silence should not be used to discredit the historicity of the offer.

Secondly, and much more significantly, Diodorus' report is corroborated by a fragment of Philochorus and by several other ancient sources.[11] According to Philochorus, the Lacedaemonians sent an embassy to Athens in the archonship of Theopompus (411/410) offering peace, which the Athenians, "distrusting" (ἀπιστήσαντες), did not accept. The second part of the fragment (139b) informs us that it was Cleophon who prevented peace with the Lacedaemonians in that year. Philochorus has the date right, against Diodorus, who put the Battle of Cyzicus and the Spartan offer of peace in the archonship of Glaucippus (410/409). The battle, as Xenophon's account implies, occurred in February or March of 410, and the Spartan embassy came to Athens shortly thereafter, probably in April.[12] In other respects, Philochorus confirms the basic outline drawn by Diodorus: the Athenians, led by Cleophon,

[10] Diodorus' account of the battle differs widely from, and adds substantially to, the picture of the battle drawn by Xenophon. The details that he reports are characterized by Busolt (*Gr. Ges.* 3: ii, 1527, n. 2) as "ein wertloses Phantasiestuck des Ephoros" and I have not thought it worthwhile to record them.

[11] F. Jacoby *Die Fragmente der Griechischen Historiker* (Berlin and Leiden 1923-   ) 328F139, actually two fragments, reports schol. Eur. *Orestes* 371 and 772. Hereafter cited as *FGrHist*. Nepos *Alcibiades* 5.5, Justin V, 4, and Aelius Aristeides, *Panathenaicus* p. 265 Dindorf are derivative and therefore of less value.

[12] Busolt, *Gr. Ges.* 3: ii, 1527, n. 2, and 1534, n. 5.

rejected an offer of peace brought by a Spartan embassy to Athens.[13]

We may thus be rather confident that, following their stunning defeat at Cyzicus in 410, the Spartans decided to ask the Athenians for peace and that Cleophon led a successful opposition to its acceptance. The details of Diodorus' picture, however, require further examination because, while they may be historically unreliable, they are nonetheless historiographically pertinent to our discussion of Thucydides' treatment of Pylos. According to Diodorus, the leader of the Spartan embassy was Endius. This family friend of Alcibiades (Thucydides 8.6.3) had served on a similar embassy once before. In the summer of 420, when the Spartans feared that Athens was about to make an alliance with Argos, they had hurriedly sent three ambassadors "who seemed to be well-disposed towards the Athenians"

[13] Cleophon's opposition to peace became a favorite motif among later ancient historians and orators, who assigned the stories of his ragings against peace to various dates and occasions: Aristotle, *Athēnaiōn Politeia* 34.1, has Cleophon, appearing drunk and corseleted in the assembly, reject peace overtures following Arginusae in 406, while Aeschines (2.76) and Lysias (13.7, 8, 12; 30.10) put his strenuous opposition to surrender in 405, following Aegospotami. The similarity of these episodes has led one scholar to call the story a "Wanderanekdote" (A. v. Mess, *Rhein. Mus.* 66 [1911] 379). But there is no such scandalous conduct attached to Cleophon's opposition to peace in 410 in Diodorus' or Philochorus' account, and thus no reason to reject its historicity on that basis. If any such incident should be suspect on these grounds, it is the *Ath. Pol.'s* placing of the story after Arginusae, when a Spartan peace offer seems illogical. See Jacoby *FGrHist* IIIbI p. 510 with IIIbII p. 410, 139 n. 3, and Grote, *History of Greece*, 8: 1, n. 1. That Cleophon engaged in bitter political struggles over Spartan peace proposals in 405 is, on the other hand, quite credible. After Aegospotami the mood at Athens was one of fear and frenzy, and there was a serious split between those who wanted peace at any cost and those who resisted surrender. The details in Lysias inspire confidence. That Cleophon opposed peace in 410, and strenuously opposed surrender in 405 is perfectly logical and consistent with our evidence and with probability. There is no need to exclude two of the three occasions, as, for example, J. Day and M. Chambers (*Aristotle's History of Athenian Democracy* [Berkeley 1962] 149) suggest. See Busolt, *Gr. Ges.* 3: ii 1535 n. 1 for discussion and bibliography.

(δοκοῦντες ἐπιτήδειοι εἶναι τοῖς Ἀθηναίοις) to Athens to prevent the alliance from being made. Endius was one of the three Spartans entrusted with that delicate mission.[14] It is quite possible that Diodorus' report that Endius led the embassy sent to Athens after Cyzicus is correct. Diodorus gives us his speech to the assembly. Its main points are: the Spartans offer peace based on the status quo; the war is far more harmful to Athens than to Sparta, since the Athenians suffer more, risk more and have inferior prospects for victory; though the Spartans are in a far better position for the war, they are still eager to end it because of the miseries that it entails for everyone.

Diodorus tells us that, following the speech, the "most reasonable" (ἐπιεικέστατοι) Athenians inclined toward peace, but that those who fomented war and derived private gain from it chose war. The latter were supported by Cleophon, "the leading demagogue of that day," (μέγιστος ὢν τότε δημαγωγός; 13.53.1-2). Speaking at length in his own fashion he buoyed up the demos by pointing to their great military victories and thus deceived them by his flattery. The Athenians, elated by their successes and putting great hopes in Alcibiades as leader of their forces, rejected the peace offer and thus committed, according to Diodorus, a blunder that they later regretted but could never overcome.

The similarity of Diodorus' (Ephorus') account of these events to Thucydides' description of the Athenian assembly in 425 (4.17-22) requires no emphasis. Thucydides too recorded the speech of the Spartan embassy, described the leader of the anti-peace forces, Cleon, in unfavorable terms (ἀνὴρ δημαγωγὸς κατ' ἐκεῖνον τὸν χρόνον ὢν καὶ τῷ πλήθει πιθανώτατος ["a demagogue at that time and most persuasive with the lower classes"]; 21.3), and portrayed the demos as elated by its present good fortune and hopeful for more conquests.[15] It is

---

[14] Thucydides 5.44.3. It appears likely that Endius was eponymous ephor in 404, the year of Athens' surrender. See Dindorf's plausible conjecture of Ἐνδίου for Εὐδίου in *Hellenica* 2.3.1 (and 10).

[15] See 4.21.2, especially the phrase τοῦ δὲ πλέονος ὠρέγοντο. Compare also Thucydides' use of the phrase τοῖς σώφροσι τῶν ἀνθρώπων to describe Cleon's enemies a few chapters later (4.28.5) with Diodorus' οἱ ἐπιεικέστατοι τῶν Ἀθηναίων (13.53.1) for the opponents of Cleophon.

possible that Ephorus modelled his picture of the assembly in 410 on Thucydides' account of the assembly of 425. They were, after all, extraordinarily similar occasions, even to the extent of the nearly identical names of the two demagogic leaders. Reality has made artistic comparison inevitable.

Indeed, when we review the parallels between Pylos and Cyzicus, we find that they are remarkably numerous. Both campaigns were planned by irregularly appointed Athenian commanders who had recently lost favor with the people and were trying to regain their prestige with ambitious, seemingly foolhardy enterprises. After his disaster in Aetolia in 426 Demosthenes had been afraid to return home to face the Athenians and had done so only after winning an overwhelming victory in Acarnania.[16] When he formed and put into practice his plan of fortifying Pylos, he was a private citizen acting under special orders from the assembly.[17] His idea of building a fort at a deserted rock in the Peloponnese was considered by the generals who accompanied him, Eurymedon and Sophocles, to be pointless (4.3.3). Similarly, Alcibiades was in a most unusual position when he planned an attack upon Mindarus in the early spring of 410. Though he had been restored to citizenship after his exile and elected general (but only by the Athenians in the fleet at Samos, not by those in the city), he still did not feel confident enough to return to Athens. He had in the previous year been in large part responsible for the Athenian naval victory at Abydus, but his failure to bring Tissaphernes over to the Athenian side meant that he needed still more striking successes to insure a return to favor with the Athenian populace. His plan to attack Mindarus' sixty ships with only forty-six of his own perhaps reveals his desire for a stunning victory.

Both Demosthenes and Alcibiades were joined by two other

[16] See Thucydides 3.98.5 and 114.1.

[17] See Thucydides 4.2.4. For Demosthenes' position, which is not precisely clear, see A. W. Gomme, A. Andrewes, and K. J. Dover, A Historical Commentary on Thucydides (Oxford 1945-1970) on 4.2.4 and 29.1. Hereafter cited as Comm. Whatever the reasons, he seems to have been without office when the campaign began, but a general by the middle of the campaign.

commanders (Sophocles and Eurymedon, and Theramenes and Thrasybulus, respectively) before fighting the major battle of the campaign. Both commanders' plans were aided by fortuitous natural phenomena: a storm forced the Athenian fleet, on its way to Corcyra and Sicily, to put in at Pylos, where Demosthenes wanted to build a fort; a calm of several days then induced the sailors to construct a fort, which Sophocles and Eurymedon had not wanted to build. In 410, a heavy rainstorm concealed the Athenian fleet's movements until the very last moment before its arrival at Cyzicus, thus insuring complete surprise of Mindarus' fleet. Both battles involved a combination of sea and land fighting, and both resulted in devastating Peloponnesian defeats in which sixty ships, virtually the entire Spartan navy on each occasion, were captured or destroyed. Following both campaigns, the Lacedaemonians sent embassies to Athens asking for peace, both of which offers were rejected by the assembly. The Athenian opposition to peace was in each case led by the leading demagogue of the day, Cleon in 425, Cleophon in 410. The parallels are numerous and readily apparent to a careful observer.

There is no reason to think that Thucydides, whose accounts of the two ten-year wars we have found to parallel one another up to this point, would have missed this opportunity for comparison and contrast between the campaigns of Pylos and Cyzicus. Scholars have already noted one clue in his narrative of Pylos indicating that he composed it some years after the campaign and with later events in mind. This consists of a remark made in 4.12.3 to emphasize the strange turn of events at Pylos, where the Lacedaemonians were attacking Demosthenes' fortified position from the sea: "*Tyche* brought matters to such a turn that the Athenians were defending themselves from land, indeed, Laconian land, against the Lacedaemonians attacking from the sea, while the Lacedaemonians were making landings from ships upon their own land, now hostile to them, against the Athenians; for at that time a great part of Sparta's reputation rested upon her preeminent continental position and her strong army, and most of Athens' reputation came from her dominance at sea and her ships." The phrase ἐν τῷ τότε indicates quite clearly that this statement was written at a time when at least one of the conditions described in the second part of the sentence no longer obtained. Some have concluded that it must, in fact, have been composed when Athens no longer had complete control of the sea. There is, of course, the expected controversy over precisely when that point was reached, but it must have been, on any interpretation, after the Athenian disaster in Sicily.[18] The passage was certainly composed after 412, probably after 407.

But rather than trying to impose a specific *terminus post quem* upon the remark we should concentrate on its real import. As de Romilly points out, the indication that the remark was made considerably later than 425 is provided, not by the phrase ἐν τῷ τότε, but "by the whole of the sentence, whose presence here implies an allusion."[19] The effect of this sentence is to draw the reader's attention, at least temporarily, toward later times and conditions. Thucydides contrasts the situation at Pylos with a later one. Moreover, he does so gratuitously. The reader of his *History* up to this point knows very well that Sparta and Athens were the greatest land and sea powers, respectively, in Greece. He has been told so on many occasions and in many ways. Why mention it again here? Because, I would suggest, Thucydides wanted to make the reader think of the position of Athens some years later, in fact, her position in the Decelean War. And if one wanted to take this contrast further, he could point out that the situation at Cyzicus was precisely the opposite of the one at Pylos. One could substitute "Athenians" for "Lacedaemonians" and "Lacedaemonians" for "Athenians" in Thucydides' sentence on the effect of *tyche* at Pylos and portray the peculiar conditions at Cyzicus quite accurately. It is difficult to know how far one should take this allusion, but it is far enough to make us certain of one thing: early in his narrative of the campaign at Pylos Thucydides

[18] See de Romilly, *Thucydides and Athenian Imperialism* (Oxford 1963) 188-189 with bibliography. Gomme's argument (*Comm.* on 4.12.3) that the passage is more easily explained on the assumption that it was written about 420 is unconvincing.

[19] Ibid., 188, n. 4.

went out of his way to "remind" the reader that conditions at Pylos were quite different from those in the later war.

Thucydides composed two speeches for the campaign at Pylos, Demosthenes' exhortation to his soldiers before the Lacedaemonians' attack upon Pylos (4.10), and the Lacedaemonian ambassadors' speech in the Athenian assembly offering peace (4.17-20). At the beginning of his address Demosthenes stresses the need for courage and blind hope (ἀπερισκέπτως εὔελπις in 10.1) in the face of great danger and overwhelming odds. The situation has reached a point of *anangke* (twice in 10.1) which does not admit of reasoning, but requires only an immediate confrontation with danger. The second part of the speech outlines a plan of defense that fits the apparently desperate situation perfectly and proves, in fact, to be eminently successful in the battle that followed. Using the suggested tactics, Demosthenes' men held their difficult position and set the stage for the ultimate Athenian victory at Pylos.

The speech that Xenophon attributes to Alcibiades before Cyzicus, though it consists of only two brief statements, nonetheless can be seen to convey a similar point: "on the next day Alcibiades convened an assembly [of the troops] and exhorted them that it was necessary [*anangke*] to fight on sea, on land and against fortifications; for, he said, they had no money, while the enemy had as much as he wanted from the King" (*Hellenica* 1.1.14). The Athenians were again in a position of *anangke*, forced to fight a critical struggle without delay, and again all three types of fighting, by land, by sea, and at a wall, were necessary. If Xenophon gives us only the gist of what Alcibiades said, it nonetheless sounds authentic enough, especially since, as we have shown, it was in Alcibiades' own interest to seek a decisive confrontation with the enemy immediately. He thus emphasized, in all probability, the necessity of following up a naval victory with a landing against the Peloponnesian position on shore. Thus the situation was, as we have just seen, similar to that at Pylos, but the combatants' roles were reversed. Now it was the Athenians who would be attacking from the sea a fortified Peloponnesian position on land. And what land was it? It was Cyzicene territory, that is, land formerly belonging to the Athenians, but now hostile to them. Was that the point of Thucydides' remark in 4.12.3? After all, *tyche* had now strangely reversed the positions of 426. This comparison of Pylos and Cyzicus may help to explain the problem, which we alluded to in note 9, of the wall Alcibiades mentions in his exhortation to the soldiers. It seems probable that the wall of Alcibiades' speech is one built by the Peloponnesians after taking the town to help forestall an expected Athenian attack. In the previous year the Athenians had easily forced Cyzicus, which had revolted, back into their alliance because, Thucydides emphasizes, it was unwalled (8.107.1). It would have been natural for the Peloponnesians, under these circumstances, to build a defensive wall. If this suggestion is right, then the parallel between Pylos and Cyzicus becomes even more striking: at Pylos the Athenians fortified a position in Spartan territory and tried to withstand Spartan attacks from sea and land. Such a strong parallelism between events occurring at similar points in the two ten-year wars might have struck Thucydides as highly ironic and might well have led him to remark on the strange twist which *tyche* had wrought. Such an explanation would account for his odd statement in 4.12.3 more satisfactorily than previous suggestions. Perhaps this suggestion goes too far, but one conclusion seems reasonable: Thucydides would have made a good deal more of Alcibiades' speech to the Athenians before the critical Battle of Cyzicus than did Xenophon, and the opportunities for comparison and contrast with Demosthenes' exhortation at Pylos were numerous.

The major emphasis of Thucydides' Pylian episode is upon the speech of the Spartans at Athens and Cleon's rejection of their offer of peace. Finley calls this speech "the dead center of the History, the point at which the earlier estimate of both Athens and Sparta is fully confirmed, and where the destructive forces analyzed since the beginning of the war seem to hang suspended before falling with their full, devastating impact."[20] This judgment may be exaggerated, but clearly the

[20] J. Finley, *Thucydides* (Ann Arbor 1963) 193.

speech that Thucydides gives the Spartans marks a critical stage in the first war. The Spartans call for real peace before it is too late, before, that is, the conflict becomes so intense that thoughts of peace are no longer possible without the total defeat of one of the two sides. The Spartans urge the Athenians to use their "good fortune" wisely and not to suffer what those men do who have unexpectedly had something good befall them: "for led on by hope, they always grasp at something more" (αἰεὶ γὰρ τοῦ πλέονος ἐλπίδι ὀρέγονται; 4.17.4). The Spartans emphasize throughout their speech that the Athenians have obtained their suddenly dominant position through good luck and the Spartans' own bad judgment, not because of any change in the balance of power. Since Thucydides' whole account of the campaign at Pylos, both before and after the speech, stresses this same point, I agree with those scholars who argue that Thucydides basically sympathized with the position taken by the Spartans in their speech.[21] This view is strengthened by the fact that he uses precisely the same pejorative language to describe the Athenians' rejection of this and later Spartan peace proposals that he gives to the Spartans themselves in 17.4: τοῦ δὲ πλέονος ὠρέγοντο in 21.2 and οἱ δὲ μειζόνων τε ὠρέγοντο in 41.4. Furthermore, he tells us in 5.14.2 that the Athenians later regretted their failure to conclude peace after Pylos. In addition, there is no doubt about Thucydides' antipathy toward Cleon, the opponent of peace whom he credits with the major role (μάλιστα δὲ αὐτοὺς ἐνῆγε Κλέων ["and Cleon especially led them on"] in 4.21.3) in the Athenian assembly's rejection of the Spartan offer. Finally, as de Romilly maintains, the fact that Thucydides gives no counter speech to Cleon or to any of the Athenians who voted against peace, but lets the Spartans' speech stand unopposed, lends weight to this conclusion: "When the Spartans put forward the reasons which should have persuaded the Athenians to

[21] Ibid., 194-195; de Romilly *Athenian Imperialism*, 172-177. Gomme, *Comm.* on 4.20.4 argues the other side quite unconvincingly, primarily because he fails to distinguish between Thucydides' view of the offer made in the speech and his own attitude toward it.

make peace, we can thus assume that Thucydides is more or less giving his own judgment of the situation."[22]

Not only does Thucydides give his own judgments to the Spartans, but he expresses them in the most general and philosophical language and tone. The speech is more a sermon to the Athenians on the fickle power of *tyche* and the consequent need for *sophrosyne* among men. Consider, for example, 4.18.4: "Moderate men are prudent enough to reckon their gains as precarious (and they would also conduct themselves sensibly in misfortune), and they recognize that war does not proceed in whatever way one wants in order to deal with it, but goes wherever *tyche* leads. And because such men do not get puffed up with confidence by their success, they are least likely to come to grief and most likely to make peace while their good fortune lasts." This is preaching, though the Spartans deny such an intention in their introductory remarks: "Our giving a rather long speech is not contrary to custom; rather, it is our habit to be brief where a few words suffice, but to use more whenever there is an opportunity to do what is necessary by teaching a useful point through words. Do not take them in a hostile sense nor as if they are lessons for the unintelligent, but consider them a reminder of good counsel to those who already know it" (4.17.2-3). The Spartans (and Thucydides) protest too much. According to Thucydides, if anyone in Greece stood in need of a lesson in moderation it was the Athenians, and if anyone in Greece was in a position to teach that lesson, it was the Spartans. The first point is made abundantly clear throughout the entire *History*;[23] Thucydides makes the

[22] *Athenian Imperialism*, 173.

[23] Compare in particular, the Corinthians' speech in Book I (especially chapter 70), Thucydides' entire description of the decision to send the Sicilian expedition (6.1-32.2), as well as 4.21.2, 41.4, 65.4. Strasburger puts it quite well: "guilt also plays its part in the fate of Athens; but even guiltiness can be a matter of fate if, as here, it rests above all upon the lack of a natural gift, which is, to be sure, the gift of a higher power: the gift of sophrosyne, which the Athenian people needed as compensation for its other excessive gifts, but did *not* receive." "Thukydides und die politische Selbstdarstellung der Athener,"

second quite directly in 8.24.4. The Spartans' speech to the Athenian assembly is thus precisely what the ambassadors say it is not: a lesson in *sophrosyne* given by knowledgeable masters to ignorant students.

How much more point that lesson has when we realize that the Athenians not only failed to learn it in the first war, but missed its meaning in the second as well! The effect of chapters 17-22 is to emphasize the Spartans' farsighted *sophrosyne* and the Athenians', and particularly Cleon's, myopic immoderateness. The reader is led, through Thucydides' artful portrait, to contrast the cautious Spartans with the grasping and unstable Athenians, and to remember the demagogic violence of the Athenian leader. After Cyzicus the same characteristics resurfaced, with the same result. Cleophon, using Cleon's tactics of making excessive demands and discrediting the Spartan ambassadors, persuaded the Athenians to refuse another Spartan peace offer.[24] In 410, however, the Athenians were even more shortsighted in rejecting peace than in 425, for their prospects at this point in the second war were far worse than those in the first war after Pylos. They were in grave financial distress, Attica was occupied by the enemy, Euboea was no longer theirs, their fleet was considerably reduced, the enemy had an unlimited source of money, and half of the empire was in revolt. In their proposal for peace the Spartans must, as Diodorus reports, have made at least some of these points to the Athenian assembly.[25] This time the Spar-

---

in *Thukydides. Wege der Forschung*, ed. H. Herter (Darmstadt 1968) 530. Hereafter cited as *Wege*.

[24] It seems safe to assume, with Busolt (*Gr. Ges.* 3: ii 1537 and n. 1), that Cleophon demanded that the Spartans return to Athens all the cities in the empire which had revolted in the preceding two years. Aristotle (*Athênaiôn politeia* 34.2) who says just that, has, in all likelihood, reported Cleophon's demands correctly, but has mistakenly moved them from 410, after Cyzicus, to 406, after Arginusae. Philochorus says that the Athenians "did not trust" (ἀπιστήσαντες) the Lacedaemonian offer. Cleophon, like Cleon before him (and Alcibiades too, for that matter [5.44.3-45]), probably succeeded in discrediting the Spartan ambassadors (see 4.22 for Cleon's tactics).

[25] Diodorus 13.52.4-6.

tans had a strong bargaining position, an advantage which was certainly not theirs in 425. Yet the Athenians, buoyed by their victory at Cyzicus, by their faith in Alcibiades as a miracle-working general, and by Cleophon's rhetoric, again "grasped after more." Thucydides has prepared the reader for this by his dramatic portrayal of the scene in the Athenian assembly in 425. The unanswered speech of the Spartans, with its wise but unheeded lesson, and the violent demagoguery of the Athenian leader remain in the reader's mind to be recalled at the proper time in Thucydides' account of the second ten-year war. What Thucydides would have made of the events in the Athenian assembly of 410 can be inferred from a look at his portrayal of the assembly of 425. There was, however, one additional reason to emphasize Cleophon's role in the decision to reject peace. The government of the 5000 was ended at this time and full democracy was restored in Athens. It is impossible to date precisely the Spartan embassy to Athens or the restoration of the Council of 500 and full democracy, but we do know that they happened almost simultaneously. The embassy occurred probably in April of 410, the restoration of the democracy in May or June.[26] One thing is clear: the victory at Cyzicus and the rejection of peace signalled the end of the government of the 5000 and the constitution that Thucydides praised (8.97.2) as the first good one Athens had in his time, and brought as well the restoration of full democracy under radical leadership. Just as Pylos raised Cleon to prominence in the first war, so Cyzicus propelled Cleophon to a leading position in the second. Each demagogue was to dominate Athenian politics for the remainder of his war. Indeed, neither ten-year war could be brought to an end until its demagogic fomentor had been killed, Cleon in battle at Amphipolis, Cleophon in stasis at Athens.[27]

[26] See Busolt, *Gr. Ges.* 3: ii 1534, n. 5; B. Meritt, *Athenian Financial Documents of the Fifth Century*, University of Michigan Studies, Humanistic Series, vol. 27 (1932) 106-107.

[27] Compare Thucydides 5.16.1 and Lysias 13: 8-13.

SPARTAN COMMANDERS: BRASIDAS AND LYSANDER

Thucydides' narrative of the last three years of the first ten-year war is dominated by the campaigns of the Spartan commander Brasidas. Almost singlehandedly this extraordinary leader removed the war from the Peloponnese, where the Spartans had suffered badly from Athenian and Messenian raids (see 4.55), and with an army of helots and mercenaries caused the revolt of several Athenian subjects in the northern Aegean, including the key city of Amphipolis. His victories gave the Lacedaemonians the bargaining power they needed to negotiate for peace in 421, as Thucydides says quite explicitly in 4.81.2. Of the three reasons that Thucydides gives (5.14.1-2) for the Athenian desire for peace—the loss of confidence occasioned by the defeat at Delium and by the loss of Amphipolis and the fear of allied revolts—Brasidas was directly responsible for two. It is no exaggeration to claim that Brasidas' campaigns in Thrace ended the Archidamian War. After his death Thucydides tells us (5.11.1) that he was honored by the Amphipolitans as a hero with games and annual sacrifices, and that, as *soter*, he was named founder of their city.

Under these circumstances it was natural to compare Brasidas with the Spartan commander who occupied much the same position in the second ten-year war. Lysander dominated the last three years of the Decelean War: he too campaigned energetically far from Lacedaemon, brought over many of Athens' allies to the Spartan side, won the victory that assured the end of the war, and received extraordinary honors for his success, including altars, sacrifices, songs of triumph, and festivals.[28] In addition, both men awakened jealousy and hostility in the government at Sparta, which was mistrustful of nonroyal commanders who enjoyed too much independence and success. But if there were very great similarities in the careers of these two commanders, there were also great differences in their personal methods and approaches. It can be shown, I think, that Thucydides intended to focus the reader's attention more upon the contrasts than the similarities between them.

[28] See Plutarch, *Lysander* 18.

Thucydides introduces Brasidas' Thracian campaigns with an unusually candid and full description of his personal character and its effects, both short-term and long-term, upon Sparta's war effort. The chapter (4.81) is worth quoting in full (Crawley's translation, somewhat modified):

> Brasidas himself was sent out by the Lacedaemonians mainly at his own desire, although the Chalcidians also were eager to have a man so thorough as he had shown himself whenever there was anything to be done at Sparta, and whose service abroad proved of the utmost use to his country. At the present moment his just and moderate conduct towards the towns generally succeeded in procuring their revolt, besides the places which he managed to take by treachery; and thus when the Lacedaemonians desired to treat, as they ultimately did, they had places to offer in exchange, and the burden of war meanwhile shifted from Peloponnese. Later on in the war, after the events in Sicily, the present virtue and conduct of Brasidas, known by experience to some, by hearsay to others, was what mainly created in the allies of Athens a feeling for the Lacedaemonians. He was the first who went out and showed himself so good a man at all points as to leave behind him the firm hope that the rest were like him.

Here we have a direct statement of a relationship between the two wars: even before he reads Thucydides' description of the campaign in Thrace, the reader is told that the reputation Brasidas gained during that campaign influenced the course of the Decelean War. What was that reputation? Thucydides gives five specific characteristics to Brasidas: he presented himself as just and moderate toward the cities; he had virtue and intelligence; he seemed in all respects to be a good man.[29] It

---

[29] That ἀρετή here means "moral virtue" rather than "martial courage" should be clear from the context. See J. L. Creed "Moral Values in Thucydides' Time," *CQ* N. S. 23 (1973) 222-224; J. Classen *Thukydides*, revised by J. Steup (Berlin Bks. I-II, 5th ed. 1914-1919, Bks. III-VIII, 3rd ed. 1892-1922) *ad loc.*; E. Lange, *Neue Jahrbücher für Philologie* 145 (1892) 827ff.

was clearly Brasidas' moral character that so impressed Athens' allies and that left a firm hope that other Spartan commanders were like him. This hope, Thucydides says, became an important factor in the Decelean War when Athenian allies began to show a strong inclination toward the Spartans.

Now it is a fact, well documented and exampled, that Thucydides uses the word ἐλπίς almost uniformly throughout his work to designate and emphasize unfulfilled expectations. Pierre Huart has analyzed this noun in Thucydides and has drawn the following conclusion about its usage: "Dans la grande majorité des cas, ἐλπίς marque l'espoir et (comme pour ἐλπίζειν) il est bien peu fréquent que ces espoirs soient réalisés."[30] The reader of Thucydides becomes so accustomed to this fact that he can be virtually assured that anyone who expresses hope in the future will soon be betrayed by the ἔργα. Ἐλπίς portends disaster for its users, whether they are the Melians, the Athenians before Sicily, or Nicias before the final disaster in Sicily. Indeed, Huart draws a parallel between 7.77.3 and our passage: "En VII, 77, 3, après la défaite athénienne, l'espérance de Nicias a beau 'être hardie' (ἐλπίς . . . θρασεῖα τοῦ μέλλοντος), elle ressemble plus en réalité à un acte de foi qu'à une vision nette de la situation; c'est aussi à un acte de foi que se livrent les anciens alliés d'Athènes, en passant du côté de Sparte, lorsqu'ils expriment l'espoir (et 'ferme!'), (ἐλπίδα . . . βέβαιον), que les autres Lacédémoniens ne peuvent manquer de ressembler à Brasidas, le seul qu'ils connaissent (IV, 81, 3)."[31]

Was this hope fulfilled? Were Lacedaemonian commanders in the Decelean War like Brasidas? The only one who might be so considered was Callicratidas, who commanded the Peloponnesian fleet for less than a year and who was totally eclipsed by the ambitious Lysander. It was the latter who won over many of Athens' allies to the Spartan side and thus reaped the rewards of Brasidas' reputation. And he used his victory and repaid those states that had revolted from Athens and joined

[30] *Le vocabulaire de l'analyse psychologique dans l'oeuvre de Thucydide* (Paris 1968) 145.
[31] Ibid., 147.

Sparta by establishing decarchies and harmosts in nearly every "allied" city, by founding a new and oppressive empire in Greece, and by maintaining an iron grip over that empire.[32] As Grote says, "The fiat of Lysander, acting in the name of Sparta, became omnipotent, not merely over enemies, but over allies."[33] Within a year after Lysander's liberation of Greece from Athens the cities of Hellas began to look back longingly at the period of Athenian dominion.

It is my contention that Thucydides wrote his description of Brasidas' character and the effect that it had on Athens' allies in the Decelean War with these events in mind. More specifically, 4.81 is a not very subtle intimation of the tyranny of Lysander. The hope that Brasidas' justice, moderation, virtue, intelligence, and moral excellence would be found in other Spartan leaders as well was not only unfulfilled, but, like most hopes in Thucydides, met with bitter and tragic disappointment. Thucydides, if he wrote these words at some time after 404, could count on the fact that a Greek audience would catch their bitter irony. The cities of Greece, eagerly hoping for another Brasidas, got Lysander instead. Thucydides fixes this unrealized hope in the reader's mind even before he begins his description of Brasidas' campaigns in Thrace. Section 4.81.3 is a signpost to the reader of historiographical intimation to come.

Thucydides does not make the reader wait long. One page later he gives us a speech of Brasidas (to the people of Acanthus), in which we find the following claims:

> I am come (said he) not to injure, but to liberate the Greeks; after binding the Lacedaemonian authorities by the most solemn oaths, that all whom I may bring over shall be dealt with as autonomous allies. We do not wish to obtain you as allies either by force or by fraud, but to act as your allies at a time when you are enslaved by the Athenians. You ought not to suspect my purposes, in the face of these solemn assurances; least of all ought any man to hold back through apprehension of private enmities, and through

[32] G. Grote, *History of Greece*, 9: 21-25.
[33] Ibid., 9: 15.

237

fear lest I should put the city into the hands of a few chosen partisans. I am not come to identify myself with local faction: I am not the man to offer you an unreal liberty by breaking down your established constitution, for the purpose of enslaving either the Many to the Few, or the Few to the Many. That would be more intolerable even than foreign dominion; and we Lacedaemonians should incur nothing but reproach, instead of reaping thanks and honour for our trouble. We should draw upon ourselves those very censures, upon the strength of which we are trying to put down Athens; and that too in aggravated measure, worse than those who have never made honourable professions; since to men in high position, specious trick is more disgraceful than open violence.—If [continued Brasidas] in spite of my assurances, you still withhold from me your cooperation, I shall think myself authorised to constrain you by force. We should not be warranted in forcing freedom on any unwilling parties, except with a view to some common good. But as we seek not empire for ourselves—as we struggle only to put down the empire of others—as we offer autonomy to each and all—so we should do wrong to the majority if we allowed you to persist in your opposition (4.86.1-6, 4.87.2, 5)

Grote, whose translation that is (*History of Greece* 9: 13-14), remarks that "the language of Brasidas, sanctioned by the solemn oaths of the Lacedaemonian Ephors, in 424 B.C.—and the proceedings of the Lacedaemonian Lysander in 405-404 B.C., the commencing hour of Spartan omnipotence—stand in such literal and flagrant contradiction, that we might almost imagine the former to have foreseen the possibility of such a successor, and to have tried to disgrace and disarm him before hand. The Dekarchies of Lysander realised that precise ascendancy of a few chosen partisans which Brasidas repudiates as an abomination worse than foreign dominion; while the harmosts and garrison, installed in the dependent cities along with the native Decemvirs, planted the second variety of mischief as well as the first, each aggravating the other."[34] Grote's

[34] Ibid., 9: 15.

juxtaposition here is quite telling but should be emended as follows: "The language of Thucydides, composed for Brasidas in 424 B.C., and the proceedings of Lysander in 405-404 stand in such literal and flagrant contradiction, that we can be nearly certain that Thucydides knew of the latter when he wrote the former and thus intended to disgrace and disarm Lysander before presenting him in his *History*." It seems probable that these words, coming as they do so soon after the implicit contrast between Brasidas and Lysander in 4.81, are meant to foreshadow the latter's actions. It can (and no doubt will) be argued that Thucydides could have written these words before 404 or even that Brasidas could have spoken them in 424. Those are safe, but unhelpful conjectures. The essential aspect of this statement is its particular relevance to Lysander's empire building. The language of 86.4-6 expresses precisely the sense of betrayal felt by the cities of Greece in 404 when the freedom-bringing Spartans subjected them to garrisons and decarchies and a rule far harsher than that of the Athenians. Furthermore, Brasidas goes on at far too great a length in formulating his hypothetical case: "I do not think we would be bringing real freedom"; "that would be worse than rule by others"; "we would be seen as meriting more hateful charges than those who make no pretensions to honesty"; "it is more disgraceful for persons of character to take what they covet by specious deception than by open force" (4.86.4-6). Here is an entire diatribe against Lysander's activities in 404, not a discussion appropriate to the issues confronting Acanthus and requisite to Brasidas' case in 424. Thucydides gives Brasidas an indictment of Lysander. They are, to Thucydides, parallel figures in the two wars with antithetical roles.

There is another passage in Thucydides' narrative of Brasidas' campaigns that looks forward in this same way to the career of Lysander. In 4.132 Thucydides tells us that the Spartans sent an army under Ischagoras to reinforce Brasidas during his second summer in Thrace. Brasidas had asked for such help in the preceding winter but it had been refused because his successes in the north had caused envy in Sparta's leading men, many of whom were at that point more eager for peace

and the return of their 292 men from Athens than for a continuation of hostilities (4.108.6-7). But now, in the late summer of 423, the Spartans recognized that the large force under
Nicias and Nicostratus that the Athenians had just sent to the
north would put Brasidas in a vastly inferior military position
and the allies of Athens who had revolted in serious danger.
The Spartan force, whose size Thucydides does not give us,
was accordingly sent to his aid, but was prevented from passing through Thessaly by Perdiccas' intrigues there. In 132.3
Thucydides concludes his account of this episode:

> Ischagoras, however, and Ameinias and Aristeus, whom the
> Lacedaemonians sent out to inspect the situation, reached
> Brasidas on their own, and brought out, contrary to *nomos*,
> some of the Lacedaemonians' own men of military age from
> Sparta, in order to appoint them archons of the cities and
> [thus] not to entrust them [the cities] to whoever happened
> to be there. And he placed Cleandidas, son of Cleonymous, in
> Amphipolis, and Pasitelidas, son of Hegesandrus, in Torone.

The emphasis in this passage is clearly upon the words τῶν
ἡβώντων αὐτῶν παρανόμως ἄνδρας ἐξῆγον ἐκ Σπάρτης. As
Grote and Beloch pointed out, here is the first hint of the later
harmosts.[35] It is, we should add, a rather broad hint. Thucydides' language is quite strong: "they brought out, contrary to
nomos, some of *their own*[36] *men of military age*[37] from
Sparta." The nomos thus broken was the Spartan custom that
only elderly men, above military age, were sent to such posts.[38]

---

[35] Ibid., 6: 227; J. Beloch, *Griechische Geschichte* (Berlin 1912-1931)
3: ii 1170-1171.

[36] Stahl emended αὐτῶν to αὐτῷ, an unnecessary and indeed harmful
change that removes the emphasis laid upon "the Lacedaemonians' *own*
men."

[37] See Grote, *History of Greece*, 6: 228, n. 1 for the proper force of
οἱ ἡβῶντες.

[38] See the scholiast: ὡς οὐκ ὄντος νομίμου ἐξάγειν τοὺς ἡβῶντας ἢ οὐκ
ὄντος νομίμου ἄρχοντας καθιστάνειν ταῖς πόλεσι τοὺς ἡβῶντας, ἀλλὰ τοὺς
προβεβηκότας καθ' ἡλικίαν. Compare 8.5.1, where Thucydides makes no
remark about the illegality or impropriety of Agis' bringing men from
Sparta intended to be harmosts for allied cities.

But παρανόμως is a very strong word with which to describe a break in custom. Thucydides uses it on only two other occasions, both times to refer to a flagrant violation of interstate moral law: the Theban invasion of Plataea in peacetime and in a holy month at that (3.65.1) and the Plataean massacre of Theban captives who had surrendered (3.66.2). The latter example is particularly instructive for the passage under discussion. The Thebans say that they do not grieve for the soldiers who were killed in battle, for they suffered what was, in a sense, lawful (κατὰ νόμον γὰρ δή τινα ἔπασχον): "But, as for those who held out their hands and whom you captured and promised us later not to kill, when you killed them παρανόμως, did you not commit a dreadful act?"

A similar promise was broken in 4.132.3. For, as we have seen, Brasidas had told the people of Acanthus (and of Torone and Scione too) that the government at Sparta had sworn to leave the cities autonomous. As Gomme says, "here were Spartan governors being sent to them, not just officers in command of troops."[39] Thucydides accentuates Spartan duplicity through the use of the strongly negative adverb παρανόμως and through the explanatory clause, "in order to establish commanders in the cities and not to entrust them to whoever was there" (132.3). Τοῖς ἐντυχοῦσιν is the antithesis of τῶν ἡβώντων αὐτῶν . . . ἐκ Σπάρτης. As Grote says, "I explain τοῖς ἐντυχοῦσιν to refer to the case of men *not Spartans* being named to these posts."[40] The Spartans did not want to rely on the native inhabitants nor on the men in Brasidas' army to govern the cities that had revolted to Brasidas. We must remember that Brasidas' force did not have any Lacedaemonians in it: it was composed of helots and Peloponnesian mercenaries (4.80). Polydamidas, whom Brasidas put in charge of Mende after evacuating that city's women and children, is often called a Lacedaemonian, but there is no evidence whatever for this.[41]

---

[39] A. W. Gomme, *Comm. ad loc.*

[40] *History of Greece*, 6: 228, n. 1.

[41] *OCT Thucydides* II index nominum *s.v.*; Pauly-Wissowa, *Realencyclopädie der classischen Altertumswissenschaft* (Stuttgart 1894-) *s.v.*; Poralla, *Prosopographie der Lakedaimonier* (Rome 1966) Studia

Thucydides, our only source for this man, calls him "archon of all" the Peloponnesians and Chalcideans (4.123.4, 129.3, 130.3) at Mende, but does not identify his country of origin. He was in all likelihood a mercenary from somewhere in the Peloponnese other than Lacedaemon. His woeful inadequacy (see especially his loss of control over the demos and its disastrous consequences—4.130.3-7) as archon of Mende against the Athenians may well have been the decisive factor in the Spartan decision to send Lacedaemonians to be archons of Amphipolis and Torone. Here then is the reason for Thucydides' stress upon the fact that the Lacedaemonians were bringing their own men out of Sparta to govern the cities. This decision, forced upon the Spartans by the special conditions created in Thrace, where an army of helots and mercenaries was operating under a nonking hundreds of miles away from Lacedaemon, ran counter to Spartan custom and to the promises of the Spartan government.

It was a most dangerous precedent that this decision set, for Sparta and for the rest of Greece. Late in the second war a Spartan commander, also of nonroyal lineage, would exercise a prolonged command over allies and mercenaries many miles from the Peloponnese. But Lysander's power went far beyond that of Brasidas. The latter had been visited by inspectors from Sparta and had been given archons for the cities without asking for them. Indeed, such appointments undermined his claims and his promises in the north. In the second war Lysander made no such claims or promises and suffered little interference from the Spartan government at home once he established himself in power with Persia and the Greek cities. He appointed his own harmosts in the cities (see Xenophon, *Hellenica* 2.2.2, 2.2.5, etc.) and became a virtual dictator of a new empire. Parallel commands, contrasting attitudes toward them—such was Thucydides' verdict on Lysander and Brasidas if, that is, we have correctly interpreted his intimations of the former in his treatment of the latter. This is not to deny that the Thucydidean portrait of Brasidas is not totally favorable

Historica, *s.v.*; W. Pape-G. Benseler, *Wörterbuch der Griechischen Eigennamen* (Braunschweig 1911) *s.v.*

(compare 4.85.7 with 4.108.5; 4.88.1 with 4.122.3 and 4.122.6; 4.123.1 with 5.16.1), but it does seem clear that, among Spartan commanders in the field for long periods of time, Brasidas stands out in Thucydides' mind for his moderation and justice. One might contrast also the portrait of Agis, another general free from the Spartan government for a considerable period of time (see 8.5.1-3).

THE MELIAN DIALOGUE: ITS PLACE IN THUCYDIDES' PLAN

There has been much discussion concerning the date of composition of the Melian dialogue, most of it centering around the question of whether or not it was written after 404 B.C. There are prominent adherents of both positions, and one suspects that there always will be.[42] One cannot prove that the dialogue must have been written at one date or another. For that we should require, one suspects, nothing short of a notarized declaration by its author of the precise date of composition. What one can do, however, is simply note that at the very outset of the dialogue Thucydides draws the reader's attention, in highly dramatic fashion, to the end of the Athenian empire. Chapters 89-91 read as follows (Crawley translation):

> ATH. For ourselves, we shall not trouble you with specious pretences—either of how we have a right to our empire because we overthrew the Mede, or are now attacking you because of wrong that you have done us—and make a long speech which would not be believed; and in return we hope that you, instead of thinking to influence us by saying that you did not join the Lacedaemonians, although their colonists, or that you have done us no wrong, will aim at what

---

[42] To give only a few examples: Before 404, see A. Momigliano, *Memorie della Accademia delle Scienze di Torino* II, 67 (1930) 11; Beloch, *Gr. Ges.* II², 2, 14. After 404, see De Sanctis, *Rendiconti della Accademia Nazionale dei Lincei*, Rome VI, 6 (1930) 299 ff.; also in *Studi di storia della storiografia greca* (Florence 1951) 73ff.; de Romilly, *Athenian Imperialism*, 275-286; K. von Fritz, *Die Griechische Geschichtsschreibung* (Berlin 1967) 721.

is feasible, holding in view the real sentiments of us both; since you know as well as we do that right, as the world goes, is only in question between equals in power, while the strong do what they can and the weak suffer what they must.

MEL. As we think, at any rate, it is expedient—we speak as we are obliged, since you enjoin us to let right alone and talk only of interest—that you should not destroy what is our common protection, the privilege of being allowed in danger to invoke what is fair and right, and even to profit by arguments not strictly valid if they can be got to pass current. And you are as much interested in this as any, as your fall would be a signal for the heaviest vengeance and an example for the world to meditate upon.

ATH. The end of our empire, if end it should, does not frighten us: a rival empire like Lacedaemon, even if Lacedaemon was our real antagonist, is not so terrible to the vanquished as subjects who by themselves attack and overpower their rulers. This, however, is a risk that we are content to take.

One can at least say that it was Thucydides' intention in these lines to make the reader focus upon the defeat of Athens. That is, he intimates, the context in which the dialogue is to be read and understood. No reader can miss the dark mention of Athens' fall in the Melians' remarks. Certainly Thucydides' Athenians did not. Without any specific prompting, they envision in their rejoinder a hypothetical defeat by Lacedaemon, with whom the Athenians are currently at peace, and correctly predict its consequence: it would be less fearful than a spontaneous uprising by members of the empire.[43] They then quite

---

[43] This last point is often missed by those like Momigliano (*Proceedings of the Cambridge Philological Society* NS 6 [1960] p. 4, with note 2) and Andrewes (*Comm.* 4: 166-167), who argue that the prediction is not wholly accurate since it was not primarily Athens' allies who in 404 demanded her destruction but rather Thebes and Corinth (see Xenophon, *Hellenica*, 2.2.19). What the Athenians say in 5.91 is that defeat by Sparta is less to be feared than a spontaneous uprising by

self-consciously correct their anachronism: "but our *agon* is not with the Lacedaemonians" (5.91.1). As Andrewes says, "the parenthesis . . . need not be taken as an attempt to retrieve the apparent anachronism by recalling us to the situation as it formally was in 416: the point may simply be that the present argument, ἀγών, is not with Sparta but with the Melians."[44] It is true that the parenthesis "need not" be taken in such a way, and the point "may simply be" such as Andrewes describes, but it nonetheless seems more likely that Thucydides wrote these lines after 404 than before that date, and it is almost certain that he meant the reader to think about Athens' fall when he wrote this first part of the Melian dialogue. That is instructive, but we may go a bit further.

Xenophon tells us that in the last months of the second war Melos was very much on the minds of the hard pressed Athenians. When word came to Athens of the devastating naval defeat at Aegospotami, "no one in the city slept that night, and they mourned not only for the dead, but much more still for themselves, thinking that they would suffer what they had done to the Melians, colonists of the Lacedaemonians, after defeating them by siege, and to the Histiaeans and Scioneans and Toroneans and Aeginetans and many others of the Greeks" (*Hellenica* 2.2.3). The Melians, described first and most fully, are uppermost in Athenian minds. "Melian famine" was already a proverbial expression: Aristophanes uses the phrase in his *Birds*, 186 (see Isocrates, *Panathenaicus* 63, 89, *Panegyricus* 100, 110, and Zenobius 94). A little later Xenophon says:

Athens' allies *alone*. (See Classen-Steup *ad loc.*: "To all appearances αὐτοί means here 'alone' [compare 1.139.3], that is, *not in league with* ἄρχοντες ἄλλων [my italics], who, in the case of a victory would have reined in the desire for revenge of the ὑπήκοοι.") The prediction is in no way vitiated by the fact that is was Sparta's allies who led the forces that demanded Athens' destruction. The Athenians in 5.91 envision two mutually exclusive alternatives, defeat by those who rule others and defeat by their own subjects. The former alternative in fact occurred and the prediction was borne out. See de Romilly, *Athenian Imperialism*, 276, n. 1.

[44] *Comm.*, 166.

Lysander went to Aegina and gave back the city to the Aeginetans, as many of them as he could collect, and did the same for the Melians and whoever else had been deprived of their land. Then he ravaged Salamis and sailed up to the Peiraeus with 150 ships and blockaded the harbor. The Athenians, blockaded now by land and sea, did not know what to do, since they had no ships or allies or food. They thought that there was now no safety, but they would suffer what they had done themselves, not in retaliation, but through hybris when they wronged men of small cities for no other reason than that they were allied with the Peloponnesians (2.2.9-10).

Then, after a first embassy asking Sparta for peace was sent back to Athens by the ephors with the demand that they return with better terms, the Athenians fell into despair, "for they thought that they would be sold into slavery" (2.2.14). Xenophon thus makes it plain that in 405/404 the Athenians thought a great deal about their treatment of the Melians and other such populations which they had annihilated. Did Thucydides not know of these things when he made the Melians say to the Athenians in 5.90, "it is expedient . . . that you should not destroy what is our common protection, the privilege of being allowed in danger to invoke what is fair and right"? Then he added "and you are as much interested in this as any, as your fall would be a signal for the heaviest vengeance and an example for the world to meditate upon."

The Athenians came perilously close to destroying τὸ κοινὸν ἀγαθόν. After a winter of starvation they sent an embassy to Sparta in April of 404 announcing their desire for peace on any terms. The Corinthians and Thebans and "many others of the Greeks" gathered at Lacedaemon urged that no peace be granted, but rather that Athens be "obliterated" (ἐξαιρεῖν). Obliterated she would have been, and with some justification, had it not been for Sparta's old-fashioned belief in ὀνόματα καλά: "but the Lacedaemonians said that they would not sell into slavery an Hellenic city which had done great good at times of greatest danger to Hellas" (*Hellenica* 2.2.20). The Lacedae-

monians gave the Athenians peace and thus spared them the
fate to which they had condemned the Melians. Is the irony
of the Athenians' harsh judgment of ὀνόματα καλά in 5.89
accidental? "Possibly," some might say. But one can look at
the matter from another perspective. Almost fifty years ago
Otto Regenbogen made a most perceptive and suggestive ob-
servation:

> How gloomy and cruel the Melian negotiations are—one
> should probably recall here that Thucydides, if he could
> have finished his work, would have had to portray the nego-
> tiations after the capitulation of Athens, which were con-
> ducted between the Spartans and their allies concerning the
> fate of the city. Plutarch gives to them in the *Life of Ly-
> sander* 15, an account embellished with novelistic details.
> In the serious presentation of Thucydides these negotiations
> at the end would have formed an impressive contrast with
> the middle (and indeed the high point) of the whole. Is this,
> then, the explanation for the singular form which Thucyd-
> ides has chosen?[45]

Given the ironic parallelism that we have found Thucydides
using at every stage in his treatment of the two wars, Regenbogen's conjecture appears remarkably acute. An Athenian
dialogue as the final dramatic episode of the *History* would
fit well into the structure of Thucydides' work as we have
analyzed it. Indeed, it might help to explain not only the form
that Thucydides chose for the Melian affair, but one other
troubling feature of the *History* as well.

Regenbogen (and a few others after him) stated that the
dialogue would stand in the middle of the work if it had been
completed.[46] These assertions have remained unsupported and,

---

[45] *Das humanistische Gymnasium* 44 (1933) 9, n. 13; and in *Kleine
Schriften*, ed. by Franz Dirlmeier (Munich 1961) 227, n. 13.

[46] See G. Deininger, *Der Melier-Dialog* (Thuk. V 85-113) Erlangen
Dissertation 1939, 80; H. Gundert, *Die Antike* 16 (1940) 111, also in
Wege, 130; F. Wassermann, *TAPA* 78 (1947) 35-36; J. de Romilly,
Budé Thucydides vol. 3 (Paris 1967) preface to Book V, xiii. I agree
completely with Wassermann when he says (p. 35) "Both Athenians
and Melians plead their cause before the audience of 404 B.C.," but it

as a result, generally neglected. How could anyone know that the Melian dialogue was the center of the projected work? It does not fall mid-way in the war (431 . . . 416 . . . 404), for example. In what sense, then, is it central? Our analysis of the work's structure helps to answer that question.

We have seen that, for Thucydides, the second ten-year war begins with the Lacedaemonian decision of 414 to invade Attica again (6.93). But he commenced his introduction to that war in 6.1, the beginning of the account of the Sicilian expedition, the ἀληθεστάτη πρόφασις of the second war. We have also seen that Thucydides alerted the reader to the fact that 6.1 was his second beginning by repeating the structural pattern of the opening of his *History* in Book VI. The last event that Thucydides describes before starting his narrative of that campaign was the Athenian siege, capture, and destruction of Melos. What better way to emphasize the fact that one era was ending and another beginning than to compose at that crucial juncture a formal dialogue, unique in the work up to that point, in which the Athenians are portrayed at the height of their power and, forebodingly, of their arrogance and hybris?[47] Thucydides warns his readers that one historical process has reached its logical end. The Athenian empire has attained its zenith, not only as a physical force but also as a moral principle: "They killed as many of the Melian men as they captured, and sold the children and women into slavery, and colonized the place themselves, sending later 500 colonists of their own to take over the place" (5.116.4). In the very next sentence Thucydides begins the latter half of his work, his account of the second ten-year war, the double war in which Athens fell from

is difficult to follow him in his conclusion that "the Dialogue was not meant to present a condemnation of Athenian imperialism" (p. 36). Why does Thucydides make the Athenians refer so arrogantly to the fall of their empire and its consequences? And why does he make them scoff at ὀνόματα καλά, when those were the very things which saved the Athenians from annihilation? (See Xenophon, *Hellenica* 2.2.20). To contrast, so clearly and so ironically, Athenian treatment of helpless Melos with Spartan treatment of helpless Athens was surely to condemn the Athenians' conduct in 416 B.C.

[47] See W. Liebeschuetz, *JHS* 88 (1968) 76-77.

power and arrogance to crushing defeat and terrified surrender. In April, 404 she held her breath while her enemies discussed her fate. The words with which the Athenians had ended their dialogue with the Melians (5.111.5) might well have been spoken by the Athenian ambassadors to Sparta as they left the Peloponnesians to render their final verdict: "Examine this matter carefully then, after we have left, and turn it over many times in your mind: you are deciding the fate of a country, one country, whose survival or ruin will be determined by this one decision."

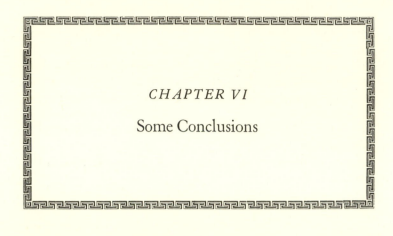

CHAPTER VI

Some Conclusions

For 100 years Thucydidean studies were dominated by one question, the so-called composition problem. From the publication of F. W. Ullrich's *Beiträge zur Erklärung des Thukydides* in 1846 until the appearance of J. de Romilly's *Thucydide et l'impérialisme athénien—La Pensée de l'historien et la genèse de l'oeuvre* in 1947, it was impossible to write about Thucydides without first expressing one's opinion on this problem, which thus became known as "die thukydideische Frage." In the latter book de Romilly summarized the effect of those 100 years of scholarship: "Exhausting by the immense bibliography which it offers, completely negative in its results, the question of the composition of the work can at present be considered as the perfect example of a vain and insoluble problem."[1] And yet even in that same book de Romilly had felt compelled to state her own view, by no means simple, on the problem in the concluding section, as she admits in her "Additional Remarks" to the English translation of the book in 1963.[2] In the three decades since the publication of *Thucydide et l'impérialisme athénien* there has developed an increasing trend of scholarly independence from this overbearing problem, and, more importantly, growing confidence in other

[1] J. de Romilly, *Thucydides and Athenian Imperialism*, trans. by Philip Thody (Oxford 1963) 6.
[2] Ibid., 370.

methods of dealing with the text. A large share of the responsibility for this healthy and productive change belongs to Madame de Romilly herself for the influence of her extremely valuable *Histoire et raison chez Thucydide*, published in 1956. Much of the rest of the credit should go to John Finley, particularly for his article "The Unity of Thucydides' History,"[3] and for his book *Thucydides*.[4] There are signs now that even in Germany the composition problem is beginning to fade in importance. In his influential and comprehensive book *Die griechische Geschichtsschreibung* Kurt von Fritz summarizes the history of the problem in these words:

> If one surveys now the whole affair, it appears to a certain degree as a perfect example of those "Penelope-works," which philology produces with some frequency and in which the results, won with great sagacity, were continually undone again by scholarly criticism, until at the end nothing is left and the whole effort, with whose published product one can in this case fill a small library, appears to have been in vain.[5]

In the course of the preceding five chapters we have purposely avoided any mention of the so-called composition problem in order to focus all the attention of the analysis upon the structure of Thucydides' work as it now stands. The point was to see whether or not there is a clearly identifiable literary plan to the *History* at all. It seems clear from the foregoing study that Thucydides not only wrote his history according to a carefully conceived plan, but that this plan shapes to a substantial degree the composition of nearly every segment in the work. Thucydides wrote his account of each ten-year war with the events of the other in mind. Now if all that could be shown was that Thucydides' composition of the second ten-year war was modelled on his treatment of the first, we should be no

[3] *Harvard Studies in Classical Philology* Suppl. vol. I (1940).
[4] Ann Arbor 1963 (originally Cambridge, Mass. 1942).
[5] K. von Fritz, *Die Griechische Geschichtsschreibung* (Berlin 1967) 573. Note, however, that von Fritz is a bit more optimistic about the value of this approach in the following pages.

further along with the composition problem than before. One could argue that Thucydides, after completing his narrative of the Archidamian War, became aware of the renewal of hostilities and patterned his description of the second war upon that of the first. But what we have in fact found is much more striking: in many cases Thucydides' handling of events in the first ten-year war seems strongly affected by the events of the later war. On several occasions our investigation produced evidence that passages in Books I to IV could best be explained by referring to passages in Books VI to VIII or to incidents that occurred in the last seven years of the Decelean War. Some of these arguments are perhaps less conclusive than others, but their overall weight is considerable: it seems difficult to avoid the conclusion that Thucydides did not compose his account of the first ten-year war, at least in the form in which we have it, until he had witnessed the second.

The major aim of scholars treating the composition problem was to determine when Thucydides wrote various segments of his *History*. In spite of the considerable amount of time and talent spent in this search few generally-accepted discoveries have been made. It has, in short, proved impossible to date individual Thucydidean passages. More importantly, since Patzer (1937) and Finley (1940), it has become nearly impossible to argue that Thucydides' work lacks unity.[6] Almost everyone who has treated the problem since then has had to grant that there are clear signs that Thucydides went over his work carefully after the end of the war and produced an artistically unified account of the Peloponnesian War. Once this is admitted, as de Romilly acutely observes, "reconstruction of Thucydides' work can offer only a curiosity interest. Among a number of equally possible solutions, it implies an almost gratuitous choice and makes no difference in the interpretation of the actual *History*."[7] This last is, I think, the most significant ques-

---

[6] H. Patzer, *Das Problem der Geschichtsschreibung des Thukydides und die Thukydideische Frage*, NDF Abt. Klass. Phil. VI (Berlin 1937) and J. Finley "The Unity of Thucydides' History," *HSCP* Suppl. vol. I (1940); also in *Three Essays on Thucydides* (Cambridge, Mass. 1967).

[7] *Thucydides and Athenian Imperialism*, 348.

tion to ask of any approach to Thucydides: does it make a contribution to the interpretation of the text. It appears that the answer with respect to the century of *Kompositionsfrage* must be no. The method founded by Ullrich and carried to a logical conclusion by Schwartz has failed, almost entirely, to help us interpret the *History* of Thucydides.

The method of analysis followed in the preceding five chapters is founded on an entirely different principle. Rather than analyzing the text with a view toward determining when individual segments were composed, it takes the text as we have it as a given and asks first how it was constructed and then why it was constructed as it was. By examining the relationships between different passages in the text, we have been able to define their function more precisely than could be done before. Books I and VI could be understood not only as introductions to the two ten-year wars, but as parallel introductory sections that Thucydides meant the reader to compare with one another. This view in turn allowed us to comprehend the function of individual passages in those books, for example the digressions on Pausanias and Themistocles in Book I and on the tyrannicide in Book VI. Each excursus was intended by Thucydides to serve as a *paradeigma* for the crucial issue on which its ten-year war was to turn. Since these digressions came at nearly identical points in the two introductions to the wars, it became clear that Thucydides meant us to compare and contrast them, and thus to discover one essential difference between those two wars. The same point holds true for the conferences Thucydides constructs in Books I and VI. The fact that Thucydides inserted parallel sets of speeches at similar points in his narrative of the two introductions enables the reader again to make effective and penetrating comparisons and contrasts between the resources and preparations of the two sides that will confront each other in the two wars. That is why Thucydides constructed and placed them as he did.

We found in the preceding chapters that this double vision extended over the entire eight books of Thucydides' *History*. Thucydides, then, seems to have planned his work as a whole, not piecemeal as he went along. Such literary architecture could not have been arranged until after the conclusion of the Peloponnesian War in 404 B.C. This view does not deny the possibility or even the probability of notes or working drafts prior to the composition of the final version. It does, however, render the search for such notes and drafts relatively insignificant. Even if earlier *Schichten* could be identified (and after 100 years that is highly doubtful), would such discoveries help us interpret the work of art Thucydides has given us? Quite the contrary: the search for earlier levels of Thucydides' *History* has actually obscured the architecture of the work. Concentration upon the composition problem has, in short, caused far more harm than good. Not only has it failed to produce any significant results; it has prevented scholars from understanding the real nature of Thucydides' compositional plans and techniques, indeed, the real nature of his art.

THE MEANING OF 1.22.4

We have attempted to identify the major criteria according to which Thucydides shaped his material. We have thus treated a different type of composition problem: not what were the steps by which Thucydides developed his work from first notes to final draft, which de Romilly calls "the perfect example of a vain and insoluble problem"; but rather according to what structural principles did Thucydides compose the draft we have. Our answer was that he intentionally and somewhat arbitrarily divided his war into two ten-year wars whose histories he composed in parallel ways. One might next inquire why Thucydides chose to write his *History* in this way? The answer to this question comes from a careful reading of Thucydides' most famous sentence, 1.22.4, which we are now in a position to understand in its fullest sense:

καὶ ἐς μὲν ἀκρόασιν ἴσως τὸ μὴ μυθῶδες αὐτῶν ἀτερπέστερον φανεῖται· ὅσοι δὲ βουλήσονται τῶν τε γενομένων τὸ σαφὲς σκοπεῖν καὶ τῶν μελλόντων ποτὲ αὖθις κατὰ τὸ ἀνθρώπινον τοιούτων καὶ παραπλησίων ἔσεσθαι, ὠφέλιμα κρίνειν αὐτὰ ἀρκούντως ἕξει. κτῆμά τε ἐς αἰεὶ μᾶλλον ἢ ἀγώνισμα ἐς τὸ παραχρῆμα ἀκούειν ξύγκειται. (Perhaps the

254

lack of the mythical in them will appear rather unpleasant for listening; but if those who will want to examine the clear truth of the past and once again of the future, which according to the human condition will reflect and resemble it, judge these things useful, that will be sufficient; for they are composed as a possession for all time rather than as a competition piece to be heard for the moment.)

His *History* will, according to Thucydides, be useful to the reader for two reasons: it will enable him to examine the past with precision; and the future will resemble and reflect the past. Inherent in this pair of statements is the implication that a study of the past helps one to interpret the future.[8] This is not a naive and simple statement asserting a cyclical view of history: Thucydides does not say that the future will repeat the past; he says only that, given the human condition, it will be similar to the past. A careful study of the past will not allow one to predict the future, but it will enable one to interpret the future more wisely.

The previous chapters of this book have shown that Thucydides performed precisely this service in his own work. He composed his own account of the Peloponnesian War in such a way as to accentuate and to shape correspondences between two periods of *History*. He divided his subject into two ten-year wars and patterned his narratives of those wars in parallel ways. In other words, Thucydides has carried out the program of 1.22.4 in his own *History*. He has enabled the reader to see clearly the similarities between past and future by his composition of past and future. Thus the statement in 1.22 has direct application to the history of the Peloponnesian War as Thucydides has constructed it.

Thucydides says that his work will be an ὠφέλιμα to the

---

[8] Note Crawley's excellent translation: "The absence of romance in my history will, I fear, detract somewhat from its interest; but if it be judged useful by those inquirers who desire an exact knowledge of the past *as an aid to the interpretation* of the future, which in the course of human things must resemble if it does not reflect it, I shall be content" (my italics). See also Adam Parry, *BICS* 16 (1969) 108, particularly "in a similar or analogous fashion."

255

CONCLUSIONS

reader who will want to investigate the clear truth (σαφές) of the past as an aid to the interpretation of the future. What he does not say is that he helps the reader make this interpretation by composing his *History* in such a way as to bring out comparisons and contrasts between different periods of history and by thus leading the reader to make Thucydidean judgments about events and decisions. We have looked in detail at many passages in which Thucydides leads the reader to interpret history by his construction of historical episodes. Two of the historiographically most instructive passages were the major digressions in Books I and VI. We argued that Thucydides wrote the excursus on Pausanias and Themistocles in order to provide for the reader a general paradigm of Spartan and Athenian leaders and the treatment of them by their respective cities and a specific model for the careers of Lysander and Alcibiades. The latter pair would, at the end of the Peloponnesian War, repeat in extraordinarily similar ways, the careers of the former two "most famous men of their time." By thus portraying in parallel biographies the lives of Pausanias and Themistocles, Thucydides was helping his reader see how "a close study of the past could aid the interpretation of the future, which will, given the human condition, be similar and parallel to the past." Thucydides later confirmed this interpretation for the reader by having Alcibiades allude to the career of Themistocles and claim that he emulated such men. It seems quite likely that in his treatment of Lysander Thucydides would, in a similar way, have referred the reader to the paradigmatic case of Pausanias. Such historiographically created pairs help the reader interpret past and future.

The digression in Book I is thus illustrative of Thucydides' historiographical method. But the excursus on the tyrannicides in Book VI is even more instructive, both historically and historiographically, because Thucydides goes even further in his use of this technique and because he is more candid about his use of it. As we saw, Thucydides not only implied that the tyrannicide was a model for the events of 415, but he said explicitly (6.60.1) that the demos' memory of the tyrannicide affected its handling of the Hermocopidae. In this case, then, not only was the "future" resembling the past, but it was strongly influenced by it. That was the historical lesson Thucydides meant to teach by his digression. But the passage is even more revealing historiographically because Thucydides ties it to his methodological remarks in 1.20-22 and thus makes it into an exemplum of his method and his aim in writing history. That such was his intention is clear first from his inclusion of a preliminary discussion of the tyrannicide in 1.20, where he used it as an example of men's habit of "accepting uncritically from each other oral tradition about the past, even concerning their own city" (1.20.1). "So little pains do the vulgar take in the investigation of truth," he adds, "accepting readily the first story that comes to hand" (Crawley translation). Thucydides goes on in 1.21 to contrast his own method of dealing with the past, which is based upon a method of discovery relying upon the "clearest possible data, given the antiquity of the events" (21.1). He then, in 1.22, outlines his method of dealing with the Peloponnesian War itself, and it is here that he makes his famous remark about readers who will want to examine the clear truth (σαφές) of the past as an aid to the interpretation of the future. Thus the reader already has a hint that Thucydides considers the affair of Harmodius and Aristogeiton to be an example of his methodological distinction between other men's treatment of the past and his own.

In his excursus in Book VI Thucydides makes this distinction in far more breadth and depth. At its beginning (53.3) he recalls his remarks in 1.20.1-2: "for the demos, knowing by oral tradition that the tyranny of Peisistratus and his sons had in the end become harsh, and furthermore that it had been put down not by themselves and by Harmodius, but by the Lacedaemonians, lived in continuous fear and took everything suspiciously." (This is almost the only part of the oral tradition which was right!) Then, throughout the excursus, Thucydides points to the errors in the oral tradition. He is particularly concerned with political misconceptions: contrary to popular belief, the tyrants were wise and moderate leaders who performed great services for Athens, while the conspirators were violent and rash men acting out of purely private mo-

257

tives; in addition and above all, Harmodius and Aristogeiton did not put an end to a harsh tyranny, but made a benevolent tyranny harsh. These fundamental errors in the oral tradition had a distrastrous influence upon the city of Athens in 415, as Thucydides makes clear at the end of the digression: "the demos of the Athenians, having these things in mind, and remembering whatever it knew about them by oral tradition, was harsh then and suspicious towards those who took the blame for the mysteries, and thought that everything had been done with an aim toward an oligarchical and tyrannical conspiracy" (6.60.1). The demos' ignorance had terrible consequences. Excellent men were imprisoned, and then an informer stepped forward with full information. Thucydides says explicitly that "no one could say, then or later, the clear truth [σαφές] about those who did the deed." But the demos "happily took, *as it thought*, the clear truth" (my italics; 60.4) and began to put to death or condemn to exile those whom the informer named, while it let him and his associates go free. Then, "when they *thought* they had the clear truth about the Herms, the Athenians were greatly strengthened in their belief that the affair of the mysteries, in which Alcibiades was implicated, had been committed for the same reason by him, as a conspiracy against the demos" (my italics; 61.1). As a result, Alcibiades and other aristocrats were called to trial on capital charges and "they wanted to put him to death" (61.4).

Thucydides' references in this digression to his critical remarks in 1.20 and his constant use of the word σαφές, so crucial for his statement of purpose in 1.22, tie the digression on the tyrannicide, inextricably and unmistakably, to the methodology. Thucydides has done everything but tell his reader the purpose of his historical excursus. If he had written for the simple-minded, which he explicitly said he did not, he might have said the following: "My digression on the tyrannicide is designed to contrast the misuse and the proper use of history. The Athenian demos misinterpreted, through ignorance, laziness, and improper historiographical method, the historical example of Harmodius and Aristogeiton, and thereby committed a serious, indeed, catastrophic, political blunder (the expulsion of their most effective military leader on insufficient grounds). The Athenian people knew from the oral tradition only that the tyranny ended by being harsh and that it was put down not by themselves, but by the Lacedaemonians (6.53.3). They feared that the affairs of the Herms and mysteries were evidence for an oligarchical and tyrannical conspiracy which would lead to an overthrow of the democracy (see 6.60.1, 6.15.4, 6.28.2). They drew the wrong analogy. By a painstaking and methodologically accurate study of the tyrannicide one can see how that episode *is* a paradigm for the Hermocopidae, aiding in its interpretation [see pp. 110-117]. The past can be used as an aid to understanding the future, but only if it is carefully and properly understood itself. That is the service which I have performed in my digression on the tyrannicide. It is also the very service which I claimed in 1.22 I would perform for those who will want to scrutinize the clear truth of the past."

In this instance Thucydides did almost all the work for the reader. That is why the digression on the tyrannicide is a paradigm in and of itself of Thucydides' method. Not only did he draw the parallels between the two historical events; not only did he set them next to one another; not only did he explicitly point out the demos' misuse of historical analogy; he even went so far as to hint, broadly and clearly, at the connection between the digression and his methodological statements in 1.20-22. Thucydides thus virtually tells the reader that he has designed chapters 6.54-59 as a paradigm of his claim that his careful scrutiny of the past will be of use to those who will want to interpret the future, which will reflect and resemble it. It is this aspect of the excursus on the tyrannicide that sets it apart from other episodes in Thucydides' *History*.

But we should be aware that it is only in this respect that this digression is different from other Thucydidean passages. It is different in degree, not in kind, from the rest. Thucydides has composed much of his *History* according to this same principle of studying historical episodes for the light they can shed on other episodes, to which he relates them historiographically. Many passages in Thucydides' *History* are related to each other in this same way; they vary only in the method by which they are related to one another. Sometimes Thucydides signals a repetition of a particular pattern of events by the use of the word αὖθις, which he used in 1.22.4 to refer to the recurrence of similar patterns in the future. In 5.25.3, for example, he uses αὖθις to point to the outbreak of the second ten-year war, which would be parallel to the first. In 7.18.3 he uses αὖθις to contrast the Lacedaemonians' feeling of guilt about having caused the first war with their confidence that "this time the same guilt would lie with the Athenians": αὖθις ἐς τοὺς Ἀθηναίους τὸ αὐτὸ περιεστάναι. In 2.48.3 he says that he will not deal with the causes of the plague, but will write his account of it in such a way that if someone scrutinizes (σκοπῶν) it, he will be able to recognize it, by knowing something about it beforehand, if it should ever come again (αὖθις). Here Thucydides claims that his own account will have not predictive value, but rather interpretive value, and the verb σκοπεῖν is, of course, the same as the one he used in his general statement about the value of his *History* in 1.22. This example is different from the first two, because Thucydides does not write an account of another similar plague, but, methodologically speaking, it points clearly to Thucydides' purpose in composing his *History*.

On occasion, then, Thucydides is explicit about the relationship between pairs of events in his history. Generally, however, there is no word like αὖθις to signal the recurrence of a particular pattern to the reader. Thucydides' most common technique for drawing the reader's attention to historical parallelism is formal or historiographical parallelism. By composing episodes in parallel forms, he leads the reader to make comparisons and contrasts between them. This is implicit, not explicit, style, and it had before Thucydides already enjoyed a long tradition in Greek literature. Indeed, Thucydides could rely upon his readers' understanding of it in order to be certain of its effect, as Schadewaldt acutely observed:

One easily grasps why Thucydides discloses only his purpose of criticizing the tradition, and leaves that of criticizing

260

the political facts to the understanding of his reader. This silence was made possible for him through the very form of the paradigm, to whose nature, since its first entrance in the Nestor/Phoenix speeches of the *Iliad* belonged the anticipation, without explicit statements, of the useful comprehension of the ethical as well as the judgmental implications. . . .

. . . Thucydides counts on readers to whom he does not need to explain his own point of view, since the form of his episodes explains it to them.[9]

Strasburger makes much the same point when he speaks of Thucydides' "skilled technique of making, without explicit words, historical interpretations apparent through literary composition."[10]

Thucydides took pains to show the reader how the future would reflect and resemble the past in his own *History* by composing it in such a way as to accentuate such similarities and parallels. The famous statement of aim in 1.22.4 is, then, an integral part of the methodological and programmatic statement that precedes it in 1.22.1-3, not a separate, or even separable claim about the work's possible value. Just after Thucydides tells us his method of writing speeches and narrative, he adumbrates his method of composing parallel episodes and the value that we may derive from it. This value is in part pedagogical: not only will Thucydides' careful research into past events give us a reliable picture upon which to base our interpretation of the future; in addition, his careful composition of those events will give us a reliable method upon which to base our interpretation of the future. We will know what to compare the future with and thus how to compare it. In this latter sense, in particular, Thucydides' work is indeed a possession for all time: once we have learned the proper meth-

[9] W. Schadewaldt, *Die Geschichtsschreibung des Thukydides* (Berlin 1929) 93 and 95.

[10] H. Strasburger, *Die Wesensbestimmung der Geschichte durch die antike Geschichtsschreibung* (Wiesbaden 1966) 73: "geübten Technik, durch literarische Komposition geschichtliche Sinndeutung ohne Wörte sichtbar zu machen."

od of analyzing and interpreting history, we shall always have the tools with which to understand its lessons.

Now it is no doubt true that as this kind of historian Thucydides not only drew his readers' attention to parallel and similar events in the past and future, but to some extent fashioned those very parallelisms and similarities. Such an historian is not only a chronicler, he is a creator. It is in part this aspect of the *History* that led R. G. Collingwood to his famous judgment about the nature of Thucydides' historiography:

> Herodotus may be the father of history, but Thucydides is the father of psychological history.

> Now what is psychological history? It is not history at all, but natural science of a special kind. It does not narrate facts for the sake of narrating facts. Its chief purpose is to affirm laws, psychological laws. A psychological law is not an event nor yet a complex of events: it is an unchanging rule which governs the relations between events. I think that every one who knows both authors will agree with me when I say that what chiefly interests Herodotus is the events themselves; what chiefly interests Thucydides is the laws according to which they happen. But these laws are precisely such eternal and unchanging forms as, according to the main trend of Greek thought, are the only knowable things. . . .

> . . . the Thucydidean speech is both in style and in content a convention characteristic of an author whose mind cannot be fully concentrated on the events themselves, but is constantly being drawn away from the events to some lesson that lurks behind them, some unchanging and eternal truth of which the events are, Platonically speaking, παραδείγματα or μιμήματα.[11]

The final sentence in particular of Collingwood's assessment appears to be a remarkably accurate summary of the findings of the preceding five chapters of this book. We have found evidence that Thucydides uses paradigms throughout his work

[11] R. G. Collingwood, *The Idea of History* (New York 1957) 29-30, 31.

in order to draw what he considers to be crucial relationships between sets of events in the Peloponnesian War. Without going into any such detailed argumentation Collingwood has put his finger upon a major feature of Thucydides' historical thought. But, we might add, the very fact that makes Collingwood's judgment so brilliant also accounts for its failure to provide an adequate description of Thucydides' historiography: Collingwood was led by his intuitively perceptive but inadequately documented insights into Thucydides to draw a penetrating but essentially misleading picture of his thought. While it is true that Thucydides was interested in teaching the lesson that lies behind events, and in discovering paradeigmata in history, his mind was always concentrated on the events themselves. His research into and presentation of patterns in history stressed not so much eternal and unchanging forms as it did contrasting and even contrary circumstances; he sought to bring out and emphasize the differences between parallel sets of events as well as the similarities. Above all, his was no simplistic cyclical view of history, in which events repeated themselves everlastingly; neither his theory, expressed in 1.22.4, nor his practice, evidenced throughout his *History*, bears this out. Rather, he held the opinion that the future would reflect and resemble the past, but would vary from it "according to the variety of the particular cases" (ὡς ἂν ἕκασται αἱ μεταβολαὶ τῶν ξυντυχιῶν ἐφιστῶνται in 3.82.2). The Athens of the second war confronts decisions similar to those faced by the Athens of the first. But instead of Pericles, she has Nicias and Alcibiades to lead her; Syracuse in place of Sparta as her enemy; division, not unity, to accompany her during the crises.

History: science and art

Herodotus, says Hermann Strasburger in a perspicacious phrase, created a "hybrid of science and art, which history has remained to the present day."[12] Modern historians are, by and

---

[12] H. Strasburger, *Die Wesensbestimmung*, 55: "Mischwesen aus Wissenschaft und Kunst, welche die Geschichte bis auf den heutigen Tag geblieben ist."

large, less than comfortable with the artistic side of history, both in their theoretical discussions of its place among the sciences and the arts and in their actual practice of it in their own histories. Most of the classical historians were, on the other hand, literary artists of the first order. That, and not simply their attention to accuracy, is why some of them are still read by the general educated public.[13] Some contemporary historians understand this requirement for great history. Note what Sir Ronald Syme, himself a master of Tacitean style, has to say about the historiographical equipment of another great stylist: "Now, of Gibbon we can say, as he ventured to say himself, 'diligence and accuracy': that was what he had. He uses the phrase more times than one. But to write history you need something more: the thing must be readable, it must have a certain unity of style and design. . . . Accuracy and style are not quite enough; surely one needs structure and architecture."[14]

Structure and architecture are aspects of Thucydides' art that have received insufficient attention. The *History* of the Peloponnesian War reads, as many have noted, like a tragedy. Historians, using (or trying to use) Thucydides as a mine for "data," find this term inappropriate, misleading, even perverse. But other readers go on employing it. The tragedy is not an individual's, but a city's. Athens in the beginning is at its height, the apex of civilization in Thucydides' political conception. By the end of Book VII (which Macaulay called the "ne plus ultra of human art")[15] her greatest venture has ended

[13] Note what Dionysius of Halicarnassus has to say about the preservation, down to his day, of the works of certain historians who were contemporaries of Thucydides: "And withal their works are invested with a certain charm and grace, greater with some than with others, but possessed by all, and it is for this reason that their writings are even now extant" (*On Thucydides* 331, trans. W. Kendrick Pritchett [Berkeley, Los Angeles, London 1975] 3).

[14] "How Gibbon came to History," *Gibbon et Rome à la lumière de l'historiographie moderne*, Université de Lausanne, Publications de la faculté des lettres 22 (Geneva 1977) 52, 53.

[15] The context is: "I do assure you that there is no prose composition in the world . . . which I place so high as the seventh book of Thucyd-

in "total ruin."[16] By the end of "Book X" the city, a political and military shambles, would await her fate in terrified surrender. It is a long way since Pericles' proud words: "you must yourselves realise the power of Athens, and feed your eyes upon her from day to day, till love of her fills your hearts" (Crawley translation, 2.43.1).[17] What gives the work its tragic cast? Certainly its subject, but Thucydides has colored it carefully: no citations of sources to break the flow of the action (that is, in modern terms, no footnotes); few digressions to disturb the movement from one episode to another (and those few, as we have seen, serve to make the reader consider the relationships between events); dramatic dialogues and debates to engage the reader himself in major decisions and crises; even direct appeals to the emotions, particularly pity and fear.[18] We have attempted to document the implicit literary devices: the rigorous standards applied to selection of material for inclusion and exclusion; the care devoted to literary emphasis that so frequently reveals historiographical decisions (the Athenian treatment of Scione, 5.32.1, receives half a sentence, while the similar events at Melos merit a full, formal dialogue —the difference in emphasis depends upon historiographical timing rather than upon historical character); finally, and most significantly, artistic juxtaposition that enhances historical parallelism and hence creates historiographical meaning, perhaps most clearly in Books I and VI, though we found evidence of similar technique throughout the work.

By means of these literary methods Thucydides unified his work. Some have felt this masterful control, particularly other

ides. It is the *ne plus ultra* of human art" (Quoted in G. O. Trevelyan, *The Life and Letters of Lord Macaulay* [New York and London 1875] 1: 387).

[16] See N. M. Kopff and H. R. Rawlings III, "Panolethria and Divine Punishment: Thuc. 7.87.6 and Hdt. 2.120.5," *La Parola del Passato* 182 (1978) 331-337.

[17] Note that Dionysius calls the funeral oration "that lofty tragic composition" (*On Thucydides*, 351, trans. Pritchett 12). Compare the analysis of the funeral speech by H. Flashar (*Der Epitaphios des Perikles* [Heidelberg 1969]), who finds it full of tragic irony.

[18] See Dionysius, *On Thucydides*, 330.

artful historians: "I suppose the Peloponnesian War has more unity than the average drama. Only perhaps you'd call it not true. I'll admit that modern history has seldom been 'composed' in the artistic sense."[19] These remarks are apposite to the current appraisal of Thucydides in more ways than one. In short, literary control engenders historical suspicion. The age-old comparison between Herodotus and Thucydides has come full circle: Herodotus, for centuries the uncritical and therefore unreliable "father of lies," has become the simple compiler of facts and therefore the guarantor of truth; Thucydides, on the other hand, is no longer the careful and trustworthy researcher he claimed to be, but rather the perversely skilled manipulator who consciously distorts the facts and thus intentionally misleads his readers. In Collingwood's words, "Thucydides is not the successor of Herodotus in historical thought but the man in whom the historical thought of Herodotus was overlaid and smothered beneath anti-historical motives."[20] For many this assertion goes too far, but it has recently met with the approbation of a new "school" of Thucydidean studies, one which has opened valuable new avenues to understanding Thucydidean historiography.

In a general historiographical essay on Thucydides W. P. Wallace quotes Collingwood's remarks with approval and then embellishes them:

> His elaborate speeches, twisted and distorted in their Greek, reflect the determination of the author to win his way through the tangle of events to the ultimate and intelligible reality which he feels must lie behind them. It is a reality which, I think, he never found. A will o' the wisp which led him, as it has led other great historians, into the bog of pseudo-explanation, the kind of explanation which has made some see in history gold, silver, bronze, and iron age cycles, or preparation for the return of the Messiah, or the patterned rise and fall of great civilizations. It is to Thucydides' credit

[19] T. E. Lawrence, *Fifty Letters, 1920-1935. An Exhibition*, University of Texas, Humanities Research Center (Austin 1962) 9.

[20] R. G. Collingwood, *The Idea of History*, 30.

that he never made explicit the explanation towards which he obviously felt that he was making his way.[21]

In a series of articles dealing with historical episodes in the fifth century B.C. Mabel Lang has consistently criticized Thucydidean historiographical principles on the grounds that Thucydides consciously manipulated his composition of the events of history for his own purposes.[22] By finding inconsistencies in Thucydidean narratives and by showing how certain features of the narratives can be explained on the hypothesis that Thucydides was "oftentimes guilty (from our point of view) of substituting the interpretation for the fact," she argues that Thucydides' accounts of several events are open to suspicion and therefore in need of "correction."[23] For example, she examines Thucydides' account of the Epidamnian affair and decides that of the two Corinthian expeditions narrated only one actually took place: "The two Corinthian expeditions to Epidamnus can most satisfactorily be thought of as one expedition which Thucydides has used twice in order to account for the variety of results which it had or might be thought to have had. This cavalier treatment of a fact can, I think, be detected from various signs."[24] Lang understands the danger of such an approach, but sees no alternative: "It is a tricky task to attempt to 'correct' Thucydides out of his own mouth, but where his account is the only one we have this is what we must do."[25]

---

[21] "Thucydides," *Phoenix* 18 (1964) 260.

[22] "The Murder of Hipparchus," *Historia* 3 (1955) 395-407; "A Note on Ithome," *GRBS* 8 (1967) 267-273; "Scapegoat Pausanias," *CJ* 63 (1967) 79-85; "Kylonian Conspiracy," *CP* 62 (1967) 243-249; "Thucydides and the Epidamnian Affair," *CW* 61 (1968) 173-176.

[23] "Thucydides and the Epidamnian Affair," *CW* 61 (1968) 175.

[24] Ibid., 175.

[25] Ibid., 176. Compare the similar caveat, also unheeded, in "Kylonian Conspiracy," *CP* 62 (1967) 249, n. 9 (from p. 248). S. Chernick has questioned the validity of Lang's methodology in "Historical Manipulation in Thucydides?" *CW* 65 (1971) 126-130. See in particular his remark on p. 126: "Yet it seems to me likely that these 'oddities' [in Thucydides' account] are more the product of preconceptions concerning Thucydides' historical and political views than the result of the historian's manipulation of facts or events."

Now this kind of rewriting of Thucydidean accounts is becoming more fashionable as scholars become more aware of the artistry of the *History*. That there is indeed a relationship between these two processes is expressed rather clearly by Lang herself:

> And this is exactly what seems most to interest Thucydides: not the facts, but what they mean. And it seems to me that he is oftentimes guilty (from our point of view) of substituting the interpretation for the fact. Nor would this be so heinous a crime (since it is one to which we are all somewhat prone) if he were not so skilled in presenting the interpretation with all the convincing circumstantiality of fact itself![26]

The last sentence is an explicit statement of the assumption that because Thucydides can be shown to have great artistic control over his material he must therefore be guilty of manipulating or distorting that material.

More recently, a pupil of both Wallace and Lang, Virginia Hunter, has published a more general study of Thucydidean historiographical technique, *Thucydides: The Artful Reporter*. In a series of well argued and clearly presented analyses of Thucydidean episodes she succeeds in exposing Thucydides' method of composing speeches and narrative in order to reveal the relationships between men's thoughts and subsequent actions. Her work thus continues that of J. de Romilly, to whom, as she acknowledges, she owes a large debt. But Hunter carries her analysis a good deal further than de Romilly:

> Granted de Romilly's close analysis, we are still uneasy. Again we ask, what *was* Thucydides doing? Why this tremendous concentration and intensity to make events turn out as they should? Surely it is insufficient to return, as de Romilly does, to the explanation, 'En effet, l'histoire de Thucydide tend à laisser le plus possible les faits parler d'eux-mêmes.' Why must 'facts speak for themselves?' . . . In the end de Romilly's explanation leaves Thucydides' work dis-

---

[26] "Thucydides and the Epidamnian Affair," *CW* 61 (1968) 175.

crete and aimless. Thus the first task of the present study will be to reconsider the historian's technique of anticipation to see if it has some larger significance.[27]

Her first conclusion is that "By means of this technique [of connected speeches and action] men are represented as learning or incapable of learning from their own and others' experiences, from *empeiria* and *paradeigma*."[28] Hunter goes on to discover larger patterns in the *History*, some of which, as I said before, anticipate my own conclusions: "A puzzling characteristic of the second half of the *History*, the events leading up to and including the Sicilian expedition (5.84-7.87), is its aura of *déjà vu*. Time and again characters, events, and even sequences of events are reminiscent of counterparts and parallels in the 'first war.' "[29] She then takes this line of argument further: "For Thucydides events happen with a definite regularity and order, and there is a pattern to history. Thus informed by pattern and cycle the facts of history are made meaningful. . . . Through the technique of foreshadowing the reader shares in the experiences of the protagonists. Not only does he see time and again which *logos* is correct and why, but as events recur he can criticize and predict himself. Having learned from the first cycle, he should find events of the second cycle all but inevitable."[30]

This summary seems to me to overstate the case. As we have seen, a careful and comprehensive study of the structure of Thucydides' *History* reveals a far greater preoccupation with contrast than with comparison, a much larger interest in comprehension of the past than in prediction of the future, and, above all, a belief in the ironic contradictions rather than in the straightforward repetitions of history. To Thucydides history consists of complex sequences of events more remarkable for their variety than for their regularity, and he has serious reser-

[27] V. Hunter, *Thucydides: The Artful Reporter* (Toronto 1973) 8.
[28] Ibid., 178.
[29] Ibid., 179.
[30] Ibid., 182-183. See pages 179 and 184, where Hunter refers to Thucydides' "recurrent type characters" and calls him "surely the least objective of historians."

vations about men's abilities to learn from the examples of others. Indeed, in most instances in his *History*, men do not; that failure is what gives the work its tragic irony.

Nonetheless, there is reason to believe that the present study will be thought to provide support and confirmation for the new school of Thucydidean criticism. To the extent that this analysis of Thucydidean architecture has revealed even greater artistic control over historical data than was seen before, the view that Thucydides composed his account according to literary, even dramatic, criteria will be further advanced. Perhaps we have even found evidence that he manipulated the beginnings of his two wars to produce epic lengths for them, and that he went a bit far, at least by our present standards, in drawing historical analogies between those wars. Such a conclusion seems to contradict the older view of Thucydides, the careful compiler of facts. Thucydides, after all, wrote a history, not a novel. And yet we know more about the last quarter of the fifth century B.C. than about any other period of Greek history, and this knowledge we owe in large part to Thucydides. He wrote a detailed, informative, and careful account. But to what extent are these two views contradictory or mutually exclusive? Wide disagreement on how to read the *History* has characterized Thucydidean scholarship for generations: Cornford thought Thucydides a dramatist, Cochrane believed him a scientist; Page saw a physician, Parry a poet.[31] Is one side completely right, the other wholly wrong, or is it possible to reconcile the two views?[32] It is difficult, I think, to improve upon Wade-Gery's summary evaluation:

[31] F. Cornford, *Thucydides Mythistoricus* (London 1907); C. W. Cochrane, *Thucydides and the Science of History* (London 1929); D. L. Page, "The Description of the Great Plague in Athens," *CQ* 47 (1953) 97ff.; A. Parry, "The Language of Thucydides' Description of the Plague," *BICS* 16 (1969) 106-118.

[32] See W. Robert Connor's essay "A Post Modernist Thucydides?," *CJ* 72 (1977) 289-298, especially 298: "It may even prove possible to restore at a higher level the old reconciliation of the artist and the historian." The remarks of a fictional historian may be particularly apposite here: "I entirely agree that a historian ought to be precise in de-

Perhaps no good historian is impartial; Thucydides certainly not, though singularly candid. . . . Such criticisms hardly detract much from his singular truthfulness. Readers of all opinions will probably agree that he saw more truly, inquired more responsibly, and reported more faithfully than any other ancient historian. That is a symptom of his greatness, but not its core. Another symptom is his style: it is innocent of those clichés of which Isocrates hoped to make the norm of Attic style; in its 'old-fashioned wilful beauty' (Dionysius) every word tells. Like English prose before Dryden and Addison, it uses a language largely moulded by poets: its precision is a poet's precision, a union of passion and candour. . . . To combine his predecessors' candour of vision with his successors' apparatus of scholarship was a necessity laid on him by his sense of the greatness of his subject: he could no more distort or compromise with what he wished to convey than Shakespeare or Michelangelo could.[33]

Thucydides tells us (1.22) that he did his research painstakingly, and we may, I think, believe him. That is one-half of the historian's task, the "scientific" half. The other side he only hints at, in his remarks, also in 1.22, on the value of his research to readers. He had a truth he wished to convey: the future will be parallel and analogous to the past. By artful representation, the ironies of history can be enhanced, past events can be controlled by the mind. "Civilization," as Wade-Gery reminds us, "is largely made up of such controls."[34] Great historians help us learn, in part by their diligent research, but even more by their inspired art. Mommsen, who invented many of our scientific methods for studying ancient history and had an unparal-

---

tail; but unless you take all the characters and circumstances concerned into account, you are reckoning without the facts. The proportions and relations of things are just as much facts as the things themselves; and if you get those wrong, you falsify the picture really seriously" (Dorothy L. Sayers, *Gaudy Night*, Avon Books [New York 1968] 21).

[33] H. T. Wade-Gery, *The Oxford Classical Dictionary*[2] s.v. Thucydides, 1069.

[34] Ibid., 1069.

leled mastery over its details, believed that "The historian perhaps belongs more with artists than with scholars."[35] The *History* of the Peloponnesian War is not the truth, it is Thucydides' truth. As a record of late fifth-century Greece, however, it is more valuable than all the inscriptions, coins, architectural remains, and artifacts that have been unearthed. It is an intelligent and passionate man's view of the tragedy of his city.

[35] *Reden und Aufsätze* (Berlin 1905) 11.

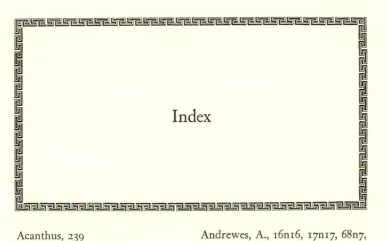

Index

LIBRARY OF CONGRESS CATALOGING IN PUBLICATION DATA

Rawlings, Hunter R.
  The structure of Thucydides' History.

  Includes index.
  1. Thucydides.   History of the Peloponnesian War.
2. Greece—History—Peloponnesian War, 431-404 B. C.
I. Title.
PA4461.R3   938'.05'072   80-8572
ISBN 0-691-03555-5   AACR2

Hunter R. Rawlings III is Professor of Classics and Associate Vice
Chancellor for Instruction at the University of Colorado, Boulder, and
Editor of *The Classical Journal.*